ALSO BY CLARENCE WASHINGTON SR.

Tools for Effective Prayer:
The Mechanics, Dynamics, and Contents of Prayer

Victory Every Day in Every Way:
Kingdom Living According to Nehemiah the Governor

HIJACKED!

*How Dr. King's Dream
Became a Nightmare*

VOLUME 1
THE DREAM

CLARENCE WASHINGTON SR.

Copyright © 2021 Clarence Washington Sr.
Cover and internal chapter and section illustrations by Donald C. Washington.

All rights reserved. No part of this book may be used or reproduced by any means, graphic, electronic, or mechanical, including photocopying, recording, taping or by any information storage retrieval system without the written permission of the author except in the case of brief quotations embodied in critical articles and reviews.

LifeRich Publishing is a registered trademark of The Reader's Digest Association, Inc.

LifeRich Publishing books may be ordered through booksellers or by contacting:

LifeRich Publishing
1663 Liberty Drive
Bloomington, IN 47403
www.liferichpublishing.com
844-686-9607

Because of the dynamic nature of the Internet, any web addresses or links contained in this book may have changed since publication and may no longer be valid. The views expressed in this work are solely those of the author and do not necessarily reflect the views of the publisher, and the publisher hereby disclaims any responsibility for them.

Any people depicted in stock imagery provided by Getty Images are models, and such images are being used for illustrative purposes only.
Certain stock imagery © Getty Images.

ISBN: 978-1-4897-3604-8 (sc)
ISBN: 978-1-4897-3602-4 (hc)
ISBN: 978-1-4897-3603-1 (e)

Library of Congress Control Number: 2021910238

Print information available on the last page.

LifeRich Publishing rev. date: 06/16/2021

All Scripture quotations in this book, unless otherwise noted, are taken from the Holy Bible, New King James Version, copyright © 1979, 1980, 1982, 1997.

Scripture taken from the New King James Version®. Copyright © 1982 by Thomas Nelson. Used by permission. All rights reserved. Scripture quotations identified as NKJV are taken from the New King James Version.

International Version®, NIV® Copyright © 1973, 1978, 1984, 2011 by Biblica, Inc.® Used by permission. All rights reserved worldwide.

The "NIV" and "New International Version" are trademarks registered in the United States Patent and Trademark Offices by Biblica, Inc.™

Scripture taken from the New American Standard Bible®, copyright © 1960, 1962, 1963, 1968, 1971, 1972, 1973, 1975, 1977, 1995 by the Lockman Foundation. Used by permission. Scripture quotations identified as NASB are taken from the New American Standard Bible.

Scripture taken from The Message. Copyright © 1993, 1994, 1995, 1996, 2000, 2001, 2002. Used by permission of NavPress Publishing Group.

Scripture quotations marked (TLB) are taken from The Living Bible, copyright © 1971. Used by permission of Tyndale House Publishers, Inc., Carol Stream, Illinois 60188. All rights reserved.

Scripture quotations identified as KJV are taken from the King James Version.

Scripture quotations taken from the Amplified® Bible (AMPC), copyright © 1954, 1958, 1962, 1964, 1965, 1987 by the Lockman Foundation Used by permission. www.Lockman.org

To my wife, Janice, and my son, Donald. They have encouraged me and helped me to write this book by confirming what living out Dr. King's dream can look like when you do it God's way. I also thank Jan for her help with editing and exposing the blind spots of the forest that an author can't see because of my in-depth engagement with the trees in the forest. And again I thank my son, Donald, for his illustration and graphic design contributions for the front and back covers and the graphic images for the chapter and section divisions.

And so on behalf of the two dreamers who have not given up on making Dr. King's dream a reality in their lives, even though they have experienced the numerous disheartening ways in which it has been hijacked, below I included the poetic epigraph "Charity" by the most notable William Cowper.

Fairest and foremost of the train that wait
On man's most dignified and happiest state,
Whether we name thee Charity or Love,
Chief grace below, and all in all above,
Prosper (I press thee with a powerful plea)
A task I venture on, impell'd by thee:
Oh never seen but in thy blest effects,
Or felt but in the soul that Heaven selects;
Who seeks to praise thee, and to make thee known
To others hearts, must have thee in his own.
Come, prompt me with benevolent desires,
Teach me to kindle at thy gentle fires,
And, though disgraced and slighted, to redeem
A poet's name, by making thee the theme.
God, working ever on a social plan,
By various ties attaches man to man:
He made at first, though placed as he sees best,
Where seas or deserts part them from the rest,
Differing in language, manners, or in face,
Might feel themselves allied to all the race …
But if unhappily deceived I dream
And prove too weak for so divine a theme,
Let charity forgive me a mistake,
That zeal, not vanity, has chanced to make,
And spare the poet for his subject's sake.[1]

CONTENTS

Preface xiii

Introduction: Who Was Dr. Martin Luther King Jr. and Why Is His Dream So Important to People of All Colors and the Survival of Our God-Given American Dream? xvii

    An Overview of the Life of Dr. King xvii

    The Reason Why Dr. King's Dream Is So Important to All Americans xxiv

    The Conspiracy to Discredit Dr. King's Dream xxxii

The Dream: What Is the Content of Dr. King's Dream—Its Methods and Goals?

Chapter 1:   The Methods Content to Be Implemented: Dream Method 1—Righteousness, Forgiveness, Perseverance 1

    Righteousness 4

    Forgiveness 10

    Perseverance 13

Chapter 2:   The Methods Content to Be Implemented: Dream Method 2—Self-Respect and Self-Control, Nonviolence, Unity 19

    Self-Respect and Self-Control 20

    Nonviolence 31

    Unity 37

Chapter 3:	The Methods Content to Be Implemented: Dream Method 3—Faith and Hope	51
Chapter 4:	The Goals to Be Achieved: Dream Goal 1—Dr. King's Dream Is Deeply Rooted in the American Dream	73
	The Biblical Worldview Chart	87
Chapter 5:	The Goals to Be Achieved: Dream Goal 2—Dr. King's Dream Is Characterized by His Intense Desire for Freedom and Justice	95
Chapter 6:	The Goals to Be Achieved: Dream Goal 3—Dr. King's Dream Is Characterized by His Intense Desire for Hateful Unforgiveness to Be Replaced with Loving Forgiveness	113
	Replacing Hateful Unforgiveness with Loving Forgiveness	116
	Traumatized Racial Groups Are Biblically and Legally Entitled to Restitution	134
Chapter 7:	The Goals to Be Achieved: Dream Goal 4—Dr. King's Dream Is Characterized by His Intense Desire for Racial Pride to Be Replaced with Humility	155
	The Dream Concluding Remarks	168

Appendixes

Endnotes	173
Table of Contents for Volume 2 — *The Hijack*	185
Table of Contents for Volume 3 — *The Nightmare*	187
Table of Contents for Volume 4 — *The Recovery*	189
List of Bible Versions Abbreviations	191
Index	193

PREFACE

Most people who have read the title of this book (and possibly the back cover) probably want to know why I undertook such a project as this with all its potential controversies. What motivated me is the great struggle that such an enormous number of Black people (and Americans in general) are still undergoing in their effort to make Dr. King's dream a reality in their lives since his death. This is particularly troubling to me when I see what is happening today in the low-income Black communities of my hometown, Chicago, Illinois.

This is most troubling when I reflect on the large number of Christian churches that marinate the Black communities of Chicago and other cities around the nation. They claim to be following the dream that Dr. King delineated for both Black communities and the nation in general. There are so many churches, so many Christian activist groups, and so many social activist groups. So many laws have been passed, and so many social programs have been instituted in the name of Dr. Martin Luther King to make his dream a reality for Black people and our nation as a whole.

But instead of the dream becoming a reality, the dream has become a nightmare for massive numbers of Black citizens of such cities as Chicago, St. Louis, Baltimore, Detroit, and Los Angeles. The murder rate, and particularly the Black-on-Black murders, is so bad for example in Chicago that the city has been given the name *Chiraq*! This relates the extremely high Black-on-Black murder rate in Chicago to the murder rate that once existed in the nation of Iraq when it was a war zone. During the first weekend of August 2018, seventy-three people were wounded in Black neighborhoods on the west and south sides of Chicago, of which twelve people died. The following Monday in these same Black neighborhoods, sixteen people were wounded, of which five died. And as I write on this day in July 2020, nothing has changed.

Therefore, there must be a concrete reason why Dr. King's dream has not become a reality in our nation over the last fifty-plus years when so many churches, so many local and federal government agencies, so many private groups, and so many individuals claim to be working to implement it. And the reason is that Dr. King's dream has been hijacked by many of the aforementioned who claim to be serious about making the dream a reality in their personal lives and the American culture in which we live. Now how do I know this for sure and for certain?

I know that Dr. King's dream has been hijacked for sure and for certain because his dream is rigidly based in the sound doctrine of God's Word. Moreover, God Himself confirmed the reality of the hijack when he said through the prophet Isaiah,

> As the rain and the snow come down from heaven, and do not return to it without watering the earth and making it bud and flourish, so that it yields seed for the sower and bread for the eater, so is my word that goes out from my mouth: It will not return to me empty, but will accomplish what I desire and achieve the purpose for which I sent it. You will go out in joy and be led forth in peace. (Isa. 55:10–12 NIV)

You see, either Dr. King's dream is not rooted and grounded in Scripture, God's Word, or we as Black people and the nation as a whole are not correctly implementing the dream. The reason why this is so absolutely true is that when the dream is correctly implemented according to the truth of Scripture, it will indeed become a reality in America. God's Word cannot return empty or without effective results. So this book was written to inform well-intentioned people—particularly the church—who genuinely don't know what part they might be playing in helping to hijack Dr. King's dream.

And so I want to give readers a glimpse forward into *Hijacked!* by saying that you don't have to live in Chicago, St. Louis, Baltimore, Detroit, Los Angeles, or any other city that is experiencing a heavy dose of the nightmare in order to be a part of the problem or a part of the solution.

Likewise, you don't have to be Black or an African American in order to be a part of the problem or a part of the solution. We are all in this thing together—Black, White, Brown, Red, and Yellow—as you will see as you read this book. For together we will stand or together we will fall! The late Dr. Martin Luther King Jr. said that there are spiritual forces or dynamics at work or in play in the world. These dynamics can simply be stated in the following way: love and live together or hate and die together. One path is the way of the wise, and the other path is the way of fools.[1]

Read *Hijacked!* and use it to examine yourself to see if you are a part of the problem or a part of the solution and to help others. The prophet Jeremiah said to Judah after they had been carried off by King Nebuchadnezzar and the vicious Babylonians—after their dream in Canaan (the Promised Land) had turned into a nightmare of captivity— "Let us search out and examine our ways, and turn back to the LORD" (Lam. 3:40).

The four-volume edition of *Hijacked!*, which explores *The Dream* (volume 1), *The Hijack* (volume 2), *The Nightmare* (volume 3), and *The Recovery* (volume 4), is thorough. All four volumes contain an authors and subjects index and endnotes to resources that will start you on a journey that will take you as deep as you desire to delve into each of the four topics of Dr. King's dream. The four volumes provide in one literary work all the significant aspects of Dr. King's dream, the obstacles concerning the inability to achieve his dream, and the process that must be employed to overcome such obstacles. The term "ignorant Christian" should be an oxymoron! *Study to shew thyself approved* means more than studying the Bible. You must be a man or woman of Issachar (1 Chron. 12:32) and a Berean who were more noble (Acts 17:11).

The nightmare that is currently being experienced in America as a result of the hijack is a spiritual problem that must be solved by spiritual means. But you must possess the vast knowledge that this book provides— the spiritual as well as the secular—for all aspects of the dream, the hijack, and the nightmare so that the recovery can be effectively implemented.

May God richly bless you as you start on the journey of reading *Hijacked!* I pray that God does this by enabling you to turn off the voices emanating from the world, your flesh, and the devil as you read, and that He will enable you to take captive every thought and feeling that you experience on this journey and make these things obedient to Christ (2 Cor. 10:5). In Jesus's name, I pray. Amen! This is the only way you will be able to examine yourself objectively and determine whether you are part of the solution to effectively implementing Dr. King's dream or part of the problem in helping to hijack it.

Now onward to the introduction and the start of partaking of the abundant blessings of knowledge, wisdom, and discernment that God has in store for you as you gain a better understanding of how to be a part of the solution and not in any way a part of the problem of hijacking Dr. King's dream.

Note: In this four-volume edition of *Hijacked!*, the table of contents of other volumes are provided in the appendix of each volume. This allows readers of a particular volume to obtain some helpful before-and-after context for a deeper understanding when other volumes have not been read. The appendix of the table of contents of the volume that you are now reading contains the page number of the table of contents of other volumes.

INTRODUCTION

Who Was Dr. Martin Luther King Jr. and Why Is His Dream So Important to People of All Colors and the Survival of Our God-Given American Dream?

An Overview of the Life of Dr. King

In order to wet the mental and spiritual whistles of the readers of this book so that you will be motivated to deeply absorb its content, I think it would help if I first said something about a few of the highpoints of Dr. King's life. I pray that his life experiences that are included will help you to better understand the importance of the content of his dream when you explore it as you read *Hijacked!* Likewise, understanding some of the highlights of Dr. King's life experience will help you to better understand how his dream has been hijacked in the past and how it is currently being hijacked today.

However, I want to say in advance that in no way am I attempting to present a complete account of all the important contributions of Dr. King. Although he only lived to be thirty-nine years of age, he accomplished more in this short period of time than most men and women will achieve in a lifetime twice as long. Such a task would require a most lengthy book to achieve, which is not the purpose of *Hijacked!* My account of Dr. King's life throughout this book will be limited to what is necessary to adequately express his God-given dream, how it was hijacked, and how we can recover from the hijack. For people who want a more thorough account of Dr. King's life, there are other books that do this. One such book is *I Have a Dream: Writings and Speeches That Changed the World*, edited by James Melvin Washington, with the foreword by Coretta Scott King, Dr. King's wife.

And so in a few words, before exploring *The Dream* (volume 1), *The Hijack* (volume 2), *The Nightmare* (volume 3), and *The Recovery* (volume 4), who was Dr. Martin Luther King Jr.? Dr. King was an African American

Baptist minister. But more importantly, he was the most visible leader, activist, and spokesperson of the civil rights movement from the mid-1950s until his assassination by a sniper on the evening of April 4, 1968. Dr. King was standing on the balcony of his room in the Lorraine Motel in Memphis, Tennessee, one day after he had delivered his last speech, titled "I've Been to the Mountaintop." The Lorraine Motel is now part of the complex of the National Civil Rights Museum. A good question to answer now is, Why was Dr. King in Memphis on April 4, 1968?

Dr. King was in Memphis at this particular time to lead another protest march to support the striking garbage workers when he was shot and assassinated by James Earl Ray. In the first march on March 28, 1968, just a few days prior to his death, Dr. King led about six thousand protestors through downtown Memphis to support the striking garbage workers. And when disorder broke out, stores were looted by some Black youth, which ended with one sixteen-year-old killed and fifty people injured.

So what happened to James Earl Ray? Ray was captured and received a ninety-nine-year sentence. James Earl Ray died of kidney failure on April 23, 1998, at age seventy while serving his life sentence in Nashville, Tennessee. Now what was Dr. King's greatest achievement before his untimely death?

His greatest achievement, although he had many others, as exemplified below, was the detailed strategy that he developed for the advancement of the civil rights movement. This worldwide renowned strategy is based on nonviolent civil activism. Dr. Benjamin E. Mays (1894–1984) was a giant in the Christian ministry and also the man Dr. King called his "spiritual mentor and intellectual father."[1] After Dr. King's assassination, Dr. Mays eulogized him on the campus of Morehouse College in Atlanta, Georgia. That eulogy included the following very insightful words that help to establish Dr. King's faith and his commitment to nonviolence in the execution of the civil rights movement. Dr. Mays said,

> Here was a man who believed with all his might that the pursuit of violence at any time is ethically and morally wrong; that God and the moral weight of the universe are against it; that violence is self-defeating; and that only love and forgiveness can break the vicious circle of revenge.[2]

Along these same lines, in Dr. King's first book, *The Stride Toward Freedom: The Montgomery Story* (1958), Dr. King said that he taught the people involved in the Montgomery civil rights movement (the 1955–1956 Rosa Parks, Montgomery Bus Company boycott) that nonviolence was the soul and heart—the lifeblood—of effective Christianity.[3] The effectiveness of this kind of Christian love, as described by Jesus in such text as the Sermon on the Mount, was empirically confirmed to Dr. King by the writings and teachings of Mahatma Gandhi. In *The Stride Toward Freedom*, Dr. King presented six points, principles, or rules that characterize the ethics of his philosophy of nonviolent resistance.[4] The six rules for nonviolent resistance can be paraphrastically summarized in the following way:

Rule 1: Nonviolent resistance replaces violence or physical resistance with a strongly active spiritual resistance to evil. Nonviolent resistance is continuously active in seeking to convince evildoers of their wrong deeds and to abolish evil laws and practices.

Rule 2: Nonviolent resistance strives for reconciliation with purveyors of evil instead of destroying or shaming them. A just and fair community for all involved is the goal of nonviolent resistance.

Rule 3: The target of nonviolent resistance is always the evil systems of our culture and not the people who are the purveyors and gatekeepers of evil. "For our struggle is not against flesh and blood, but against … the powers of this dark world and against the spiritual forces of evil in the heavenly realms" (Eph. 6:12 NIV).

Rule 4: Nonviolent resistance is a commitment to suffer to make social and economic justice a reality and not to impose suffering on others.

Rule 5: Nonviolent resistance is a commitment to love purveyors and gatekeepers of evil with forgiveness, grace, and mercy instead of being filled with bitterness and hatred toward them. Hatred of people absolutely does not have any role in the deployment of nonviolent resistance whatsoever.

Rule 6: Nonviolent resistance is composed of courageous actions against evil that are motivated by faith that it will be overcome and social and economic justice will prevail in the end.

It should be carefully noted from the above six rules that Dr. King's philosophy of nonviolent resistance is an activity that seeks to win an opponent to friendship rather than to humiliate or defeat him.[5]

Therefore, this demonstrates that his strategy for civil disobedience was truly based on his Christian faith. In his "Letter from Birmingham Jail," Dr. King expressed the significant principle of how the Christian faith should be employed to process acts of civil disobedience. He said that when a person's conscience compels them to break a law that they sincerely believe is unjust (Acts 4:18–20), they must be willing to accept the penalty (Rom. 13:1–5).[6]

In summary of the above, Dr. King described his chronicle of the Montgomery bus boycott (*The Stride Toward Freedom*) as being the story of fifty thousand Negroes who made a gallant, heartfelt effort to employ the principles of nonviolence, which was motivated by genuine Christian love.[7] These people put on and employed the whole armor of God as their weapons of warfare. And in the process, God gave them the understanding of how to obtain significance, self-worth, and social and economic justice reforms when they recruit Him—through prayer, nonviolence, and love—to be their battlefield commander. Benjamin Mays, the distinguished Atlanta educator, president of Morehouse College (1940–1967), literary critic, and friend of Dr. King, expressed the importance of this chronicle with these highly motivational and stirring words:

> Americans who believe in justice and equality for all cannot afford to miss the book. Negroes cannot afford to miss it because it tells us again how we can work against evil with dignity, pride and self-respect.[8]

So it's easy to see that all the disrespectful, undignified, and violent civil disobedience that is occurring in places like the University of California, Berkeley, is definitely part of the hijacking of Dr. King's dream, which is also occurring in several other forms. It should be noted that in 1968,

Coretta King founded in Atlanta, Georgia, the Martin Luther King Jr. Center for Nonviolent Social Change, better known as the King Center. The King Center contains a library and archives of the original source materials for Dr. King's works and more than two million American civil rights movement documents. It is used by more than five thousand scholars and researchers each year.[9]

Now what are some other significant things that would be helpful and interesting to know or to expand on about Dr. King, the great American minister, patriot, and civil rights activist, before moving on to the dream, the hijack, the nightmare, and the recovery? Well, inquisitive minds might want to know the following about Dr. King before moving on to the meat of this book. And others might feel that they need even more information before moving on. So here it is. He was born Michael King Jr. on January 15, 1929. But in 1931 after a trip to Germany, his father, the second-generation Baptist pastor, the Reverend Michael King Sr., changed his name and his two-year-old son's name to Martin Luther. Dr. King's father did this in honor of the great sixteenth-century German theologian and reformer Martin Luther.

However, I have to believe that the process by which Dr. King was renamed from Michael to Martin Luther and his upbringing by his parents were supervised by the LORD God Almighty Himself. The reason why I say this is that Dr. King was born to be a great, zealous man of God, just like the German reformer Martin Luther. Jeremiah the prophet said,

> The word of the LORD came to me, saying, "Before I formed you in the womb I knew you, before you were born I set you apart; I appointed you as a prophet to the nation." (Jer. 1:4–5)

You see, I thoroughly believe that neither his father nor his mother realized what this name change would mean to their first son or how it might motivate him later on in his life. When he was two years old, I don't believe they were thinking much about how Dr. King's name change would affect him, but God was. He was born for such a time as this—the climax of injustice and the civil turmoil it produced in the fifties and sixties. The divine timing of Dr. King's birth was no accident.

He was born in the Jim Crow South—a time of openly flaunted, in-your-face racism and mandated segregation in all public facilities, exactly when God had preordained him to be born. Blacks could not drink from the same public water fountains as Whites; or use the same public toilets; or sit in the same area in movie theaters; or eat in the same restaurants as Whites; or live in the same motels as Whites; or go to the same schools as Whites; or ride in the front of public buses. And besides all this, Blacks were lynched and raped and experienced all kinds of injustices for any and all reasons at the whims of Whites on a regular basis.

Case in point, there was the racially motivated massacre of Black people and the destruction of their little town named Rosewood that took place in rural Levy County, Florida, in January 1923. Eyewitness accounts say that the death toll was as many as 150 people.[10]

And then in 1955 a fourteen-year-old African American, Emmett Louis Till, from Chicago, while visiting some relatives in the South was beaten, mutilated, shot in the head, and weighted down. Then his dead body was thrown into the Tallahatchie River near Money, Mississippi. A twenty-one-year-old White woman's husband and his half brother did this because the woman said that she was offended by young Emmett Till's flirting with her in her family's grocery store.[11] You see, Dr. King was born for times such as the above and was given the divinely supervised name of Martin Luther.

Moreover, besides the name change to one of the greatest Christian rebels in history, Dr. King's middle-class, college-educated parents nurtured and helped their son to develop to his fullest potential emotionally, educationally, socially, and above all spiritually. In other words, it was a God-thing from the beginning to the end of Dr. King's life. The psalmist said in his praises to the LORD, "All the days ordained for me were written in your book before one of them came to be" (Ps. 139:16), which applies to Dr. King's life and everyone else born of a woman. Dr. King's steps were indeed ordered by the LORD as the psalmist infers in Psalm 139 and others.

Additionally, it might be interesting to know that he was not a tall man. In fact, Dr. King was a relatively short man, about 5'7", with a medium frame.

Also, he married the very lovely, well-educated, and artistic Coretta Scott in 1953, with whom he had four children (two sons and two daughters). Now what about Dr. King's educational background? I think this will help in better understanding who he was and what motivated him.

After passing the college entrance exam to Morehouse College in Atlanta, Georgia, at age fifteen, he left Booker T. Washington High School in Atlanta, Georgia. He then received a bachelor of arts degree in sociology from Morehouse (1944–1948), a bachelor of divinity degree from Crozer Theological Seminary in Pennsylvania (1948–1951), and earned a doctor's degree in systematic theology from Boston University (1951–1955).

Furthermore, it was at Boston University that Dr. King met Coretta Scott. He later married her in 1953 in Marion, Alabama. Prior to his graduation from Boston University, Dr. King, in 1954, became the pastor of the Dexter Avenue Baptist Church in Montgomery, Alabama.

However, this was not Dr. King's first pastoral experience. For in 1947, at age eighteen, he was licensed to preach and became the assistant to his father at the Ebenezer Baptist Church in Atlanta. In 1960, Dr. King moved back to Atlanta from Montgomery and became the copastor with his father of the Ebenezer Baptist Church. He was a busy man, moving wherever God called him and allowing God to groom and prepare him for the special calling that God had on his life.

Moreover, concerning who Dr. King the man was, in December 1955, after Mrs. Rosa Parks was arrested and put on trial for refusing to relinquish her seat on a bus to a White man, a bus boycott movement was established and given the name the Montgomery Improvement Association (MIA). Dr. King was unanimously elected as the president of MIA.

Then in 1957 after the Montgomery bus boycott had ended, Dr. King cofounded and was elected to be the first president of the Southern Christian Leadership Conference (SCLC), which is still active today in community and civil rights issues. The other cofounders were Ralph Abernathy, Bayard Rustin, Fred Shuttlesworth, and Joseph Lowery.

In addition to this, Dr. King was named Man of the Year by *Time* magazine in 1963. On October 14, 1964, Dr. King was awarded the Nobel Peace Prize for his nonviolent resistance to racial prejudice in America. I should also note before moving on that Dr. King gave the prize money of $54,123 to the civil rights movement.

Also, after the arduous work of his wife, Coretta Scott King, and others in several attempts at procuring a national holiday, on November 2, 1983,

President Ronald Reagan signed a bill making the third Monday in January an official holiday to honor Dr. King. But it was not federally observed for the first time until January 20, 1986. And when this happened, Coretta Scott King made the well-known proclamation that Dr. Martin Luther King Jr. Day was not a Black holiday but a holiday for all the people of America.

There are many other things that could be said about the life of Dr. Martin Luther King Jr., such as his unwavering commitment to his family through all the trials and tribulation that he experienced. For example, the thirty times he was arrested for civil disobedience; the four times he was assaulted, which included a stabbing in his chest; assaults and deaths of civil rights activist supporters (e.g., Unitarian minister James Reeb and Mrs. Viola Liuzzo in 1965 in Selma, Alabama); the many threats on his life, the lives of his family, friends, and supporters, which include the bombing of his home and an unexploded bomb that was found on his front porch; the more than six million miles he traveled; the more than twenty-five hundred speeches he gave to protest injustice; the five books and numerous articles he somehow found time to write and promote; and so many other things that would take volumes to write about. But I think that what I have said about this great American will give you a better understanding of how awesomely outstanding he was—for the glory of God.

The Reason Why Dr. King's Dream Is So Important to All Americans

So it is now time to make the transition to his dream for Black Americans—or I should say for all Americans. For his dream was indeed inclusive. Now that you know something about the man, Dr. Martin Luther King Jr., it is time to introduce the question, Why is Dr. King's dream so important to people of all colors and the survival of the God-given American dream?

Well, the best way I can start to answer this most significant question is through a simple insight provided by Dr. King. It was given to a crowd of about 1,500 people on the evening of July 28, 1960, in Tulsa, Oklahoma. People squeezed into the First Baptist Church of North Tulsa to hear a thirty-one-year-old pastor who was changing America. One of the topics that Dr. King spoke on that evening was titled "On the Need for

Unity." And one of the things he said on the importance of unity has been proclaimed around the globe.

More importantly, what he said is most significant in describing the importance of his dream to the people of America. Dr. King said on the importance of unity that summer evening in Tulsa that America was at the crossroads of life and death. He said that we had to make the choice to love one another and live together as brothers and sisters or to hate one another like the fools that we had been in the past and die. Love and live together, or hate and die together![12]

That says it all! Unity is the key! It's not rocket science! It's not hard to understand, but America has not been able to do a very good job of creating unity among its people. We have not been able to implement the foundation of Dr. King's dream over the fifty-plus years since he was assassinated.

You see, that's what Dr. King's dream teaches us how to do. It proclaims the basics of unity or peace, joy, success, prosperity, and respect for all America's people. It gives us a very simple plan of how to live together without destroying one another or how to keep from dying together as fools. Jesus said it this way:

> Every kingdom divided against itself will be ruined, and every city or household divided against itself will not stand. (Matt. 12:25)

It's not rocket science! United we stand! Divided we fall! Nikita Khrushchev. who led the former Soviet Union during the first part of the Cold War (1953–1964) as the first secretary of the Communist Party, said the following about the division that exists in our nation:

> We do not have to invade the United States. We will destroy you from within.[13]

During the time of Khrushchev's Soviet leadership, he knew that all the Communist Party had to do was to persevere in racial propaganda and thus sabotage or hijack our unity, and we would eventually destroy ourselves. And so the implementation or the injection of the principles of Dr. King's dream to improve our unity as a nation was of the utmost importance during the Cold War times of 1947 and the fall of the Soviet Union in 1991.

But today in America, we are facing another period of crisis or the danger of dying together as fools! Our nation has reached another high point of hatred and disunity. Identity politics is the order of the day. More and more people are forming exclusive political allegiances according to religion, race, social background, and so forth, and this results in them hating anyone who doesn't believe the same as they do.

And so there is division along racial lines; division between the rich and the poor; division among the Democrats and the Republicans like this nation has never seen before; and division promoted by the mainstream media like we have never seen before. Fake news— conspiracies and lying—abounds to bring down a president, a political party, or influential powerful people who don't agree with the ideology supported by a heavily biased news media. Hateful speech and violence is increasingly being supported by the mainstream media to silence people with opposing views.

Consequently, in no time in America has the importance of Dr. King's dream and its principles of unity been more necessary than it is today for restoring unity back into our nation. At no time in America has it been more important to take note of those simple but powerful words of Dr. King, who said that we must love and live together or hate and die together.[14] We need a strong injection of the dream into America today. Nobody can get along with anybody else. And a lack of unity in any nation will eventually cause its destruction.

You see, the side effects of a lack of unity in a nation or a people that progress to the point that they no longer have enough things in common to motivate them to come together for the good of their nation. This will destroy the genuine love that people have for it. And the loss of the love of a nation by its people will eventually lead to the self-destruction of such a nation.

More simply stated, without love of country, America will die by suicide! America cannot survive without our love.[15] Walt Kelly, the American creator of the comic strip *Pogo*, famously said in 1970 on an Earth Day poster:

We have met the enemy, and he is us.

This is why such things as athletes kneeling during the playing of the national anthem is so destructive to the survival of America, particularly at this fragile time in the history of our country. Dr. King never kneeled during the playing of the national anthem and/or the presentation of the American flag. He understood that we must remain unified as a nation and love America in the midst of the process of transforming her into what the Constitution and Declaration of Independence clearly state that the nation should be. The alternative is that we will be destroyed from within and die like fools.

This is the reason why Dr. King never took a knee during the playing of the national anthem. He never disrespected or dishonored the national anthem or the American flag, which symbolizes the American dream in which his God-given dream for America is so deeply rooted. The reason for his patriotic behavior is that one of Dr. King's deeply held beliefs was that the end never justifies the means. Such thinking is a major precept of the ideology of Marxists, neo-Marxists, and men like Saul Alinsky, who wrote the well-known book *Rules for Radicals: A Pragmatic Primer for Realistic Radicals*, first published in 1971. Saul Alinsky said the following in stating his antichrist ideology (1 John 2:18) relating means to ends:

> Life and how you live it is the story of means and ends. The end is what you want, and the means is how you get it. Whenever we think about social change, the question of means and ends arises. The man of action views the issue of means and ends in pragmatic and strategic terms. He asks only whether they are achievable and worth the cost; of means, only whether they will work. To say that corrupt *means* corrupt the *ends* is to believe in the immaculate conception of ends and principles.[16]

However, if you think about Dr. King's "Six Rules of Nonviolent Resistance" and his dream methods and dream goals that are explored in chapters 1 and 2—which are rooted and grounded in Scripture—the fallacy of Alinsky's ideology is conspicuously obvious. Alinsky's ideology is the antithesis or the complete opposite of the strongly biblical beliefs of Dr. King.

You see, Dr. King never took a knee during the playing of the "Star-Spangled Banner" or the presentation of the American flag because he knew that dishonoring and disrespecting the national symbols of the God-given American dream would sabotage or hijack his God-given dream for America. For the two of them are inseparably connected through the Almighty above. The only images available of Dr. King taking a knee were when he was praying!

And I submit for your consideration that if football players and other millionaire athletes would spend more time on their knees praying to the Almighty for wisdom and guidance, they would spend less time on their knees disrespecting and dishonoring the things that symbolize what God inspired the establishment of America to be! There are numerous images of Dr. King marching in protest events with several American flags in his convoy of followers. His niece Alveda King said that Dr. King *insisted* on the American flag being with them during the civil rights marches.

Along those same lines, Frederick Douglass, the renown African American social reformer, abolitionist, orator, writer, and statesman, is known by everyone of his time to have loved the "Star-Spangled Banner." In the years after the Civil War, he frequently played the "Star-Spangled Banner" on his violin for his grandchildren. Douglass said the following in 1871 in a speech at Arlington National Cemetery:

> If the Star-Spangled Banner floats over free American citizens in every quarter of the land, and our country has before it a long and glorious career of justice, liberty, and civilization, we are indebted to the unselfish devotion of the noble army.[17]

So, discerning Americans—Black and White and all the other colors—must "not become weary in doing good, for at the proper time we will reap a harvest if we do not give up" (Gal. 6:9). The very wise and spiritually discerning King Solomon said it this way in Proverbs 22:28 (NASB):

> Do not [hastily] remove the ancient boundary which your fathers have set.

Therefore, if you truly believe in the effectiveness of Dr. King's dream to reconcile all men and women to one another and heal the nation, then you must examine your talk and your actions with the following questions: (1) According to Dr. King's "Six Rules of Nonviolent Resistance" and the rest of his dream methods described in the upcoming chapters, will my behavior hijack or promote the dream? (2) According to Dr. King's "Six Rules of Nonviolent Resistance" and his dream methods, am I selfishly blowing off steam with expressions of hate toward America, or is my behavior working effectively toward solving the problem of injustice? In other words, are my actions part of the solution or part of the problem? Am I acting like a hijacker or a supporter of the dream?

That's why we must remember that without the genuine love of country in our hearts, America—and Dr. King's dream—will surely die by suicide! This means that we must look before we leap into the deceptive traps that have been set by those who are propagating the idea that the end justifies the means. We must not throw the baby out with the dirty bathwater!

Such thinking is a concept that has been rejected by the unbelieving culture in which we live or by those who traffic in the politics of hate in their ill-fated attempts to promote their humanistic version of Dr. King's dream. Christian believers must accept and support sound biblical doctrine, which clearly states that we must hate the sin and love the sinner or hate the game and love the player—less we all die as fools! The process of such a death through the hijacking of Dr. King's dream is explored in the four volumes of *Hijacked!*

In the process of exploring such a death, the readers of *Hijacked!* will see in vivid detail why unity or getting along with one another is so difficult to accomplish in America today. In preview, the reason is that Dr. King's dream has been hijacked for many years, allowing disunity and hatred to be engrained and planted within our political, social, and religious institutions of worship and higher learning like weeds in a garden. And so hijackers are most difficult to root out of our culture. Today, hijackers are as numerous as they have ever been! The weeds have almost taken control of the garden because the watchmen on the walls, the pastors and other spiritual leaders of our nation, have fallen into a spiritual stupor—knowingly or unknowingly supporting the hijackers.

And so in many cases, because of the lack of discernment by the church, the hijacking political-social-civil activists and liberal-thinking religious institutions are determining the thinking of the people who claim to be the blood-bought body of Christ.

A good example of this is that the majority of Black Christians who attend traditional Black churches in America are confused about the spiritual content and substance of Dr. King's dream. They are confused about what it means and how they should apply it to their daily Christian lives and their politics in particular. And so they are disconnected from the effective spiritual meaning of Dr. King's God-given plan of how to make his dream an effective reality in their lives and an effective reality in the American culture. Dr. King's dream has been hijacked by spiritual leaders and the political, social, and civil activists who believers have allowed to influence their thinking. And if this is true for Black Christians, it is for sure and for certain true for Blacks who are not Christians, which is to be expected.

However, the sad thing is that many Black Christians don't seem to have any more spiritual discernment about the fact that Dr. King's dream has been hijacked in the past and is currently being hijacked than unbelievers or Blacks who are not Christians. Many Black believers don't have any more discernment than unbelievers about the hijack of Dr. King's dream that has turned his dream into a nightmare in our culture. They look at all the churches in cities where the hijacking is so obvious and don't realize that the reason is that Dr. King's dream is not being implemented according to the sound doctrine of the Word of God in those cities. They say that institutional racism is the cause of all the Black-on-Black murders, crime, and poverty instead of the institutional hijacking of Dr. King's dream. This is what has really turned those cities into a nightmare, which is spreading like a cancer into the rest of the American culture.

And the reason why I know that this is absolutely true—for sure and for certain—is that, as the LORD said through the prophet Isaiah,

> My word that goes out from my mouth: It will not return to me empty, but will accomplish what I desire and achieve the purpose for which I sent it. (Isa. 55:11)

We must walk by faith and not by sight until what God has promised us becomes a reality. This is the shocking truth that I have experienced during my years as one who has both Christians and unbelievers as associates and friends, some of whom are pastors like myself.

Likewise, a similar spiritual stupor and a lack of spiritual discernment can be attributed to White or other non-Black believers. In a nutshell, the traditional Black church is not the only part of the body of Christ that has participated in the hijack of Dr. King's dream. And this will indeed lead to the destruction of the American dream that Dr. King held so dear to him and proclaimed with love in numerous sermons and speeches. The virtual destruction of both Dr. King's dream and the American dream will occur, for sure and for certain, if the Black church and the White church—if the church—doesn't recover from the hijack of Dr. King's dream.

You see, we have all played a part in turning Dr. King's dream into a nightmare, either by the sin of omission or commission, due to a lack of discernment and permitting the infiltration of humanistic and worldly ideologies and philosophies into the congregations of the body of Christ.

So, it can be most accurately stated that it is *not* structural, institutionalized, or systemic racism in America that caused the nightmare that many are experiencing in America today. The nightmare is clearly the result of both the intentionally and unintentionally structural, institutionalized, or systemic hijacking of Dr. King's dream. This is demonstrated either explicitly or implicitly in the exploration of *The Dream, The Hijack, The Nightmare,* and *The Recovery.*

But briefly, the reason why this is true is that there are some very strong political and ideological (and spiritual) forces that exist in our nation that can't afford to allow Dr. King's dream to become a reality if they want to stay in power and maintain control over America and its people. What I am saying is that the reasons for the hijack and the forces behind the hijack are deeper or more complex than most of the American people are capable of perceiving. This is true because of the limited knowledge of the history of our nation and current events that most Americans possess. There are some evil, wicked, and godless forces at work in our nation that are trying to fundamentally change America not for God's glory but for theirs. And they are not willing to let Dr. King's God-given dream for America get in their way of doing this without a fight. The Apostle Paul said the following, which should help motivate readers to partake of the journey that is explored in *Hijacked!*

> And do this, understanding the present time: The hour has already come for you to wake up from your slumber, because our salvation is nearer now than when we first believed. The night is nearly over; the day is almost here. So let us put aside the deeds of darkness and put on the armor of light … clothe yourselves with the LORD Jesus Christ, and do not think about how to gratify the desires of the flesh. (Rom. 13:11–12, 14)

The Conspiracy to Discredit Dr. King's Dream

It is now time to move on and start exploring the details of Dr. King's dream. But before doing that, there is one thing that remains to be done. And that is this. As you might have known, that old ancient serpent Satan, who is called the devil, is always going to do everything and use everybody that he can to hijack Dr. King's dream by trying to discredit its validity. That's where he starts, just like he did with God's Word way back in the book of Genesis. And the way that Satan has done this in relation to Dr. King's dream is that he has used influential people—people who are believed to be trustworthy by others—to propagate a big lie about Dr. King's dream.

And that lie is that there are some things that people got wrong about Martin Luther King Jr., that he became more radical or, for example, that he approved of riots toward the end of his life. But this is a lie straight from the pit of hell, and the devil is its author! This is the lie that people tell when they don't want to follow the principles that God provided for America through Dr. King for making his dream a reality. This is the lie that people propagate when they want to lean on their own understanding in the conduct of civil rights activities to change America and do it in the name of Dr. King. They want to use their methods—in Dr. King's name—to give credibility to their godless feelings, behavior, and thinking.

For example, during the riots after the torturous, sadistic murder of George Floyd by a Minneapolis White policeman, there was a protestor/

rioter who said, "Dr. King said, 'A riot is the language of the unheard.'" But that was only a small part of what Dr. King said about riots. A more complete expression of Dr. King's sentiments about riots is given in his speech titled "The Other America,"[18] which was delivered on April 14, 1967, at Stanford University, a little less than a year before his death. In this speech, not only did Dr. King say what was said by the protestor/rioter, but before he said this, Dr. King said that riots are destructive and self-defeating to the cause of seeking social reforms.

More specifically, what Dr. King said was that riots thwart—hinder or prevent—the objectives of social and economic reforms. They defeat the very objectives or purpose that the participants in riots claim to be attempting to achieve. Dr. King stated in this speech that he was still convinced that the most effective weapon that people can employ for achieving social and economic justice is nonviolent resistance.

So, whether you are a person who acknowledges the great advancements that African Americans have made in America over the past fifty years since Dr. King's death or you are in denial about this or think that things are progressing too slowly, there is no evidence that Dr. King ever abandoned his view on nonviolent protest. Dr. King's dream contains the *goals* that must be achieved and the *methods* that must be employed to fix what is wrong with America. He maintained, until his death on April 4, 1968, that nonviolent protest was the only solution to making his dream a reality in America. And he had good reasons for believing this because his nonviolent resistance was the only way that has ever succeeded. Groups such as the Chicago branch of Black Lives Matter want to reclaim Dr. King "under a different image: the image of a forceful radical"[19] (#ReclaimMLK hashtag on Twitter).

Nonetheless, there is a simple question that will thwart the conspiracy to discredit Dr. King's dream methods so that evil methods can be employed in his name. You simply need to ask the question, "Would Dr. King support the tactics, for example, that Black Lives Matter (BLM) employs in its attempts to bring about social justice?"

In other words, would Dr. King support Black Lives Matter protestors against police brutality carrying signs that said and chanting, "Pigs in a blanket, fry 'em like bacon" in St. Paul, Minnesota, in 2015 and "What do we want? Dead cops! When do we want them? Now!" in New York City in

2014 and Baton Rouge, Louisiana, and Dallas, Texas, in 2016? No! I don't think that the "radical" Dr. King would support such behavior!

What this means is that young and old activists, Black and White, want to embrace the more forceful, determined Dr. King who demanded justice for the oppressed. But they want to reject the loving forgiveness of Dr. King that prompted him to say in July 1967, in response to the Detroit riots, that violence not only begets or reaps violence in return, but when you sow the wind, you reap the whirlwind (cf., Hosea 8:7). In response to the Detroit riots, Dr. King was provoked to warn that violence magnifies or proliferates violence. And this multiplication of violence causes the problems that were trying to be resolved, to intensify and produce a state of affairs that is much worse than it was before the riots.[20]

Also, as recorded in David J. Garrow's *Bearing the Cross: Martin Luther King, Jr., and the Southern Christian Leadership Conference*, Dr. King said that he would take his stand for nonviolent resistance with him to his grave.[21]

Likewise, a few months later—on the night before his death—Dr. King said the following as a strong confirmation of his irreversible nonviolence stand before a jam-packed audience in Memphis, Tennessee. He said that the crossroads that America faces is not the choice between nonviolence or violence but the choice between nonviolence or no longer existing as a blessed or exceptional nation of people that possess the favor of God upon them.[22]

Now pause and think about what you have thus far read in this section of the introduction. There are people who embrace Dr. King's tough love, but they reject his tender love—which is the same thing that these people do to the two sides of God's love. As you explore Dr. King's dream, the above unchanging statements on his feelings, behavior, and thinking for bringing about change will become crystal clear. The Holy Spirit will make it clear that throughout Dr. King's entire life, until the moment of his death, he proclaimed his belief that violence cannot destroy hate or eliminate darkness. It only increases these things. Only love and light can destroy hate and eliminate darkness. Only love and light can change enemies into friends and make the dream a reality in America.[23]

David Chappell, a professor of history at the University of Oklahoma and author of *Waking from the Dream: The Struggle for Civil Rights in* the Shadow of Martin Luther King, Jr., made an insightful comment on this. He said the following in an article printed on January 15, 2018, in the *Washington Post,* titled "The Radicalism of Martin Luther King, Jr.'s Nonviolent Resistance":

> Each year, Americans remember the Rev. Martin Luther King Jr. as an inspirational orator who exhorted them to live up to their most generous ideals. Guardians of King's legacy—such as the radical sociologist and activist Michael Eric Dyson—cringe at this depiction. They complain that the media focus on anodyne excerpts from King's famous "Dream" speech, which distort his true message and legacy: an urgent demand for long-overdue economic justice and power ... But even their more radical interpretation of King's message tends to dull and displace the great power that King's life properly symbolizes. *What distinguished King is not the ends he articulated, but the means he created, tested and perfected in pursuit of those ends* ... supporters and critics ... at the time recognized that "nonviolence"—which was a method rather than a goal—was the heart of his work and his rhetorical appeals.[24]

Note that just like today, even though most of the people of Dr. King's time recognized that nonviolent protest was the focal point of his work, either they did not understand how and why it was successful or they did not except it. This was definitely the case with some of his African American rivals for Black leadership, which included such men as Black Panther leaders Huey Newton and Eldridge Cleaver. But nobody could deny that his tactic of nonviolent protest worked and that it brought about "revolutionary" changes in America.[25]

So, what all this tells us is this. There is the Dr. King that some people want him to be. And then there is the Dr. King who is what he is and was always that way. Don't buy into the deceitful lies of those who have hijacked the dream in their attempts to justify leaning on their own futile understanding. Swift social changes occurred before Dr. King's death.

However, after Dr. King's death, lesser men occupied Black leadership positions. Men with lesser spiritual integrity arrived on the political and social scene of America to take Dr. King's place. These men rose to leadership positions in the Black community, accompanied by their conspiracies and hidden agendas of personal wealth, power, and a more radical approach or methodology for civil rights actions. They replaced the strict adherence to Dr. King's dream methods with their own ideas about the methods that should be employed to make the dream a reality. They tried to fix something that wasn't broken and implemented their fix in the name of Dr. King. And to this day, they have not figured out what they are doing wrong or how they have hijacked Dr. King's dream!

You see, a dream that is received from God, as was the case with Dr. King's dream, does not change with time.

Thus the hijack started and snowballed out of control after Dr. King's death, not yet to be recovered from. One such hijacker who has propagated the narrative that Dr. King became more radical and abandoned some of his core beliefs toward the end of his life is Michael Eric Dyson. Dyson is a professor of sociology at Georgetown University and the author of *Tears We Cannot Stop: A Sermon to White America*.

And I must say that the reason why the tears of some Black people can't stop is that they refuse to obey Dr. King's dream methods and abandon their angry, unforgiving, hateful spirits. You would think that such a man as Dyson, who has been an ordained Baptist minister for thirty-five years, would know—as Dr. King surely did—that what God gives you will stand the test of time. Wow! This is such a basic truth of the Christian faith. Dr. King did not have the option of abandoning any part or portion of what he received from God, regardless of whether it seemed to be effective or not. Dyson and others do not seem to understand this spiritual principle.

Along these lines, in a video produced by Emmanuel Ocbazghi,[26] Michael Eric Dyson made some accusations that appear to be an attempt to show how his image of Dr. King as a radical has been "whitewashed."[27] To Dyson's general accusation that people are in denial about some supposed radical aspects of Dr. King's character, again I say the following. There is the Dr. King that some people want him to be, and then there is the Dr. King who was what he was and maintained his God-given core values expressed in his dream until the day he died.

Also, to Dyson's accusation in the video transcript that Dr. King did not, as most Americans believe, maintain the same beliefs that he delineated in his 1963 "I Have a Dream" speech throughout his entire life—"As if we had already in America come to a point where we were no longer judging people by the color of their skin but by the content of their character" [28]—I say this. This is a typical example of what I previously mentioned about those who are trying to radicalize Dr. King's latter years. Dr. King and everyone who heard him knew that his dream was an aspiration and definitely not an achievement. Why would he say, "I have a dream," if it was already an achievement instead of an aspiration? Why Dyson would say this, I really don't know. Taking into consideration Dyson's undisputable knowledge and intellect, the only reason that is plausible is that it was said to deceive, manipulate, and discredit Dr. King's original dream and thus promote the idea of the need for a more radical dream.

So, it should be noted that if you read Dr. King's writings from the beginning of his civil rights activities to his death, you will see that neither his dream goals nor his dream methods (volume 1, chapters 1–7) changed in their essential nature. In the transcript of this video, Dyson spoke of a speech in which Dr. King said that his dream had turned into a nightmare. But even though this is true, it doesn't not mean that Dr. King sought to change either his God-given dream goals or the God-given dream methods God gave him to achieve them. Again, this seems to be, in my opinion, another clear attempt by Dyson to justify his dream-killing behavior and that of others. This appears to be an attempt to discourage people so that they would use other methods in their efforts to bring about change in America, none of which has worked or will ever work, because God is not in them.

Other attempts by Dyson in this video that have the appearance of an intense effort to get people to abandon Dr. King's ideology of nonviolence and to embrace him as a radical are his accusations that America has not acknowledged the humanity of Black people. Along with this is his biased and incomplete commentary on a portion of a speech in which Dr. King expressed riots as being the language of the unheard. My response to these accusations is that, number one, neither of them prove that Dr. King was more radical at the end of his life than he was when he gave his "I Have a

Dream" speech in 1963. And number two, if you read Dr. King's speech titled "The Other America" (which I mentioned on page XXXIII), it is obvious that he was merely making an observation and not proclaiming a justification for riots or violence. Just prior to making the statement that riots were the language of the unheard, Dr. King had made it unmistakably clear—with many words—that riots were destructive and self-defeating and that they created more problems than they solved.[29]

Furthermore, to the accusation that conservatives and right-wingers have attempted to whitewash Dr. King's memory of the "social context of his racial ideas,"[30] my rebuttal is the following. Dyson is accusing others of distorting Dr. King's memory by whitewashing it, which is the exact thing that he himself is doing. The difference is that, in Dyson's vernacular, he is "blackwashing" Dr. King's memory, which has the effect of bringing Dr. King's dream down to the spiritual level of others like himself who have chosen not to seek Dr. King's dream goals or to employ Dr. King's dream methods to fix what is wrong with America.

The final Dyson accusation in this video is that there came a point in Dr. King's life when he began to say that most Americans were unconsciously racists. Dyson planted the seed that in later years, Dr. King believed that most Americans were subconsciously programmed to be racists. And again, this appears to be an attempt to prove that a more radical approach than Dr. King's original God-given goals and methods, which he wrote about so abundantly, was needed to bring about change in America.

However, if you read the numerous writings of Dr. King up until the time that he took his last breath of air on this earth, what will be revealed to you is this. Dr. King began to more and more understand the depth of the race problems in America. And this increased his understanding of how radically obedient he must be in employing the methods that God gave him to effect change in America.

Thus, contrary to Dyson's analysis, Dr. King's increased understanding of the race problem in America did not make him want to be more radical in a worldly or ungodly manner and start leaning on his own understanding. Dyson believes that the acceptance of Dr. King as a radical—or that he no longer fully believed in his six rules for nonviolent resistance in later years—is the effective way to fix what is wrong with America. But the truth is that only when you start *radically* executing Dr. King's dream methods toward the achievement of his dream goals will Black people specifically and Americans in general become successful in making Dr. King's dream a reality in America.

The deception of angry, unforgiving, hateful influential people in America, who delusionally believe that they have a plan for bringing about changes in America that is better than Dr. King's God-given plan, is one of the chief methods by which the dream that is explored in this four-volume literary work is being hijacked! And all this is done in the name of Dr. King. In his book *Tears We Cannot Stop: A Sermon to White America*, Dyson appears to attempt to lay a foundation that would convince people that Dr. King had become a radical toward the end of his life. In doing this, it appears that Dyson attempted to justify the employment of feelings, behavior, and thinking for bringing about positive change in America that are substantially inferior to the spiritual and moral high ground delineated by Dr. King's dream. The exploration of Dr. King's dream methods and dream goals (primarily in *The Dream*, volume 1) reveals just how severely Dyson and others have hijacked the dream by not adhering to Dr. King's teachings for civil rights activism to achieve social justice.

So my prayer is that the foregoing discussion will make you watchful for those who have hidden agendas to discredit Dr. King's powerful and effective dream methods and dream goals that are explored in the four volumes of *Hijacked!*

Now onward to a journey—starting with *The Dream*, volume 1, chapter 1—that will forever change your feelings, behavior, and thinking about Dr. King, the power of his dream, and a solution for making it a reality in your life and America in particular—like you probably have not imagined.

Note: The table of contents of the other three volumes of *Hijacked!* are provided in the appendix of this volume. This allows readers of *Hijacked!* to obtain some helpful before-and-after context for a deeper understanding of this volume when some of the other three volumes have not been read. The table of contents of this volume contains the page number of the table of contents of the other volumes that are located in the appendix.

THE DREAM: WHAT IS THE CONTENT OF DR. KING'S DREAM—ITS METHODS AND GOALS?

1

THE METHODS CONTENT TO BE IMPLEMENTED: DREAM METHOD 1—RIGHTEOUSNESS, FORGIVENESS, PERSEVERANCE

What is the content of Dr. King's dream? This is where you are right now in the process of discovering whether you as a reader of *Hijacked!* are contributing to the process of making the dream a reality or contributing to the hijack. So let's start the process of exploring the content of the dream by first examining Dr. King's most well-known speech, in which he proclaimed to the world that he had a dream for Blacks and for America in general. And that speech of course was titled "I Have a Dream"!

This speech was given during the March on Washington, DC, on August 28, 1963, at the Lincoln Memorial before what looked like a sea of people (about 250,000) and the entire nation via Television cameras. The March on Washington was the first large march of Blacks and Whites, people of all colors, together for a common cause. It took place on the steps of the Lincoln Memorial after Dr. King and other civil rights leaders had met with President John F. Kennedy.[1] So what are the elements of Dr. King's dream that can be gleaned from this message to the nation? Also, what are the principles that Dr. King revealed in this speech for effectively implementing the dream?

You see, the dream is no good unless it is effectively implemented. And so the dream and its implementation are the two sides of the dream coin—if you will. This means that you cannot separate one from the other. You cannot split the coin. It's a unit.

Therefore, when I talk about the content of the dream, I am referring to the elements, the various aspects, or the goals of the dream. But I am also referring to the methods or the actions and attitude that must be employed to make the goals of the dream a reality. Carefully note that Dr. King's dream was given to him by God. This means that God's will must be done His way or by using His methods, which is what Dr. King's dream is all about.

So, again I say, What are the elements of Dr. King's dream that we can glean from his message to the nation? And what are the principles that Dr. King provided in his speech for effectively implementing the dream?

Well, the speech or message "I Have a Dream," can be broken into three parts: (1) the introduction, in which Dr. King started where the American people were spiritually and then brought them to where God wanted them to be so that he could tell them what God told him to tell them; (2) the methods of implementation of the dream, where Dr. King proclaimed to the American people the God-given essential actions and attitudes of daily life for making the dream or dream goals a reality; and (3) the goals of the dream, where Dr. King proclaimed to the American people the God-given goals that they should strive to achieve with an expected guarantee of being successful if they diligently used or employed the methods given to them by Dr. King for daily living.

Dr. King provided a stirring, momentous introduction of the dream to get his massive audience on board as to exactly why the March on

HIJACKED!

Washington, DC, was so absolutely necessary. He talked about what happened one hundred years ago or "five score years ago," which was a direct reference to the year 1863 when President Abraham Lincoln delivered the Gettysburg Address and signed the Emancipation Proclamation. Dr. King noted that one hundred years later after signing that document, it had still not been fulfilled and that this was the reason for the occasion—to dramatize the disgraceful dilemma of the Negro that still existed. He said that the Constitution and the Declaration of Independence were a promissory note whose obligations to Black people had not been executed.[2]

Furthermore, in the introduction to "I Have a Dream," Dr. King dramatically stated that Negroes refuse to believe that America's default on its promissory note was due to the bank of justice being bankrupted of opportunities. And that until the words "insufficient funds" that had been falsely written on the promissory note to the Negro since 1863 was resolved, there would be neither a breather from protest nor the quietness of serenity in America.[3]

Now this small portion of the introduction to "I Have a Dream" doesn't carry with it the full heart-tugging effect as Dr. King presented it. But I think that it is enough to give readers of *Hijacked!* somewhat of a feeling for the moment on that day, August 28, 1963, when one of the world's greatest orators stood before 250,000 people and prepared them to hear what God had put on his heart to tell them. Dr. King told this massive crowd of Black and White Americans that stood before him (and the nation) that it was long overdue for America to become the people that we professed to be. He said that there was really no justifiable excuse for the shameful, hypocritical condition that existed in such a prosperous nation that bragged to other nations about its love for freedom.

So what did Dr. King tell us about how his dream must be implemented in order for the goals of the dream to become a reality? What did Dr. King tell us about the methods or the behavior and attitudes of people and groups that must be employed in order to achieve the various goals of his dream? After the introduction to "I Have a Dream," Dr. King put forward what I am calling three "dream methods"—dream methods 1, 2, and 3. These implementation methods can be used to determine whether you are a part of the solution for fulfilling the dream or a part of the problem that is working to hijack the dream.

Dr. King said, from which can be extracted the contents of dream method 1, that in the process of getting the promissory note to Black people fulfilled, we must do it in a way that is beyond reproach or in the most *righteous* way. He said that it must be done without bitterness or hatred, which means that we must bestow *forgiveness* to America and everyone that we feel participated in the failure to fulfill the promissory note to the Negro.[4] So, from this, Dr. King gave us the two elements of *righteous* and *forgiveness*.

And then he added a third element to dream method 1 when he said after this that some people are asking the enthusiastic followers of the civil rights movement about when they will be satisfied with the plight of Negroes in America. In answering this question, Dr. King recited a list of things that included an end to police brutality, not having access to motels and hotels, ghetto living in the North and "For White Only" signs in the South, and not having voting rights or a reason to vote.[5]

He then summarized this list with the text of Amos 5:24, which says, "But let justice run down like water, and righteousness like a mighty stream." Dr. King's answer from Amos 5:24 to the question of when will the devotees of the civil rights movement be satisfied with the plight of Black people in America was—not until "justice rolls down like waters and righteousness like a mighty stream."[6] So we have the third element, which is *perseverance*.

Thus, the three elements of dream method 1 are *righteousness, forgiveness,* and *perseverance*.

Righteousness

Dr. King proclaimed first of all in dream method 1 that *righteousness* must be maintained in the pursuit of justice and any other goals of the dream. This means that the end (the goals of the dream) can never be legitimately used to justify the means or the methods used to make the dream a reality in our lives and the nation.

In other words, the means/methods by which we attempt to make the dream a reality must be rooted and grounded in the sound doctrine of God's Word. Simply put, what God hates we must hate and not support in any way whatsoever. That's righteousness! Solomon said under the unction of the Holy Spirit in expressing some of the things that God hates,

> These six things the LORD hates, Yes, seven are an abomination [detestable] to Him:
> A proud look,
> A lying tongue,
> Hands that shed innocent blood [abortion/prochoice supporters],
> A heart that devises wicked plans,
> Feet that are swift in running to evil,
> A false witness who speaks lies,
> And one who sows discord [stirs up conflict, disunity] among brethren. (Prov. 6:16–19)

And note that in the Beatitudes, Jesus promised great blessings to those who hate what God hates, to those who pursue righteousness. He said,

> Blessed are those [Oh, the favor of God that those will receive] who hunger [like someone starving] and thirst [like someone in a dry desert] for righteousness [God's righteousness instead of their own self-righteousness]. For they shall be filled [with what they are seeking]. (Matt. 5:6)

Even more specifically, Jesus expressed to His disciples and some onlookers the priority of seeking righteousness or why it was so absolutely important to seek it first—above all other things! He proclaimed to them this most important biblical principle in chapter 6 of the Sermon on the Mount. He said in expressing this sole method by which anyone can be blessed and have all their needs met all the time:

> But seek first the kingdom of God and His righteousness, and these things [the things of life that are needed to fulfill Dr. King's dream] shall be added to you. (Matt. 6:33)

In other words, God's will, His way, and His Word must be number one. Righteousness must have the priority or be the filter in determining the methods that we use to make the dream a reality. For without the element of righteousness, the dream can never become a reality in the lives of either Black, White, Brown, Red, or Yellow Americans.

Therefore, it becomes most obvious why Dr. King said in dream method 1 that we must not be satisfied in America until "justice rolls down like waters *and* righteousness like a mighty stream"[7] (Amos 5:24). Justice is undeniably connected to righteousness in an unbreakable bond. The two are inseparable. In a nation where there is no righteousness, there will not be any justice. So, one could very appropriately say, "No Jesus! No justice!" In a nation where the people don't hate what God hates, there will not be any consistent and long-term justice. Paul said it this way:

> Now the LORD is the Spirit; and where the Spirit of the LORD is, there is liberty [There is freedom—there is justice.]. (2 Cor. 3:17)

Digging even deeper into the relationship that exists between justice and righteousness, what all this means is that justice and righteousness are supernaturally connected together by the power of God. And so justice cannot exist without the existence or the practice of a righteous standard of living by the people of a nation.

Likewise, the practice of a righteous standard of living cannot exist without justice also existing for all the people of a nation. You can't genuinely have one without the other.

Furthermore, take note that justice and righteousness feed on each other. What I mean by this is that *the more of one of them that a nation possesses the more of the other one that exists within a nation.* This is what is called the turbocharger effect between sanctification and the blessings of God or between righteousness and justice in regard to the subject matter at hand. Take note that the turbocharger effect applies to the individual people of a nation, and thus it also applies to the particular nation that such individuals populate. Dr. Henry Holloman, professor of systematic theology at Talbot School of Theology at Biola University in La Mirada, California, talked about the turbocharger effect in the following way in his book *The Forgotten Blessing: Rediscovering the Transforming Power of Sanctification*:

> When we study and practice sanctification [spiritual growth], we receive God's blessings. These blessings benefit our sanctification much as a turbo charger benefits a car. The engine's exhaust powers the turbocharger, and the turbocharger greatly boosts the engine's power. So when you accelerate your sanctification, you boost your blessings, and in turn they boost your sanctification. This win-win cycle between spiritual growth [sanctification] and spiritual blessings should encourage us to grow more in Christ.[8]

The turbocharger effect tell us, without any doubt, that when righteousness flows throughout our nation "like a mighty stream," then justice will roll down throughout our nation "like waters."[9] Justice and righteousness feed on each other. One supernaturally begets the other.

However, carefully note that you must start the sanctification-blessing turbocharger engine—the righteousness-justice turbocharger engine—by seeking righteousness *first*, as we are told in Matthew 6:33. *You absolutely cannot start the righteousness-justice turbocharger engine by first seeking justice!* Now why is this so absolutely true?

The reason why this is so absolutely true is that justice cannot be maintained or perpetuated—no matter how hard you might try—without righteousness. "Justice without righteousness" is somewhat like an oxymoron. It is a concept that is made up from contradictory elements, like the expression "He is a wise fool." For you cannot be a fool and wise at the same time. And neither can a nation possess perpetual justice without righteousness. Seeking to establish justice in a nation without righteousness as the foundation of the nation is a moronic endeavor of the highest order, which has been proven by the fall of mighty nations in the past. And sadly, I must say that this is the major source of the hijack of Dr. King's dream as well as the hijack of the American dream.

You see, where there is little or no or an anemic state of righteousness, there is nothing for justice to feed on to keep it alive. Sin starves out justice. Solomon was spot-on when he said this:

> Righteousness exalts a nation, but sin condemns any people. (Prov. 14:34)

So, what does a righteousness-justice engine look like that is trying to be started by seeking justice first instead of by seeking righteousness first (Matt. 6:33)?

Well, such an engine will just spit fire, sputter, emit smoke, move the nation herky-jerky down the road, and break down on frequent occasions. It will never make justice roll down throughout our nation "like waters," because righteousness won't be given the first priority so that it flows throughout our nation "like a mighty stream."[10] C. S. Lewis said so appropriately in commenting on Matthew 6:33,

> Aim at heaven and you will get earth thrown in; aim at earth and you will get neither.

So whose responsibility is it to be the salt and light in setting the example to pursue justice by aiming at righteousness first?

This is not a trick question. But it needs to be explored just a little bit because so many believers don't seem to have any more discernment about the methods that should be employed in pursuing justice and other aspects of the dream than unbelievers. The world has infiltrated the church to the extent that the church has allowed the unbelieving world to set the standards or to establish the methods by which the dream is pursued.

However, this was clearly rebuked by the Lord when He appeared to Solomon in the temple in Jerusalem and said this to him:

> When I shut up heaven and there is no rain, or command the locusts to devour the land, or send pestilence among My people, if My people who are called by My name will humble themselves, and pray and seek My face, and turn from their wicked ways, then I will hear from heaven, and will forgive their sin and heal their land. (2 Chron. 7:13–14)

This text makes it clear that it is the responsibility of the blood-bought church to set the example of pursuing justice by aiming at righteousness first. This text also helps to explain why Peter said that judgment will "begin at the house of God" (1 Pet. 4:17). For God has clearly revealed Himself to us in His Word. The church therefore has no excuse for not pursuing the dream by seeking righteousness first and for not being the salt and the light of the earth by encouraging others to do this also.

Moreover, I think that it is most appropriate to say that Black Christians have an even greater obligation for setting the example to pursue justice—or any other goals of the dream—by aiming at righteousness first. Now, why do I say that? Am I trying to put a guilt trip on Black Christians for the slow pace at which the dream is being achieved? No!

But the reality is that the dream came through Dr. King specifically and through Black people in general, just like the Bible came into the world through Israel. God used Israel, His chosen people, to accomplish His sovereign plan for the whole world. And to whom much is given, much is expected.

So think about this. Black people are not God's chosen people, but we are His special people. And He has given us the dream—its methods of achievement and its goals—to pass on to the rest of the world. There are no other people so distinctively marked physically as a means of setting a people apart so that such people would have the ability to be a showcase for demonstrating the dream—its methods of achievement and its goals—to pass onto the world.

Therefore, this means that God expects much from Black Christians—more from us in the process of setting the example to pursue justice by aiming at righteousness first than from other members of the body of Christ. We must set an excellent example of hating everything that God hates—first—and not just injustice. We cannot hate just some of the things that God hates and turn a blind eye to or overlook some other things that God hates in an attempt to receive justice. Think deeply about that, my Black Christian brothers and sisters. When you are God's chosen people, like the Jews, or God's special people—like I sincerely believe that African American Christian people are—then much, much more is expected from you!

Much, much more is expected than the formality of going through the motions of being a faithful Christian by going to church on Sunday and then living like Satan himself in other areas of life when you leave the church house. The LORD said through the prophet Amos in what was evidently a passage of Scripture that spoke to Dr. King's heart because he used a portion of it in his "I Have a Dream" speech:

> I hate, I despise your feast days, and I do not savor your sacred assemblies. Though you offer Me burnt offerings and your grain offerings, I will not accept them, nor will I regard your fattened peace offerings. Take away from Me the noise of your songs, for I will not hear the melody of your stringed instruments. *But let justice run down like water and righteousness like a mighty stream.* (Amos 5:21–24; italics added)

Thus, it is obvious that the Lord was not just talking to White Christians but to Black Christians as well in the Amos text. This text in Amos concerning the fact that genuine worship—true worship—must be an overflow of holiness or righteousness is for the entire body of Christ. This is true regardless of whatever kind of pain or suffering or oppression a particular part of the body of Christ might have experienced in the past. If anything, it applies much more to those whom God has chartered with the task of leading the efforts of passing on the dream to the rest of the world.

Forgiveness

Moving on, in addition to the above, Dr. King implied in dream method 1 that *forgiveness* is not optional! Although forgiveness is a part of what it means to be righteous, it is important that it is emphasized by expressing it as a separate element apart from righteousness.

You see, we must forgive everybody of everything! We unequivocally must not drink from "the cup of bitterness and hatred." And genuine forgiveness is the only cure for bitterness and hatred. Paul confirmed this when he said,

> Let all bitterness, wrath, anger, clamor, and evil speaking be put away from you, with all malice. And be kind to one another, tenderhearted, forgiving one another, even as God in Christ forgave you. (Eph. 4:31–32)

Dr. King said the following in helping to explain the importance of working hard until forgiveness has been installed in a person's heart, mind, and soul. He said that forgiveness is a permanent state of mind and not something that is characterized by random or sporadic behavior that depends on which way the political winds are blowing on a certain day.[11] Walter E. Jacobson, MD, stated this dream method principle of forgiveness this way:

> Forgiveness needs to be a Way of Life. It needs to be who we are. Day by day. Minute by minute ... The world needs each and every one of us to practice forgiveness in some form as best we can [neuroplasticity—Romans 12:2] ... It behooves each and every one of us to do the best we can today and every day to dislodge even a smidge of our anger and judgment by extending a forgiving thought to another ... It requires you and I making a conscious effort to extend compassion, acceptance and forgiveness despite any unwillingness to do so.[12]

From the above, it is clear that we must fake it until we make it. And for Christians, this means that we must *faith* it until we make it. We must exercise forgiveness to whatever extent that we can so that a forgiving spirit or the attitude of forgiveness can grow within us and become a natural part of us. The scientific principle of neuroplasticity that Paul describes in Romans 12:2 tells us that the brain, the part that is described as the subconscious mind where automatic flight-or-fight instructions are generated, molds or reprograms itself in response to what it experiences. And so we must exercise our brains with as much forgiveness as we can right now. In this way, over time, we will reprogram our brains to have a permanent state of mind or attitude of forgiveness for the things done to us in the past, present, and future. Paul said in Romans 12:2,

> Do not conform to the pattern of this world [Do not practice the behavior and customs of this world], but be transformed by the renewing of your mind [by the reprogramming of your mind through the mechanism of neuroplasticity]. (NIV)

So many people are stuck with an attitude of unforgiveness because of what was done to them or their ancestors. But over and over again, Scripture makes it clear that if we don't forgive others, God will not forgive us of our sins (Matt. 6:14–15). In other words, the presence of God and the blessings that His presence can bring into our lives for our success and prosperity and to heal our wounded, broken hearts and spirits—this won't be possible when we are not willing or don't have a desire to forgive everybody of everything. This is true regardless of how heinous a thing someone might have done to you or your ancestors—like the dastardly, shameful deeds of slavery that were perpetrated against Black Americans; the deeds of the Jim Crow era in the South; and the insensitive, evil deeds of racism in other parts of the nation!

In other words, the sin of unforgiveness is just as evil in the eyes of God as the most heinous thing that was done to you by someone. And so it doesn't take much imagination to understand that unforgiveness is a major contributor—if not the most significant contributor—of the hijack of Dr. King's dream in America today. The dream buster of unforgiveness is occurring in the Black community and other ethnic communities as well. Thus all Americans must be forever mindful that we must forgive everybody of everything. For, together we will stand, and divided we will surely fall. Paul said,

> Do not repay anyone evil for evil. Be careful to do what is right in the eyes of everyone … Do not take revenge, my dear friends, but leave room for God's wrath, for it is written: "It is mine to avenge; I will repay, says the LORD. On the contrary: "If your enemy is hungry feed him; if he is thirsty, give him something to drink. In doing this, you will heap burning coals on his head [You will bring a sense of guilt and shame to such people because of the hate that they have in their hearts for you]." Do not be overcome by evil, but overcome evil with good. (Rom. 12:17, 19–21)

The well-known life and leadership coach and author of *Born to Win*, Dr. Promod Batra (1936–2016), said the following very wise comment about forgiveness and revenge:

> An eye for an eye sounds good, but it leaves everybody blind! ... Revenge is like biting a dog because the dog bit you. You should not forget it only [to] ensure that you are not bitten again; but instead of biting back, learn from the incident.[13]

I see a whole lot of angry Black people who are "biting the dog" because of what was done to Blacks in the past in America. But they won't admit it. However, their feelings, behavior, and thinking tell another story. Sadly enough, some of these people claim to love the LORD thy God with all their heart and mind! Still yet, such people don't seem to realize that "biting the dog that bit them" is hijacking Dr. King's dream.

You see, hate and unforgiveness or revenge do not do anything but cause damage to the hearts and minds of the people of our nation—both Black and White—damage to the dream of making us one. People who are willing to bite the dog that bit them seem to be willing to cut off their noses in order to spite their faces.

The reason why such people are so willing to engage in hijacking, dream-busting behavior—such as biting the dog that bit them—is that they have been greatly wounded by the American experience. Their woundedness and/or the lack of spiritual discernment has made such people extremely vulnerable to the deception and manipulation of many in our culture—both Black and White elitists. Both Black and White elitists are using or playing such dog-biting people—both Black and White—to promote their hidden agenda of personal gain and/or the advancement of a destructive ideology. And this elitist ideology is destructive to both Dr. King's dream and the American dream, which are inseparably connected, as you will see in the exploration of dream goals.

Perseverance

Now, there is still one more element in dream method 1, which tells us that we must persevere in order to make the dream a reality in our lives and the nation in general. When Dr. King and the civil rights activists were asked when they would be satisfied, Dr. King's answer was not until "justice rolls down like waters and righteousness like a mighty stream"

(Amos 5:24). Therefore, it is most obvious that *perseverance* is a key element in dream method 1.

Simply put, perseverance is indeed a key element that must be employed in every method used in the process of making Dr. King's dream a reality in the lives of the people of our nation. You can't be blessed if you don't persevere in dream methods 1, 2, and 3. The writer of Hebrews said it this way in encouraging believers to persevere:

> For we know Him who said, "Vengeance is Mine, I will repay," says the LORD. And again, "The LORD will judge His people." It is a fearful thing to fall into the hands of the living God. But recall the former days in which, after you were illuminated [received the light], you endured a great struggle with sufferings: partly while you were made a spectacle both by reproaches [insult] and tribulations [persecution], and partly while you became companions of those who were so treated; for you had compassion on me in my chains, and joyfully accepted the plundering [confiscation] of your goods, knowing that you have a better and an enduring possession for yourselves in heaven. Therefore do not cast away your confidence, which has great reward. For you have need of endurance [you need to persevere in the dream methods], so that after you have done the will of God, you may receive the promise [you will receive the dream goals that God has promised]. (Heb. 10:30–36)

Before moving on to dream method 2, I think it is most important that I say just a little bit more about why perseverance is so important. And let me start out by saying that "a new level always means a new devil!"[14] A new level of achievement in making Dr. King's dream a reality in our personal lives and in the American culture will always mean that Satan will take his resistance against the people in America to a new level.

For example, when Satan sees that we are making significant process in making Dr. King's dream a reality in our culture, he will use a higher level of deceptive and manipulative schemes to stir up hatred and division among the American people. He will try to stir up more people, for example, to bite the dog that bit them. He will use more deceptive and manipulative schemes to create more division or more hatred between Black people and White people; between rich people and poor people; between men and women; between young people and old people; between Christians and Jews; between Protestants and Catholics; between Democrats and Republicans. So we must be determined as a nation to persevere in the dream methods through all the obstacles that the enemy is going to put in our path when he sees that we are making progress in making the dream a reality in our nation.

This must be promoted, exemplified, and sustained by both Black and White Christians in America, because unbelievers don't have the spiritual discernment to do this. Christians are the salt and the light of the world. A new level of achievement will always mean a new level of opposition by Satan and his demons to try to make us lose whatever ground we have achieved. What all this means is this:

> We do not wrestle against [our battle is not against] flesh and blood [human forces], but against principalities, against powers, against the rulers of the darkness of this age, against spiritual hosts of wickedness in the heavenly places [Satan and his demon spirits]. (Eph. 6:12)

Note that it may look like we are struggling against human beings or human forces to make Dr. King's dream a reality in America.

However, because of America's special God-given, blessed nation status to be a force for revealing His Son, Jesus Christ, to the world and drawing the people of the nations of the world to Him (cf. Ezek. 16:6–14), Satan has put a target on our back. This means that he is going to do everything that he can to prevent Americans from making Dr. King's dream a reality in our nation. It is Satan who is encouraging and motivating people of all colors in America to possess attitudes of bitterness, hate, unforgiveness, and revenge. It is Satan who uses wicked people and groups, as well as weak and spiritually undiscerning people and groups, to encourage people of all colors to bite the dog that bit them. Satan is going to do everything that he can to prevent justice from rolling down like waters and righteousness from being like a mighty stream in America.

So I say again that we must be determined as a nation to persevere in the dream methods through all the obstacles that the enemy is going to put in our path. For this will surely happen when he sees that we are making progress in the process of making the dream a reality in America.

This is very clearly demonstrated in the book of Nehemiah when he started to make significant progress in rebuilding the broken down walls of protection around the temple and the city of Jerusalem. The wall was needed to enable the Jews to maintain a faithful lifestyle of worship and service—for the glory of God—in the midst of their enemies, which surrounded them. Nehemiah said in his diary,

> So we rebuilt the wall till all of it reached half its height, for the people worked with all their heart. But when Sanballat, Tobiah, the Arabs, the Ammonites and the people of Ashdod heard that the repairs to Jerusalem's walls had gone ahead and that the gaps were being closed, they were very angry. They all plotted together to come and fight against Jerusalem and stir up trouble against it. But we prayed to our God and posted a guard day and night to meet this threat. (4:6–9)

When the Jews took their achievement in rebuilding the wall to a higher level, Satan took his opposition against the Jews to a higher level.

But when Satan did this, the Jews persevered by taking their determination to rebuild the wall to a higher level. And then, as we are told later on in Nehemiah's diary, Satan took his opposition to an even higher level—and so did the Jews until they had completely rebuilt the wall.

Likewise, we must persevere in the dream methods and endure this same dynamic in America until Dr. King's dream is a reality. In other words, no person or nation can be blessed if that person or that nation is not willing to persevere. Jesus expressed the certainty of the results of a person or group or nation that perseveres in the following text:

> Then Jesus told his disciples a parable to show them that they should always pray and not give up. He said: "In a certain town there was a judge who neither feared God

nor cared what people thought. And there was a widow in that town who kept coming to him with the plea. 'Grant me justice against my adversary.' For some time he refused. But finally he said to himself, 'Even though I don't fear God or care what people think, yet because this widow keeps bothering me, I will see that she gets justice, so that she won't eventually come and attack me!'" And the LORD said, "Listen to what the unjust judge says. And will not God bring about justice for his chosen ones, who cry out to him day and night? Will he keep putting them off? I tell you, he will see that they get justice, and quickly. However, when the Son of Man comes, will he find faith on the earth?" (Luke 18:1–8)

If Blacks persevered through the horrors of slavery, Jim Crow in the South, and overt racism in the North and have become the strong people that we now are in spite of all this, surely with God's help we can persevere in the use of Dr. King's dream methods until his dream goals are a reality in our lives and in the lives of all Americans. Now onward to dream method 2.

2

THE METHODS CONTENT TO BE IMPLEMENTED: DREAM METHOD 2—SELF-RESPECT AND SELF-CONTROL, NONVIOLENCE, UNITY

Now what new methods or ways can we obtain from the implementation section of the "I Have a Dream" speech in which Dr. King delineated some other methods or actions and attitudes for making the dream a reality? Dr. King expressed the elements of self-respect, nonviolence, and unity in another portion of "I Have a Dream." He said that we must always strive to achieve the goals of civil rights on the high grounds of "dignity and discipline" or self-respect and self-control.[1]

Thus, we must never allow imaginative or innovative protest efforts to sink to the level of either physical violence or the spiritual violence of hate. Dr. King said that we must repeatedly seek the high ground and meet force with "soul force" or the spiritual energy of nonviolent resistance.[2]

Moreover, he emphasized the fact that one of the goals of this process or this dream method is to create unity by helping our White brothers realize that their freedom is inseparably connected to and undeniably dependent upon our freedom.[3]

CLARENCE WASHINGTON SR.

Self-Respect and Self-Control

Dr. King noted that self-respect and self-control, which he described as "dignity and discipline," are important elements in making the dream a reality. So why is this true? One most important reason why self-respect and self-control or a good reputation are so important is that when a person, group, or organization starts proclaiming the message of the dream and becoming successful in implementing it, Satan will oppose such efforts. And the day will come (which is already here in America) when the only way to destroy the message of the dream and its effectiveness is to destroy the messengers through slander and false witness.

Therefore, you must develop self-respect and exercise self-control so that you can maintain a good reputation of being a dignified and disciplined human being. You will need this so that the people who know you will vouch for you and say, "No! What you said about John or Jane Doe was not right! I know this man or this woman, and you are lying on him or her!" Satan will inspire some people, groups, and organizations to bear false witness against you to try to discredit the message of the dream and its implementation by trying to discredit the people, groups, and organizations that are promoting and supporting it. This is an old, old trick that Satan has used since the beginning of time. When he can't discredit and thus destroy the message, he will then do all that he can to discredit and destroy the messenger by discrediting his or her character.

You see, this is what happened to Dr. King over and over by various people and organizations until his death. For example, on November 19, 1964, the *New York Herald Tribune* carried the following article by the *United Press International*:

> Washington.
>
> FBI director J. Edgar Hoover said yesterday that the Rev. Dr. Martin Luther King Jr. was "the most notorious liar in the country" for claiming FBI agents in Albany, Ga. would take no actions on civil rights complaints because they are Southerners.

Caryl Rivers, Washington correspondent of the San Juan, Puerto newspaper, El Mundo, reported that Mr. Hoover made the statement in a group interview with 20 women reporters who arranged periodic meetings with Washington officials.

So, the message is clear: when a nationally known, influential person calls you "the most notorious liar in the country" to a group of twenty reporters, your self-respect and self-control—your reputation for being a person of dignity and discipline—had better be in order. When this happens, you must be a person who is above reproach (above being justifiably accused of being a liar, 1 Tim. 3:2). This is absolutely necessary if you are serious about persevering in the advancement of the methods and the goals of the dream throughout the nation (or throughout your family, workplace, church, neighborhood, and local community if you don't have national recognition).

However, if you choose not to live a life that is above reproach—a life that is demonstrated to be full of self-respect, self-control, and committed to the continuous development of a good reputation before the people in your sphere of influence—you will be an easy kill. You will not be much good for the advancement of the dream if you live a reckless life, not caring much about how you live and what others know and think about how you are living. Reckless rebels who are committed to "doing you" are an easy kill for slander or false witness, drug and alcohol addictions, and a waste of your life and time incarcerated for doing crimes. You are therefore not of much use for helping to promote the goals of the dream.

Also, I should note that reckless or careless rebels, people with no commitment to a good reputation who carelessly take chances by doing things that could destroy their reputation—these kind of people fall into all social, economic, and academic categories. There are white-collar and blue-collar careless rebels; high school graduates and college graduates; well-to-do people and poor people; Democratic leaders and Republican leaders who are careless rebels; pastors, ministers, and lay people who are careless rebels and of little or no value to the process of making the dream a reality in America. Their feelings, thinking, and behavior—hidden (so they think) or done in public—demonstrate that they have no self-respect and self-control, no genuine dignity and discipline. I said "so they think" because what is done in the dark will eventually be brought to the light of day by God for everyone to see (Luke 8:17).

Along these lines, I am reminded of a well-known pastor who carelessly demonstrated his lack of self-respect and self-discipline when he was caught recruiting a prostitute on the streets of Los Angeles. And then there was a former president of the United States who was exposed nationally for having sex in the Oval Office of the White House with a female intern.

These things demonstrate that a lack of self-respect and self-control—the careless and reckless regard for the commitment to maintain a good reputation by men and women—can happen in the outhouse, the penthouse, the church house, and the White House. It does not just happen in the lives of everyday, ordinary people or people of lower social or economic status. A nationally well-known married Black leader was exposed for having a child by another woman while he was vehemently speaking out against the hijacking of Dr. King's dream that is caused by single-parent households or the lack of Black fathers in the home.

Moreover, this well-known Black leader then had the audacity to try to use the Bible to justify his hypocritical immoral actions.

You see, when you mess up—fess up! And don't add anything to your confession to defend or rationalize your acts that demonstrated a lack of self-respect and self-control. God opposes the proud, but He gives an abundance of grace for cleansing and restoration to the humble (cf. 1 Pet. 5:5).

Other well-known Black leaders and congresspersons have hijacked the dream by being caught and exposed, for example, with $90,000 in his freezer. He was sentenced in prison for thirteen years for taking bribes.

Still another high-ranking Black congressman, whose net worth was several million dollars, was convicted by the House Ethics Committee of several counts related to tax evasion.

Now guess what? It was not beneath the dignity of these leaders that I have mentioned to lie, steal, and cheat. But I would not dare to say that all the crooked and immoral acts that the people above did—and I only named a few of the people and a few things that they did—these things would not be admitted by them as hijacking Dr. King's dream. Note that almost all of them have invoked the name of Dr. King and mentioned the dream at one time or another for their own personal benefit or gain or in reference to the benefit or gain of Black people. There are a lot of genuinely wise and good Black leaders in America. But there are also a lot of weak and easily persuaded Black leaders and false prophets or wolves in sheep's clothing who are hypocrites, some of them claiming to be called by God, but—

> Do not be deceived, God is not [God cannot be] mocked; for whatever a man [or woman] sows, that he [or she] will also reap. For he [or she] who sows to his [or her] flesh will of the flesh reap corruption, but he [or she] who sows to the Spirit will of the Spirit reap everlasting life [everlasting abundant life, which will begin on this earth while we are still in our bodies]. And let us not grow weary while doing good, for in due season we shall reap [an abundant harvest] if we do not lose heart. Therefore, as we have opportunity, let us do good to all, especially to those who are of the household of faith. (Gal. 6:7–10)

You see, there are so many things that the enemy can use to tempt people, especially those with a special calling on their lives, to get them to give up or put in jeopardy the quest for a good reputation, the quest to be a dignified and disciplined person. Such things are employed by the enemy to put in jeopardy the key elements that are a must to develop and exercise in order to make the dream a reality in our lives and in the nation.

However, there is nothing new under the sun, for the things that Satan uses to tempt and trick people into giving up the quest to achieve and maintain a good reputation are the things that he has been using since the beginning of time—power, status, money, and sex.

But he also takes advantage of us by encouraging us to give up our self-respect and self-control—our dignity and discipline, which are needed for a good reputation—by tempting us to use alcohol, drugs, and/or pornography to medicate the pain of our woundedness that result from being raised in a dysfunctional family environment.

Satan likewise uses for his purposes the low self-esteem and inferiority complex that he sees in people or that he anticipates that one might possess because of the real and the perceived racism that exists in America. Satan uses feelings of worthlessness or the lack of hope in a bright future to motivate people to give up the pursuit of dignity and a disciplined life. But we should not fall into that trap because what looks like something that might medicate our pain will only cause shame and more pain after the temporary relief is over, after the high has dissipated.

What all this tells us is that nothing is off-limits or out of bounds in spiritual warfare when the stakes are high. And the stakes don't get any higher for Satan than the downfall of the two dreams—the American dream and Dr. King's dream.

Besides those things that I have already mentioned, when I look around America, I see the following things that tell me that we are now at an all-time low in self-respect and self-control, dignity, and discipline:

- mutilation of our bodies with tattoos and all kinds of piercings on almost every part of our bodies
- sloppy dress styles by both young people and adults
- high rate of obesity and unhealthy people
- high rate of drug and alcohol addictions of all kinds and illicit and legal prescriptions
- willingness to show our bodies in porno movies and other venues, with the rate of people watching pornography being just as high in the church as it is in the unbelieving culture
- rap music that disrespects and encourages hatred of women and promotes violence
- high rate of single-parent and fatherless households
- high rate of divorce in both the church and the unbelieving culture
- high rate of abortions in both the church and the unbelieving culture
- high rate of serial killings
- high rate of Black-on-Black crimes and murders in communities that are highly populated with all kinds of Christian churches

Dr. Jim Taylor, who is an international authority on the psychology of sports and parenting and the author of about fifteen books, provided some food for thought in describing why America is no longer the nation that she was in the past. He said the following in the article written for the *Huff Post*, "Has America Lost Its Self-respect?":

> If America were a man today, he would have lost respect for himself ... America was once built on compassion, yet our country now demonstrates a shameful disregard for the most vulnerable citizens ... our politicians' prioritizing their own ideologies and ambitions over the needs of their constituents are just a few signs of a cold-heartedness that has gripped America ... If America were a man, he would be an angry and self-righteous ideologue ... If America were a woman, she would be a narcissistic [self-absorbed, conceited] spoiled diva ... without respect for our fellow citizens, America can never have respect for itself.[4]

In the above quote, Dr. Jim Taylor said, "without respect for our fellow citizens, America can never have respect for itself." This statement and others can more simply be stated more personally as "without respect for others, we can never have respect for ourselves." The Apostle Paul explicitly implied this relationship between respect for others and self-respect or how we develop a healthy self-respect within ourselves when he said,

> Let nothing be done through selfish ambition or conceit, but in lowliness of mind let each esteem others better than himself. Let each of you look out not only for his own interests, but also for the interests of others. (Phil. 2:3–4)

And Paul put the cookies on the bottom shelf for anyone who is genuinely seeking a strong and healthy conscious sense of self-respect when he said,

> For I say, through the grace given to me, to everyone who is among you, not to think of himself more highly than they ought to think, but to think soberly, as God has dealt to each one a measure of faith. (Rom. 12:3)

What all this means is that Christian believers must deliver the dream to the unbelieving culture in a winsome way that they can understand and want to implement it. But we must stand firm and never try to change the truth of how God told us through Dr. King to make the dream a reality in our lives and in the American culture in general. We must never compromise the dream methods or the dream goals. For they are both rooted and grounded in the Word of God, which is the only way that either can be effective.

Therefore, we must never forget that in the process of making the dream a reality, we must work hard to evangelize the culture—Black, White, Brown, Red, and Yellow people. We must do this through genuine personal relationships with the unbelieving culture. But we must never compromise our faith! We must be as "wise as serpents and harmless [gentle] as doves" (Matt. 10:16) in our involvement with unbelievers who are committed supporters or trying to live the dream. Paul said in explaining how to live winsomely (attractively) among unbelievers and serve all men and women for the purposes of the glory of God,

> Though I am free and belong to no one, I have made myself a slave to everyone, to win as many as possible. To the Jews I became like a Jew, to win the Jews. To those under the law I became like one under the law (though I myself am not under the law), so as to win those under the law. To those not having the law I became like one not having the law (though I am not free from God's law but am under Christ's law), so as to win those having the law. To the weak I became weak, to win the weak. I have become all things to all people so that by all possible means I might save some. I do all this for the sake of the gospel, that I may share in its blessings. (1 Cor. 9:19–23 NIV)

We must become all things to all men, but we must not allow any man or woman to cause us to stray from the dream methods or the dream goals. This is the reason why the progress in making the dream a reality in the lives of the American people—both Black and White and all colors—has been so slow. This is a prime reason why the dream has been hijacked so devastatingly! Christian believers have allowed the unbelieving world to take over the leadership of the dream movement and set the course of actions or the dream methods for achieving dream goals. You can't achieve God's will your way! The reason is that worldly, carnal, or humanistic ways absolutely won't be effective. God absolutely takes His hands off of such ungodly methods or ways and lets us and our nation receive the due results of our humanism, which will always be failure in the end.

Digging deeper yet, there is something else that I need to say concerning self-respect and self-discipline that should be carefully noted by all readers of this book, which is this. Maintaining your self-respect and self-discipline, or your dignity and discipline, is more about what you and God think about you than what others think about you.

Likewise, racial dignity is more about what you and God think about Black people or White people or Brown people than it is about what others think about a particular race or ethnicity. And so it is God first and then ourselves that we should be trying to impress or to please. The apostles very clearly demonstrated this in the text below when they were brought to appear before the Sanhedrin, which was Israel's supreme court.

> And when they [captain of the temple police and his officers] had brought them, they set them before the council [Sanhedrin]. And the high priest asked them, saying, "Did we not strictly command you not to teach in this [Jesus'] name? And look, you have filled Jerusalem with your doctrine, and intend to bring this Man's blood on us!" But Peter and the other apostles answered and said: "We ought to obey God rather than men [We must please and impress God rather than men. (cf. 2 Sam. 6:14–23)]." (Acts 5:27–29)

And finally, I want to give readers of *Hijacked!* something to seriously ponder on this subject matter that could be a great help in implementing the dream. Genesis 1:26–27 tells us that mankind is made in God's image. And so what this means is that a lack of self-respect, a lack of dignity, is disrespect or a lack of respect and love of God. Paul said in Ephesians 5:29,

> For no one ever hated his own flesh, but nourishes and cherishes it, just as the LORD does the church.

Therefore, in light of Ephesians 5:29, a lack of respect for one's self, which is a lack of respect for God, since we are made in His image, really means the following from God's point of view. A lack of self-respect really means that we have an excessive amount of love for ourselves and not enough love for God and others. And as a result of our excessive love for ourselves, our focus is always on ourselves. People with a lack of self-respect are focused on whether someone respects or respected them; or what they didn't get or don't possess; or whether someone noticed them or ignored them.

You see, a person with a healthy self-respect has a love for God that compels, constrains, or coerces him or her to think about God and others more than themselves. Paul said in 2 Corinthians 5:14–15,

> For the love of Christ compels us, because we judge thus [because we are confident] that: if One died for all, then all died; and He died for all, that those who live should live no longer for themselves, but for Him who died for them and rose again.

Dr. King helped us to understand the process of developing self-respect or dignity by loving God and others in a message that he preached. On February 4, 1968, from the pulpit of Ebenezer Baptist Church in Atlanta, Georgia, Dr. King preached the well-known message "The Drum Major Instinct." This message helps us understand how a person can develop a healthy self-respect by taking their focus off themselves by demonstrating their love for God. The message is based in the text of Mark 10:35–40. It is the text where James and John came to Jesus, and in this particular proud, self-seeking request, they asked Him to "Grant us that we may sit, one on Your right hand and the other on Your left, in Your glory." Dr. King said in expounding this text, as he started the conclusion of this message, you would think that Jesus would have rebuked James and John. You would think that Jesus would have accused them of being selfish for asking such a question.[5]

But instead, Dr. King said that Jesus told James and John that such an instinct to be first, important, recognized—or to possess self-respect— was commendable if they desired to be first in love, moral excellence, and generosity. Thus, Jesus, in a nonconfrontational way, reordered their priorities and gave these men a new awareness and understanding of what it meant to be great or to possess self-respect. Dr. King said that Jesus told James and John that greatness, dignity, or self-respect could not be bestowed upon them by Him or anyone else, but it had to be earned by being a servant. And since everybody can serve, everybody can be great and possess dignity or self-respect.[6]

Also, Dr. King concluded "The Drum Major Instinct" by dramatically stressing that neither a college degree nor the knowledge of Einstein's theory of relativity nor the knowledge of the second law of thermodynamics is needed in order to be a servant—in order to be great or possess self-respect. The only thing that is needed is a heart full of grace and love.[7]

Along these same lines, Dr. King deeply held the belief that internalizing the attitude that whatever was worthwhile doing was worthwhile doing well was a key component in possessing and displaying self-respect to everyone who observes your lifestyle. In other words, he believed that striving for excellence or a commitment for continuous improvement in everything that a person does is critical for possessing self-respect. In his address "Facing the Challenge of a New Age" that he presented before the First Annual Institute on Non-Violence and Social Change on December 3, 1956, at the Holt Street Baptist Church in Montgomery, Alabama, he provided some valuable insight concerning this. He said that since the Negro must compete with people of all ethnicities and cultural backgrounds; we must have the mindset of doing whatever task is set before us better than anyone else could do it. In this address, Dr. King quoted a college president that said,

> A man should do his job so well that the living, the dead, and the unborn could do it no better.[8]

Dr. King went on to say that whatever the Negro does, he must do it like Michelangelo painted pictures, Shakespeare wrote poetry, and Beethoven composed music. He said that he would rather live the life of a free pauper than a slave living in opulence without self-respect.[9]

Similarly, the American author, poet, and short story writer Douglas Malloch (1877–1938) stressed the importance of servanthood, maximizing your potential, and excellence in everything one does. He said in his poem "Be the Best of Whatever You Are,"

> If you can't be a pine on the top of the hill,
> Be a scrub in the valley ... but be
> The best little scrub by the side of the rill [brook];
> Be a bush if you can't be a tree ...
> If you can't be a highway, then just be a trail,
> If you can't be a sun, be a star;
> It isn't by size that you win or you fail ...
> Be the best of whatever you are![10]

So think about the above if you are a blood-bought believer or struggling with self-respect and self-control or dignity and discipline. I pray that this will bring some balance to the struggle for dignity and discipline that you might be experiencing. You see, whoever is the servant of all is the greatest of all. Whoever is the servant of all has more dignity and discipline—more self-respect and self-control, because of the respect that his disciplined faithful servanthood will coerce or demand from others. The author Sonya Parker said, "Martin Luther King had a dream, but he also worked hard to make his dream come true, you have to do the same." Are you up to the task? Are you willing to make the sacrifice of being a disciplined person who is committed to living a dignified life—a person whose lifestyle is full of self-respect and above reproach, a person whose character is unquestionable, a person who is committed to excellence or continuous improvement in everything that you do?

You see, telling people to just do the minimum that they can to get a paycheck is one of the most severe forms of hijacking the dream! And I stress this because I personally know of a pastor—a Christian pastor—who made it his mission to tell his Black coworkers that they should do this. He told them that they should slow down and do the minimum. And he said this in the name of Dr. King and his dream of freedom and justice.

So you see, it is essential that we never forget that it is a significant part of Dr. King's very biblical dream philosophy that the way that one determines whether any form of labor has dignity or produces self-respect, and thus is important, is if it elevates, improves, or strengthens humanity. And if it does, then such labor should be undertaken with a commitment to excellence, with a commitment to continuous improvement.[11] So it's not rocket science. There are very clear and easy-to-understand reasons why the dream has not made more progress than it has over the past fifty-plus years. The dream has been hijacked in many ways. This is clearly demonstrated in volume 2.

Now for an even deeper look into the issues of life that might be hindering your ability to possess a healthy sense of self-respect, buy a copy of my book *Victory Every Day in Every Way: Kingdom Living According to Nehemiah the Governor*. This book is particularly effective in helping people to overcome the serious issues of life, the hurts and wounds people experience in their quest to enjoy the abundant life of peace, joy, success, and prosperity. These are the things that Christ promised everybody who believes that He died for the forgiveness of their sins and asks Him to come into their hearts, forgive them of their sins, and take complete control of their lives.

In closing this element of dream method 2, I want to leave readers with a very brief insight that was gleaned from Dr. King's speech "The Rising Tide of Racial Consciousness," which he delivered at a National Urban League conference in 1960. It shows the universality of the struggle for dignity. He said to an overflow crowd that the battle or the pursuit for human dignity is a drama that is being performed on the worldwide stage with actors and an audience from every continent on the globe.[12]

Nonviolence

In expressing his beliefs on the subject of nonviolence, which is the most essential dream methods element, Dr. King said in his speech "I Have a Dream" that we must never allow imaginative or innovative protest efforts to sink to the level of either physical violence or the spiritual violence of hate. He said that we must repeatedly seek the high ground and meet force with "soul force" or the spiritual energy of nonviolent resistance.[13]

And as I expressed in the introduction in describing who Dr. Martin Luther King Jr. was, he emphatically stated, until the very end of his life, that violence in any form for the achievement of the goals of his God-given dream was morally wrong. To observe the depths, extent, or the intensity of his conviction and commitment to nonviolence, take note of what Dr. King said in his first book in 1958, *Stride Toward Freedom: The*

Montgomery Story. He said that the devotees of the civil rights movement should never forget their commitment to a lifestyle of nonviolence. He further emphasized this by saying that nonviolence means to avoid both physical violence and spiritual violence by refusing to hate anyone.[14]

Dr. King dug deeper and expounded on this in much greater detail earlier in *Stride Toward Freedom: The Montgomery Story*. He delineated his philosophy of nonviolent resistance with six points or characteristics.[15] I paraphrased his six characteristics of this philosophy on page XIX under the title "Six Rules for Nonviolent Resistance." It is obvious from those six rules for nonviolent resistance that Dr. King aggressively believed that violence is indeed one of the most effective ways that the dream can be hijacked! Therefore, it does not take much discernment to realize that inciting violence in civil complaints is one of Satan's primary methods in his various schemes for hijacking the dream.

And so now the question that might be on the minds of the readers of *Hijacked!* is this. How did Mahatma Gandhi come to have such a great influence on Dr. King and motivate him to possess such a determined stand on nonviolence as being the center piece of his quest for civil rights in America?

First, think about this. Dr. King was thoroughly schooled in the teachings of Jesus Christ on turning the other cheek and loving your enemy in personal relationships. There was no doubt that this worked in personal relationships. But he had some degree of skepticism when it came to employing these teachings or principles on personal relationships to social reform on the vast stage of America. He had seen all the overt, deeply ingrained, in-your-face hate, violence, and segregation that existed in the South and its more hidden and subtle counterpart that existed in the North. But would the love ethics or oughtness of Jesus be powerful and effective in the transformation of America? For he had no example of the love ethics of Jesus being successful on such a large stage as America, with its hostility and indifference that seemed to be so comfortably accepted by most Whites. That was the question that haunted him! Would such an ideology or methodology be effective in America?

Well, it was a sermon on the life and teachings of Mahatma Gandhi by Dr. Mordecai Johnson, president of Howard University, after Dr. Johnson's return from a trip to India that gave him hope. This sermon motivated Dr.

King to purchase several books on Gandhi's life and works and delve deeply into his nonviolence resistance teaching. Dr. King said in *Stride Toward Freedom* that Gandhi provided him with an understanding that the love ethic of Jesus could be employed not just with the relationships between individuals but also as a force for social change on an unlimited larger scale.[16]

You see, Gandhi challenged the then awesome might of the British Empire. And he won independence for the people of India by using as his weapons nothing but truth, nonviolence, courage, and "soul force," or the spiritual power of love.[17] Dr. King called nonviolent resistance "Christianity in action."[18] He said that Christ provided the spiritual power of love and the motivation, and Gandhi provided the method or a successful example of the ethics of Jesus employed on a large scale.[19]

What all this is telling us is that Dr. King had taken up the double-edged sword of the Spirit, which is the Word of God (the rhema of God). And it had been sharpened with the belt of truth (the Logos) as Paul tells us to do in Ephesians 6:14–17. Therefore, God gave him some rhema or spoken Word of God through Mahatma Gandhi. He gave Dr. King a spoken word of wisdom through Mahatma Gandhi for the particular situation of segregation and the hardened hearts that existed in America.

Digging deeper. What about this thing called soul force that Dr. King used in describing nonviolent resistance? Soul force can be described in its simplest form as spiritual energy or the energy or power that lives within our souls or our inner being. For believers, soul force is the power of the Holy Spirit that lives within us that energizes or enables us to do the will of God. It is confronting hate and violence with love and truth, instead of with the hate and violence that was given or shown to us by others. Dr. King said that hate paralyzes, confuses, and darkens life, whereas love energizes, harmonizes, and illuminates life.[20] And so soul force is being strongly active spiritually when confronted with physical force. Soul force is meeting the forces of hate with the forces or power of love. Jesus expressed His supernatural (or soul force) love this way in Luke 6:27–28:

> But I say to you who hear [His genuine disciples]: Love your enemies, do good to those who hate you, bless those who curse you, and pray for those who spitefully use you [Overcome evil with good—Romans 12:21].

With the above in mind, it is obvious that the riots that have taken place in cities like Atlanta, Baltimore, Minneapolis, Chicago, St. Louis, Los Angeles, Seattle, and Portland and college campuses like Berkeley. These things did indeed hijack the dream. These types of civil disobedience and violent actions are always self-defeating and a severe stumbling block for years later to the reality of the dream. Satan rejoices—he has a party—when he sees Americans, Black and White, not implementing the dream methods' elements, nonviolence and the others, to settle our issues. For he knows that violence is a hijack—a severe setback, a takeover and destruction—of the dream methods that must be employed to make the dream a reality. And so we end up doing the two-steps-forward-two-steps-backward cha-cha-cha in our efforts to make the dream a reality in America, making steps but getting nowhere.

Before moving on to the dream method's element of unity, I should say something about the Martin Luther King Jr. Center for Nonviolent Social Change, which is referred to as the King Center. Located in Atlanta, Georgia, it was founded in 1968 by Coretta Scott King to educate and inspire brotherhood and sisterhood around the globe. You can visit the King Center online at www.thekingcenter.org. The mission statement that appears on the website is the following:

> The King Center serves as the premier resource dedicated to educating a global network of allied individuals and organizations working collectively using the philosophy and methods of nonviolence to create the Beloved Community that Dr. Martin Luther King, Jr. envisioned.

To promote the transition of Dr. King's envisioned world of global brotherhood and sisterhood from a dream to the actual state of mankind, the King Center developed a nonviolent conflict-resolution process. So in addition to Dr. King's six rules, principles, or characteristics of his philosophy of nonviolent resistance that he delineated in *Stride Toward Free*, the King Center developed from this "Six Steps for Nonviolent Social Change" that are provided on its website. The six steps can be paraphrased as shown below:

HIJACKED!

Step 1: *Gather information* and thoroughly research and investigate the problem from all viewpoints—yours and the opposition's.

Step 2: *Educate the opposition* and others about the issues and your viewpoint concerning the problem in an effort to win them to your way of thinking to whatever extent is possible.

Step 3: *Personally commit* and daily affirm your belief and confidence in the values and prescribed means of nonviolent resistance. This will help to eliminate hidden motives and prepare you for whatever suffering may be required.

Step 4: *Negotiate with the opposition* in an intelligent, graceful, positive manner that does not humiliate them, and use whatever humor that might seem appropriate as you confront them with a list of injustices and a plan for resolving them.

Step 5: *Direct actions* that supply moral and economic pressure on the opposition are required when they refuse to enter and remain in negotiation until the list of injustices are resolved.

Step 6: *Reconciliation* with the opposition should be sought through a well-reasoned agreement so that the nonviolent resistance process for solving injustices does not defeat the opponent and create a gulf between you and them. The nonviolent resistance process of solving injustices should work toward creating a sense of a unified community in which the opposition feels that they are genuinely welcomed and belong.

Through the late Dr. King Jr. and his family, God has provided all the tools, all the dream methods that are needed by a people or a nation to make the dream a reality in America if we are willing to do so.

Along this line of thought, most impressively, Dr. Alveda King (MLK's niece) wrote the book *King Rules: Ten Truths for You, Your Family, and Our Nation to Prosper*. Dr. Alveda King is a Gospel minister, prolife advocate, former college professor, stage and screen actress, Georgia state legislator, presidential appointee, and much more. In her book *King Rules*, Dr. Alveda

King provided an excellent exposition of both Dr. King's six characteristics of his philosophy of nonviolent resistance and the King Center's Six Steps for Nonviolent Social Change. This book is an excellent resource for helping to better understand her uncle and how to implement the dream that he envisioned for Black people, America, and the world.

In closing the discussion on the all-important dream method's element of nonviolence, there is an aspect of nonviolence that many are in denial about. And that is the subject of abortion. So think about this! The dream method's element of nonviolence must start to be implemented in a mother's womb. You can't say that you are pro-choice or neutral, which is the same as being silent about a moral evil, and say that you are implementing the dream method's element of nonviolence. This is the same as saying that you don't care about the violent killing of a baby by a doctor in its mother's womb. You don't care whether this form of violence against another human being happens or not. It's most heartbreaking that people who so vocally speak out and support gun control to prevent the killing of innocent high school students are also so silent, indifferent, or neutral when it comes to supporting pro-life or preventing the killing of innocent unborn children in their mother's womb. So why is this?

The obvious reason is that some people, both believers and unbelievers, have falsely perceived that there is some political gain by killing unborn babies that does not exist once the baby exits its mother's womb. It is politically correct, according to these people, to kill unborn babies. But the real concern should be that it is not spiritually correct.

You see, my brothers and sisters, being pro-choice is not consistent with the dream method's element of nonviolence that is a must to make the dream a reality in the Black community and in America in general. Dr. Alveda King, the civil rights activist, pro-life advocate, and the niece of Dr. Martin Luther King Jr., proclaimed a powerful word for America about abortion and her uncle. She is also the author of several books, including *How Can the Dream Survive If We Murder the Children*. Dr. Alveda King said the following in an article for Human Life Alliance titled "The Meaning of the True Dream":

> If Dr. King's Dream is to have true meaning, babies' civil rights must also be respected. Dr. King once said, "The

Negro cannot win if he is willing to sacrifice the futures of his children for immediate personal comfort and safety." Although Dr. King once accepted an award from Planned Parenthood, his positions on non-violence would lead us all to question the violence of abortion, and to indeed cry out today, "We shall overcome ... abortion."[21]

Violence in or out of the womb in an effort to achieve some sort of perceived political advantage to advance the reality of the dream is self-defeating. It is self-defeating because it hijacks the dream. Solomon said in Proverbs 6:17 that the LORD hates "Hands that shed innocent blood."

What this means is that God will never bless anything or allow anything to prosper that is done at the expense of shedding innocent blood. And there is nothing more innocent than a defenseless unborn baby in its mother's womb. Dr. King so aptly said on a couple of occasions that Americans will not only have to repent of their cruel and heartless words that were spoken and actions that were done concerning such things as abortion, but good people will also have to repent and give an account for their silence while these things were being done.[22] He also said that there is a place reserved in hell, the hottest place, for people who remained neutral or were indifferent while great moral battles were being fought in America.[23]

Unity

Self-respect and self-control, nonviolence, and now we come to the third element of this second group of dream methods, which is unity. Dr. King said the following in explaining the importance of unity in what has become known as one of the most important and memorable speeches ever given by an American, "I Have a Dream." He said that the Negro community must stop distrusting all White people and seek unity with them. Dr. King said that the reason is that many White people have come to realize that their destiny and freedom are inseparably connected to and undeniably dependent upon the destiny and freedom of the Negro. He said that this was evidenced by all the White supporters of the civil rights movement who were present when he delivered this momentous speech on the steps of the Lincoln Memorial.[24]

Thus, we must never allow imaginative or innovative protest efforts to sink to the level of either physical violence or the spiritual violence of hate. Dr. King said that we must repeatedly seek the high ground and meet force with soul force or the spiritual energy of nonviolent resistance.[25]

Moreover, he emphasized the fact that one of the goals of this process or this dream method is to create unity by helping our White brothers realize that their freedom is inseparably connected to and undeniably dependent upon our freedom.[26]

Along these same lines, Dr. King said that there are some spiritual forces or dynamics at work or in play in the world. These dynamics can simply be stated in the following way: love and live together, or hate and die together. One path is the way of the wise, and the other path is the way of fools.[27] He said this in Oklahoma to a crowd of 1,500 people on the evening of July 28, 1960, at the First Baptist Church of North Tulsa. If you know anything about the contentious race relations between Blacks and Whites in Tulsa in the sixties, then you know why this was so significant at that time.

You see, race relations in Tulsa had been almost irreparable, unrepairable, since 1921, which was the year of the Tulsa race riot. Wikipedia describes the incident in the following way:

> The Tulsa race riot ... occurred between May 31 and June 1, 1921, when a white mob started attacking residents and businesses of the African-American community of Greenwood in Tulsa, Oklahoma, in what is considered one of the worst incidents of racial violence in the history of the United States. The attack ... destroyed more than 35 blocks of ... at the time the wealthiest black community in the nation. More than 800 people were admitted to hospitals and more than 6,000 black residents were arrested and detained, many for several days. The Oklahoma Bureau of Vital Statistics officially recorded 39 dead, but the American Red Cross estimated 300.

The riot began over a Memorial Day weekend after a young black man was accused of raping a young white female elevator operator at a commercial building. After he was taken into custody, rumors raced through the black community that he was at risk of being lynched. A group of armed African-American men rushed to the police station, to prevent a lynching, where the young suspect was held and a white crowd had gathered. A confrontation developed between black people and white people; shots were fired, and some white people and black people were killed. As this news spread throughout the city, mob violence exploded. Thousands of white people rampaged through the black community that night and the next day, killing men and women, burning and looting stores and homes. About 10,000 black people were left homeless ... Some black people claimed that policemen had joined the mob; others said that National Guardsmen fired a machine gun into the black community and a plane dropped sticks of dynamite. In an eyewitness account discovered in 2015, Greenwood attorney Buck Colbert Franklin described watching a dozen or more planes, which had been dispatched by the city police force, drop burning balls of turpentine on Greenwood's rooftops.

Many survivors left Tulsa. Both black and white residents who stayed in the city were silent for decades about the terror, violence, and losses of this event. The riot was largely omitted from local and state, as well as national, histories: "The Tulsa race riot of 1921 was rarely mentioned in history books, classrooms or even in private. Blacks and whites alike grew into middle age unaware of what had taken place."

With the number of survivors declining, in 1996, the 75th anniversary of the riot, a bi-partisan group in the state legislature authorized formation of the Oklahoma Commission to Study the Tulsa Race Riot of 1921 ...

The Commission's final report, published in 2001, said that the city had conspired with the white mob against the Tulsa black community; it recommended a program of reparations to survivors and their descendants. The state passed legislation to establish some scholarships for descendants of survivors, encourage economic development of Greenwood, and develop a memorial park in Tulsa to the riot victims. The park was dedicated in 2010.[28]

You see, America has some wounds that must be healed through forgiveness so that genuine unity can be achieved, which is an essential dream method element, in order for Dr. King's God-given dream to become a reality. The reason why this is so true is that it is a biblical principle that no divided people can stand or survive as an influential and prosperous nation. Together we stand, and divided we fall. We are all in the American experience together! And the sooner we realize this, the better off we will be as a nation and as individual ethnic groups.

Moreover, it's really far more important than that. For where there is division, disunity, dissension, and strife among the ethnic groups of a nation, God's glory cannot be maximized. And the blessings of a nation and the ethnic groups that compose it cannot be abundant and cannot have the favor of God working on their behalf. God abundantly amplifies the efforts of the people of a unified nation. But He abundantly attenuates the efforts of a nation whose ethnic groups are indifferent toward one another or are at one another's throats—always trying to get the advantage over the other rather than working for the common good of the nation and one another. As Jesus so famously said,

> Every kingdom divided against itself is brought to desolation [ruined], and every city or house divided against itself will not stand. (Matt. 12:25)

This is the reason why Satan uses politics as a vehicle for hatred, because hatred divides. He also uses skin color, ethnicity or culture, economic status, social status, and church denomination differences as vehicles for hatred. He uses differences and diversities of all kinds to promote hatred for one another, which results in disunity.

Along similar lines, today, 2020, one of the most intense propaganda warfare strategies that Russia, under the leadership of Vladimir Putin, is using against America is the promotion of division or strife of every kind among our people. The Russians do this by promoting criticism, distrust, and dislike of the system of democracy that we have in America. For example, the Russians have attempted to cause disunity among our people by destabilizing our election process, which seems to have enjoyed some degree of success.

So as I unfold the details of the dream in the next chapter, I think that readers will most heartily agree that it does not take a rocket scientist to understand that disunity is a powerful agent for hijacking Dr. King's dream.

Now to dig deeper into the dream method's element of unity for a better understanding of how a lack of unity will most assuredly hijack the goals or the dream for a people, a nation, or any group or organization, I want you to think as seriously as you can about the story that I am about to tell you. The story is by an unknown author. It's about a man who visited an insane asylum. It goes something like this:

> A man who visited an institution for the mentally sick was astonished when he saw that only one attendant was guarding about one hundred inmates. And this one attendant was armed with only a small stick. So the visitor said to the attendant: "Aren't you afraid that all these insane people will get their heads together and plan to attack you!" The attendant answered him very quickly. He said: "Ah, but what you fail to realize sir is that these people are in this asylum because they were not able to get their heads together and work cooperatively with the people they were associated with before they were sent here."[29]

This brief story helps to explain why a house divided cannot stand! Note also that a house divided makes it very difficult for the individual people who make up the house to stand or to be effective in whatever they do. When the Pharisees tried to give Satan the credit for what the Spirit of God had done to deliver a demon-possessed man, Jesus said to them,

> Every kingdom divided against itself is brought to desolation [ruined], and every city or household divided against itself will not stand. If Satan casts out Satan, he is divided against himself. How then will his kingdom stand? (Matt. 12:25–26)

You see, unity is serious business! It is a key element of the dream method that must be deployed to make the dream goals an effective reality. When there is no unity or when there is a shortage of unity, our personal lives and the corporate life of America will be just like a mental institution, which is exactly where we are today. A house divided cannot stand, because the inmates who inhabit the house can't get their heads together long enough to establish some common goals and then strive cooperatively toward achieving those goals.

Another lesson that can be drawn from this simple little story about the mental institution is that division, disunity, disharmony, or the lack of the ability of people to get their heads together and work cooperatively is a form of mental illness. It is a subtle form of insanity that will change your house, your group, your organization, your church, your family, or the nation into a mental institution, an insane asylum.

Now think about this. The Spirit of God revealed through Paul the detailed principle that must be deployed to develop unity among not only members of the church but among any group of people who are willing to zealously pursue and install this principle in their lives. It is definitely not an easy principle to embrace for unbelievers who do not have the Holy Spirit to enlighten and empower them. However, unbelievers can use this principle to enhance their ability to promote unity, depending on their willingness to do so.

So what is this principle that God gave Paul to give to the church to maximize His glory through the practical reality of unity among the members of the church? Paul said in stating the principle of unity in Ephesians 4:1–3:

> As a prisoner for the LORD, then, I urge you to live a life worthy of the calling you have received. Be completely humble and gentle; be patient, bearing with one another

in love. Make every effort to keep the unity of the Spirit
through the bond of peace.

Paul said that as you develop a bond of peace with others by *making every effort* to be completely humble, gentle, patient, and bearing with one another in love, the Holy Spirit creates unity between or among you and other people. Making every effort to be a peacemaker by being humble, gentle, patient, and persevering in love through the bad as well as the good situations of life is the principle for establishing the groundwork for developing unity among people, ethnic groups, and nations.

More specifically, Paul is telling us in this text that the bond that will maintain or preserve unity of purpose (or the glue that keeps unity from falling apart) so that the dream can be effectively pursued until achieved by our nation is peace among the people.

Paul further warned about the importance of peace in promoting unity "by bearing with one another in love" (Eph. 4:2) when he said to the newly established church in Rome,

> Do not repay anyone evil for evil. Be careful to do what is right in the eyes of everyone. If it is possible, as far as it depends on you, live at peace with everyone. (Rom. 12:17–18)

You see, you may be able to speak in tongues in your private prayer life and experience so much ecstasy that you feel as though you have been raptured to the right hand of the Father. But if you are not committed and dedicated to being successful at doing your part to maintain unity in all your relationships through the bond of peace, then you won't be able to promote the dream that God gave to Dr. King for America—Black and White. The power of the dream and its worthiness to be promoted is demonstrated in the fact that it inspired Dr. King to zealously pursue it to the point of being willing to die in order to make it a reality in America.

Digging further yet, I feel the need to say a few more things about the dream method's element of unity because it is so important to the process of making dream goals / the dream a reality.

First, let me say again in maybe a little bit different way that you must be a peacemaker so that God can create a *relational spirit of unity* among you and the people with whom you are associated or connected—to whatever extent is possible.

Second, you won't be able to maintain the unity of the Holy Spirit (Eph. 4:3) with everybody you are associated or connected with. And the reason for this is that the unity of the Spirit is based on the truth of the essentials of Scripture associated with salvation ("one faith [one Gospel]," Eph. 4:5; cf. Gal. 1:6–9).

But on the other hand, through the bond of peace, you can still create a relational spirit of unity, or *a relational spirit of agreement,* for the glory of God between you and people for whom it is impossible to possess and maintain the unity of the Spirit. Again, this is consistent with what Paul said in his instructions to the Romans on how to live the supernatural life: "If it is possible, as far as it depends on you, live at peace with everyone" (Rom. 12:18). And when you do this, unity, if it is possible, will be the result. Unity to whatever extent is possible will be the result.

Third, there is a dynamic between unity and peace that should be an encouragement to you to seek unity and peace to whatever extent is possible. And that is this. Peace begets unity, and unity begets peace. They feed on each other. The more blessings of unity that being a peacemaker brings into your life, the more you will be inspired to be a peacemaker. This will then bring even more unity and its blessings into your life, which will then produce even more of a desire to maintain unity through the bond of peace—etcetera.

Fourth, Leviticus 26:8 reveals the fact that *unity will greatly amplify* a nation's ability to make the dream a reality because the favor of God will work disproportionately with the people to achieve it. The reason is that a nation of unified people will bring God an abundant of glory in how they live. So how does this work? How does God help or work disproportionately with or in favor of a nation that is working in unity to achieve the God-inspired goals of the dream?

Well, the LORD provided a very clear example of how this works when he said through Moses in Leviticus 26:3, 6–8,

> ³If you [Israel] walk in My statutes and keep My commandments, and perform them … ⁴then I will give you rain in its season … ⁵you shall eat bread to the full …

> ⁶I will give peace in the land ... I will rid the land of evil beasts ... ⁷You will chase your enemies, and they shall fall by the sword before you. ⁸Five of you shall chase a hundred, and a hundred of you shall put ten thousand to flight; your enemies shall fall by the sword before you.

This text tells us that the amount of help that God will supply America to fight its battles or to achieve the goals of the dream is greatly influenced by the amount of effort that Americans put forth to create unity and harmony in their various relationships with one another. And so it is most important that your relationships with others be as harmonious as possible.

However, unity or being harmoniously on one accord in the pursuit of the dream is even more important than what I have described thus far. And the reason why it is even more important to make every effort to seek unity through the bond of peace is this: *the relationship between unity and the help that the people of America will receive from God to achieve the goals of the dream works on the principle of leveraging.* Now, what do I mean by leveraging?

Leveraging means that 20 x 100 no longer equals 2,000—but instead it equals 10,000 (Lev. 26:8) or five times more than it would equal without some supernatural help from God. The text of Leviticus 26:8 and the context in verses 3 and 7 support the principle of leveraging in regard to the help that a unified people will receive from God for achieving any goals that will bring glory to Him, which the dream was so obviously designed by God to do when He gave it to Dr. King.[30]

Now let's dig a little bit deeper into this before we move on by thinking about the following. In the text that I quoted above that is recorded in Leviticus 26, the LORD promised the Israelites that if they faithfully followed His statues and commandments (26:3), the following three things would happen: (1) they would have an abundance of crops and eat all they wanted (26:4–5); (2) there would be no savage beast or war in their land (26:6); and (3) they would have victory over their enemies if they were attacked (26:7). All these things would be the blessings that the people would receive for their faithfulness to Jehovah God.[31]

And then in verse 8, the LORD expanded on how the blessing of victory over their enemies would be guaranteed. He said in verse 8, "Five of you shall chase a hundred, and a hundred of you shall put ten thousand to flight; your enemies shall fall by the sword before you."[32]

The LORD said in verse 8 that if five of His people act in harmonious unity, their efforts would be amplified or multiplied by twenty (100/5). But if one hundred of His people act in unity, their efforts would be multiplied by one hundred (10,000/100). This means that 20 x 100 no longer equals 2,000—but instead it equals 10,000. *This is called leveraging, which is the God-given spiritual dynamics of unity.* More vividly, leveraging can be described as the awesome change-producing or victory-producing spiritual dynamics of unity.[33]

And so we can say that unity is like the fulcrum or the pivot point of a lever, the lever being the symbolic representation of the power of God's presence. And the greater the number of people who come together in unity in prayer and other activities for the glory of God, the closer the fulcrum or the pivot point is moved along the lever toward the obstacle that a group of unified people are trying to remove or resolve to achieve their goals or the dream.[34] Figure 1 on the next page contains a diagram that demonstrates more clearly how this works.

In other words, the greater the unity in both the number of people and the amount of agreement of purpose that exists among them for the glory of God—which is what the dream was designed for—the greater is the multiplying factor or the leveraging of their effectiveness in achieving their goals. God blesses our unity by amplifying the efforts of a unified group. Consequently, the authority and power or effectiveness of the prayers and actions of the unified, harmonious group is far greater than the sum of the prayers and other efforts of the individual members of the group. And the greater the number of people who come together in harmonious unity, the greater God amplifies and leverages their efforts.[35]

Oh!—how awesome is the victory-producing spiritual power of the dynamics of unity to enable a nation of people to stand firm in the will of God and make the dream a reality. Peace begets unity, and unity begets peace—all of which is amplified and leveraged through the dynamics of unity, providing a nation of people with an awesome, enhanced ability to achieve Dr. King's dream goals. "Five of you shall chase a hundred, and a hundred of you shall put ten thousand to flight; your enemies shall fall by the sword before you" (Lev. 26:8).[36]

HIJACKED!

The Victory-Producing Leveraging Dynamics of Unity

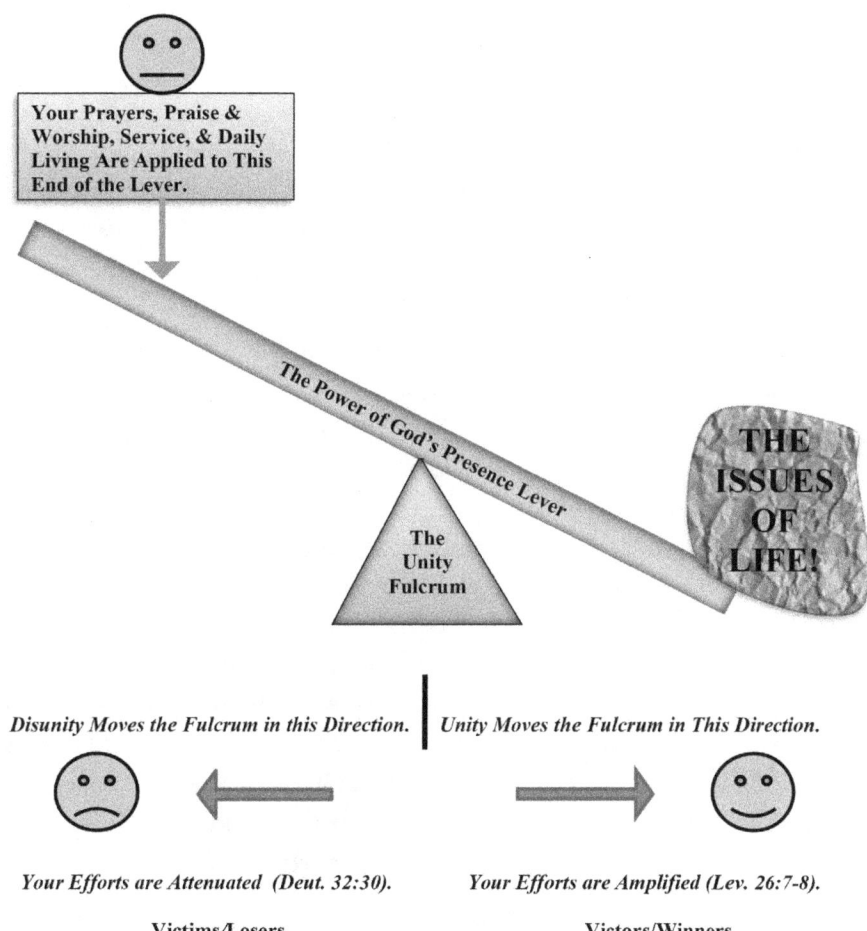

Figure 1

But guess what? As I previously stated and as demonstrated in figure 1, Deuteronomy 32:30 reveals the fact that *disunity will greatly attenuate* or reduce a nation's ability to make the dream a reality. The reason is that the favor of God will work disproportionately with such a nation's enemies or against a nation in which there is nationwide disunity, division, and strife of many kinds among the people. And such is the case with America today.

There is division and strife between various ethnic groups, division and strife between the rich and the poor, the educated and the uneducated, the liberals and the conservatives, and the list goes on and on. This seemingly never-ending list is hijacking the dream with each of its many forms of contention, conflict, and rivalry.

So how does the hijacking of Dr. King's dream occur according to Deuteronomy 32:30? The LORD said in a portion of the Song of Moses recorded in Deuteronomy 32:28–30,

> They [Israel] are a nation without sense, there is no discernment in them. If only they were wise and would understand this and discern what their end will be [Verses 28–29 could also be said about America today.]! How could one man [one of Israel's enemies] chase a thousand [a thousand Israelites], or two [of Israel's enemies] put ten thousand to flight [Israel's enemy's efforts against them were disproportionately multiplied], unless their Rock had sold them, unless the LORD had given them up?

So what does this text tell you? A principle for disunity is proclaimed by the LORD through Moses in Deuteronomy 32:30. This text tells you that if the LORD had not provided a special blessing for the unified efforts of two of Israel's enemies in Deuteronomy 32:30, they could scare and run off only two thousand Israelites—and not ten thousand.[37]

You see, God blesses unity by disproportionately increasing the effectiveness of unified, harmonious prayers and the other efforts of people for His glory. But also, God curses disunity by disproportionately decreasing—even to the point of nullifying—the effectiveness of prayers and other efforts born out of division, disharmony, strife, or other acts of rebellious disobedience to His Word. God does this by allowing Satan to have his way in the lives and efforts of people who traffic in disunity or disobedience in any form.[38]

In summary of the principles of unity for making the dream a reality, there is no doubt that the victory-producing dynamics of unity are clear. It's not rocket science. *Unity amplifies the efforts of a nation, and disunity attenuates them—disproportionately in both cases.* In other words, just a little bit of disunity has a devastating effect on prayers and other efforts to make the dream a reality. The dynamics of unity are irreplaceable in maintaining the divine strategy—the dream methods—for making the dream or the dream goals a reality in America. Without genuine unity in the achievement of a common purpose in America, all the other elements of the dream methods are useless.

Take note that this author's book *Victory Every Day in Every Way: Kingdom Living According to Nehemiah the Governor* contains a more in-depth exploration of the importance of unity in achieving goals.[39]

And once again, in closing this section and moving on to dream method 3—faith and hope, remember the warning from Dr. King on the importance of unity. He reminded us that we might have come across the oceans of the world to America on different ships, but we are today all in the same boat!

Therefore, we must learn to live together as brothers and sisters, regardless of our race, creed, or color, or we will indeed die together as fools! United we stand! Divided we shall surely fall!

3

THE METHODS CONTENT TO BE IMPLEMENTED: DREAM METHOD 3—FAITH AND HOPE

It is most significant that the last dream method's elements that Dr. King grouped together for exposition were faith and hope. The reason why this is significant is because faith and hope in God are the glue that hold together all the other dream methods' elements. It is the pinnacle, the summit, or the high point in the implementation or the execution of the dream methods for achieving the dream goals and thus making the dream a reality. The Hebrew writer said in chapter 11, verses 1 and 6,

> Now faith is the substance of things hoped for, the evidence of things not seen ... But without faith it is impossible to please Him, for he who comes to God [for any reason] must believe that He is [that He exists], and that He is a rewarder of those who diligently seek Him.

So, what is the Hebrew writer telling us about faith and hope in this text? What the Hebrew writer is telling us is that faith is the substance or what we hold onto when what God has promised us is not yet a reality in our lives. And faith is the evidence or the proof that what God has promised us is still on the way when it is yet too far away to be seen. In other words, faith is the for sure and for certain confirmation that what we are expecting or hoping to receive from God is a done deal!

Dr. King's take on this is that faith, which is the cradle or birthplace of hope, is taking one step at a time up a staircase without being able to see where it is leading you to. He said that without a never-ending, unlimited hope and the faith that births it, we won't be able to accept the inevitable, predictable disappointments of life. For hope is the energy source, motivation, and courage that keeps you moving on down the road—indifferent to all or in spite of it all—through it all. Thus Dr. King could say that he still had a dream.[1]

Moreover, Dr. King expressed the essential importance of faith and hope in making the dream a reality in his "I Have a Dream" speech like this. He said that we must endure in the faith that undeserved, unfair, or unjustified suffering is emancipating—capable of releasing the power of God to make the dream a reality. Dr. King said that since this is true, we must not wallow in the basin of hopelessness or self-pity but instead be hopeful in the promises of God.[2]

So what is undeserved or unearned suffering? What do serious MLK dreamers need to know about unearned suffering, and what did Dr. King mean when he said that it was redemptive or emancipating? Unearned suffering is suffering that a person does not deserve because of something that he or she did. Unearned suffering is suffering that is a result of deploying the nonviolent approach that people will experience while in the process of making the dream a reality. The Apostle Peter said this to help explain the importance of unearned suffering and the blessings that are associated with it:

> And who is he who will harm you if you become followers of what is good? But even if you should suffer for righteousness' sake, you are blessed [you will experience the favor of God in your life as a result of suffering for righteousness]. "And do not be afraid of their threats, nor be troubled." But sanctify [revere or be in awe of] the LORD God in your hearts, and always be ready to give a defense [an answer] to everyone who asks you [for] a reason for the hope that is in you, with meekness and fear; having a good conscience, that when they defame you [maliciously talk about you] as evildoers, those who revile [slander] your

good conduct in Christ may be ashamed. For it is better, if it is the will of God, to suffer for doing good than for doing evil ... Beloved, do not think it strange concerning the fiery trial which is to try [test] you, as though some strange thing happened to you; but rejoice to the extent that you partake of Christ's sufferings, that when His glory is revealed [at Christ's second coming], you may also be glad with exceeding joy ... But let none of you suffer as a murderer, a thief, an evildoer, or as a busybody in other people's matters ... Therefore, let those who suffer according to the will of God commit their souls to Him in doing good [commit yourself to Him in striving to achieve the dream according to the dream methods], as to a faithful Creator. (1 Pet. 3:13–17; 4:12–15, 19)

And so when Dr. King said that unearned suffering is redemptive, he was giving words of encouragement to the people deploying the nonviolent approach (as well as the other dream methods' elements) so that they would know—for sure and for certain—that this approach would reap a harvest of the dream goals if you persevered. But also, the Apostle Peter tells us that there will be great eternal or heavenly rewards (4:13) associated with unearned suffering for righteousness's sake, which includes the furtherance of the dream. To cut a long story short, let me say that the eternal rewards for those who experience unearned suffering for the glory of God will be unimaginably greater than the temporal rewards of the dream, even though that may be hard for many dream seekers to understand or believe.

Moreover, to demonstrate Dr. King's personal commitment to unearned suffering and the absolute certainty of its effectiveness in moving forward in the process of making the dream a reality, he said this. He said that if his death was the price that was required to rescue the White people from spiritual death that opposed the moral goals of the civil rights movement, then what could be more redemptive or emancipating?[3]

To dig deeper into the effectiveness and importance of unearned suffering, think about rule four of Dr. King's six rules for nonviolent resistance, which is described in the following way on page XIX: "Nonviolent resistance is a commitment to suffer to make social and economic justice a reality and not to impose suffering on others." What this rule is telling us is that serious MLK dreamers must be willing to resist their opponents by accepting unearned suffering when necessary without retaliating. Jesus said in explaining the principle of unearned suffering,

> You have heard that it was said, "An eye for an eye and a tooth for a tooth." But I tell you not to resist an evil person. But whoever slaps you on your right cheek, turn the other to him also. If anyone wants to sue you and take away your tunic, let him have your cloak also. And whoever compels you to go one mile, go with him two. Give to him who asks you, and from him who wants to borrow from you do not turn away. (Matt. 5:38–42)

You see, the dream movement initiated by Dr. King must indeed be led by Holy Ghost–filled believers who are full of faith and hope in order for it to become a reality. Secular leadership of the dream movement absolutely cannot make it a reality. And that is a big part of the reason why the movement has been so impotent. Secular thinking dominates its leadership. So exactly how is Jesus telling us to respond to unearned suffering in the above text? What does it mean to turn the other cheek in verse 39?

Well, first of all, in this text, Jesus deals only with matters of personal retaliation. It does not apply to crimes or criminal offenses that are done against a person. And it does not apply to acts of military aggression against a nation. Jesus applied this principle of not retaliating to the following four areas of a person's life: (1) unearned assaults against a person's dignity, (2) unearned violations of a person's liberty, (3) unearned violations of a person's property rights, and (4) unearned lawsuits to gain a person's personal assets.

In other words, to maximize the redemptive power of unearned suffering that God will bring to the dream movement to make it a reality requires MLK dreamers to totally surrender all their personal rights. So again it becomes obvious why the reality of the dream has stumbled, fluttered aimlessly at times, and in general been delayed or hijacked. The dream has been hijacked so many times by so many individual people and the various civil rights groups that MLK dreamers belong to because unearned suffering is a hard saying! Jesus said to His disciples,

> Most assuredly, I say to you, unless you eat the flesh of the Son of Man and drink His blood, you have no life in you. Whoever eats My flesh and drinks My blood has eternal life, and I will raise him up at the last day ... Therefore, many of His disciples, when they heard this, said, "This is a hard saying [a hard to understand teaching]; who can understand it?" (John 6:53–54, 60)

You see, the redemptive power of unearned suffering is a hard saying! It is a hard teaching. It requires lots of faith in God and an infinite amount of hope in His promise that unearned suffering is truly redemptive! And the degree to which MLK dreamers submit to the principle of unearned suffering—this determines the magnitude of the redemptive power of unearned suffering that God will bring to the dream movement to make it a reality. A little bit of unearned suffering means a little bit of the supernatural power of unearned suffering will be available to make the dream a reality. A whole lot of unearned suffering means a whole lot of the supernatural power of unearned suffering will be available to make the dream a reality. It's not rocket science.

In explaining the power of unearned suffering, which is described in rule four of six rules for nonviolent resistance, in his treatise "An Experience in Love," Dr. King used a quote by Mahtani Gandhi to show the depths of the meaning of unearned suffering. Gandhi said to his countrymen:

> Rivers of blood may have to flow before we gain our freedom, but it must be our blood.[4]

Dr. King said that during his time, some people were probably asking, What is the nonviolent resister's motive for employing the ancient biblical teaching of turning the other cheek that he and Gandhi applied to the political arena for social change? Dr. King's answer was simply that unearned suffering is redemptive or emancipating or transforming whether it was employed on the personal level or the much larger political level for social change.[5] Gandhi explained it this way:

> Things of fundamental importance to people are not secured by reason alone, but have to be purchased with their suffering. Suffering is infinitely more powerful than the law of the jungle for converting the opponent and opening the ears which are otherwise shut to the voice of reason.[6]

Again, this is not rocket science, but it is still a hard saying. The reason is that the principle of unearned suffering so clearly stated by Jesus, Dr. King, and Mahatma Gandhi is this: you must give up what little that you possess of something so that you can get all that there is of something. Black people in the late fifties and early sixties had to be willing to totally surrender all the limited civil rights that they possessed as US citizens in order to move forward in gaining all their civil rights that were due them as citizens. That's what the principle of unearned suffering tells us.

You see, telling someone that you must give up all that you have so that you can get all that there is or all that someone owes you is indeed a hard saying, a hard teaching to understand, a puzzling and seemingly inconsistent principle. Or saying that yet another way—telling someone that in order to win at making the dream a reality, they must lose all the little bit that they already possess is indeed paradoxical. This might seem like a principle that has no chance of being successful or at best illogical to most people. And so this kind of a teaching can only be employed in the struggle to make the dream a reality through faith in God and hope in His promises. Jesus similarly expressed the importance and power of the paradoxical hard saying of unearned suffering yet again when He said to His disciples about winning by losing,

> If anyone desires to come after Me, let him deny himself, and take up his cross, and follow Me. For whoever desires to save his life [for himself to live as he pleases] will lose it [lose opportunity for eternal life], but whoever loses his life [willing to live a life of unearned suffering] for My sake will find it [eternal life]. (Matt. 16:24–25)

The principle of unearned suffering for achieving very difficult and challenging goals is puzzling and illogical or seemingly contradictory to many people. It therefore becomes more obvious that an excellent understanding of the dire importance of the role that unearned suffering plays in the quest to make the dream a reality is absolutely essential. The reason is so that you will understand the absolute importance of the need of a strong faith in God and an unrelenting hope in the promises of God. This kind of faith and hope is so desperately needed so that you can persevere in the quest for the dream while you are in the midst of experiencing the severe trials of unearned suffering that might be necessary. To aid in a better understanding of the importance of unearned suffering, think about Dr. King's personal testimony.

Dr. King shared some of his personal experience with unearned suffering and how it affected him. He said the following in explaining how important it is to be willing to embrace unearned suffering in the "Suffering and Faith" article that he wrote for the April 27, 1960, issue of *Christian Century*. He said that when he became involved in the civil rights movement, he had only a few days of peace and quiet over the couple of years after that. Dr. King said that the way he coped with this was by realizing that unearned suffering was a virtue. This rescued him from feelings of bitterness and allowed him to see it as an opportunity for self-transformation and the desperately needed healing of the Negro people. Dr. King said that as a result of his experience with the redemptive power of unearned suffering, he knew—for sure and for certain—that it was the power of God that was needed for both social change and the personal salvation of those who opposed it.[7]

Digging and plowing deeper yet into the paradoxical principle of redemptive power through unearned suffering, I must say that this principle also implies that a stumbling block will most likely occur as it is successfully executed. The likely hindrance, which I am convinced already exists in the culture of the oppressed people who have executed unearned suffering in the past, is this. As more and more oppressed people become more and more successful, prosperous, and well educated, they will possess more that they must be willing to lose in order to win the dream for all oppressed people. This is somewhat similar to the dilemma that the rich, young ruler was confronted with by the LORD in Luke 18:18–25. So as a result of this, the oppressed who are successful, prosperous, and well educated will seek a substitute power to replace the redemptive power of unearned suffering.

Therefore, there will be—as we see in the culture of the oppressed today—a stagnation, delay, or not much advancement of the dream in large segments of oppressed people in America. The more successful and prosperous oppressed people tend to seek and employ principles other than the redemptive power of unearned suffering. They tend to use such substitutes that have no chance of working, such as political, social, and economic means and methods, which will cause them to compromise their faith in God and their hope in His promises.

Such substitutes will always hijack the dream in many ways because they are not of God. The God-given dream methods that were revealed to Dr. King must always be employed to achieve dream goals. There are no replacements for any of the dream methods' elements, and the redemptive power of unearned suffering through faith in God and hope in His promises as a unit is one of them. Anything else other than the dream methods is an ineffective, impotent, broken cistern. The LORD said through the prophet Jeremiah,

> Has a nation [ever] changed its gods, which are not gods? But My people have changed their Glory [Me] for what does not profit ... For My people have committed two evils: They have forsaken Me, the fountain of living waters, and hewn themselves cisterns—broken cisterns that can hold no water. (2:11, 13)

This text tells us that the people abandoned God as the source of all their needs and turned to useless, impotent idol objects.

Likewise, this is what people do when they depend on the government or political, social, and civil rights groups for the ways, means, or the source of satisfying their needs and making the dream a reality. The LORD compared what the people did to storing water underground in broken containers, which allowed the water to seep out into the ground, thus making it useless. So is there any modern-day examples of unearned suffering and its redemptive power, its power to advance the goals of the dream? The account below of the Charleston, South Carolina, church massacre answers this question with a resounding yes!

> The Charleston church shooting was a mass shooting in which white supremacist Dylann Roof murdered nine African Americans at the Emanuel African Methodist Episcopal Church in downtown Charleston, South Carolina, on the evening of June 17, 2015. Roof, a 21-year-old domestic terrorist and white supremacist, killed nine people (including the senior pastor, state senator Clementa C. Pinckney) during a prayer service. Three other victims survived. The morning after the attack, police arrested Roof in Shelby, North Carolina. Roof confessed to committing the shooting in the hope of igniting a race war. The shooting targeted one of the United States' oldest black churches, which has long been a site for community organization around civil rights.[8]

Now if you were not familiar with this story, you might envision riots, looting, setting buildings on fire, and violence of all kinds resulting from the Charleston, South Carolina, church massacre by a young White man. In other words, you might envision that the dream would be hijacked like it was in August 2014 after the fatal shooting of Michael Brown in Ferguson, Missouri. Or you might envision that the dream would be hijacked like it was in April 2015 in Baltimore, Maryland, after Freddy Gray died of a spinal injury a week after being in police custody. Or more recently, you might envision the rioting that hijacked Dr. King's dream that occurred after the brutal murder of George Floyd by a White police officer in Minneapolis in May 2020.

However, what occurred in Charleston, South Carolina, after the church massacre is a most descriptive depiction of how Dr. King said that we should respond to unearned suffering in order to release its redemptive power to further the goals of the dream. So what was the response of the church and the Black community in Charleston, South Carolina, to their unearned suffering? And what did the redemptive power of their unearned suffering accomplish to further some of the goals of the dream?

Well, first of all, there were Black and White people protesting peacefully together in unity all over Charleston. But there was no rioting, looting, burning buildings, or violence. Black and White protestors had signs that said such things as "Fight Racism," "The Whole World Is Watching," "How Many More," "We Are All Human," "Black Lives Matter," "How Does a Gun Enter the House of God," and "Take Down the Confederate Flag." But there was no rioting, looting, burning buildings, or violence.⁹

Also, the relatives of the people slain inside the church spoke directly to the captured gunman at his bond hearing. They talked to him about what he had taken from them, but none of them expressed any anger. And those who chose to offered him forgiveness and said that they were praying for his soul, while he remained unresponsive.

In addition to this, the local community surrounding Charleston held prayer vigils in churches, parks, and other public places. Fundraisers were held for the families of the slain victims. A mass unity rally of an estimated twenty thousand people was also held on the Arthur Ravenel Bridge. And several dozen boats joined in the unity procession under the bridge.

So what about the redemptive power of the unearned suffering that the church and the Black community experienced? What kind of progress was made toward solving some very difficult race issues that advanced the goals of freedom and justice or the dream because of the way in which the Black community responded to their unearned suffering? Well, at a statehouse press conference held five days later on June 22, the governor, who was Nikki Haley at the time, plus US Republican senators Lindsey Graham, Tim Scott, and the former Republican governor Mark Sanford called for the state flag, which was the Confederate flag, to be removed by the state legislature. They said that while the flag was "an integral part of our past, it does not represent the future" of South Carolina.

And as a result of this, on July 6, 2015, the South Carolina Senate voted to remove the Confederate flag from display outside the South Carolina State House. Likewise the House voted to remove the flag, and on July 9, 2015, Governor Nikki Haley signed the bill. And then the very next day, on July 10, 2015, the Confederate flag was taken down for the last time.

But that's not all the story because Wal-Mart, Amazon.com, Sears Holding Corporation (which owns Sears and Kmart), and eBay—all of these retailers announced that they would stop selling merchandise that had the Confederate flag on them. Also, Warner Bros. announced that they were stopping the production of the General Lee car toys, which had a Confederate flag on its roof. And in addition to this, many of the major flag manufacturers of the Confederate flag decided to stop manufacturing the flag on a large scale for profit.[10]

Taking all this into consideration, I feel most confident through the encouragement of the Holy Spirit to agree totally with Dr. King on the subject matter of unearned suffering and its associated power of God. That is to say that unearned suffering resulting from the nonviolent approach in conjunction with the other dream methods' elements will assuredly reap a harvest that will advance toward victory the various highly contested struggles for freedom and justice. Paul so confidently said to the Galatians and to those today who have put their faith in God and their hope in His promises:

> And let us not grow weary while doing good, for in due season we shall reap [a harvest] if we do not lose heart [if we do lose hope and give up]. Therefore, as we have opportunity, let us do good to all, especially to those who are of the household of faith. (Gal. 6:9–10)

You see, without faith in God and the hope that the dream that God gave Dr. King will become a reality in America one day, we will grow weary and lose the vitality to keep on striving vigorously to achieve it. So we *must* keep our faith, our hope, keep on executing the dream methods in our quest to make the dream goals a reality, and keep on remembering the awesome promise below that God made through the prophet Isaiah to those who put their faith and hope in Him:

> As the rain and the snow come down from heaven, and do not return to it without watering the earth and making it bud and flourish, so that it yields seed for the sower and bread for the eater, so is my word that goes out from my mouth: It will not return to me empty, but will accomplish what I desire and achieve the purpose for which I sent it. You will go out in joy and be led forth in peace. (Isa. 55:10–12)

And one Christian author (J. MacArthur Jr.) put it this way about the absolute certainty of God's promises coming true:

> Faith is not wistful longing that something may come to pass in an uncertain tomorrow. True faith is an absolute certainty, often of things that the world considers unreal and impossible. Christian hope is belief in God against the world—not belief in the improbable against chance. If we follow a God whose audible voice we have never heard and believe in a Christ whose face we have never seen, we do so because our faith has a reality, a substance, an assurance that is unshakable [Heb. 11:1]. In doing so, Jesus said, we are specially blessed (John 20:29).[11]

Before moving on, there is still one more thing that must be addressed in a bit more depth concerning the dream method's elements of faith and hope as it relates to the use of unearned suffering in the process of making the dream a reality. To do that requires refreshing our remembrance that in the article "Suffering and Faith" that Dr. King wrote for the April 27, 1960, issue of *Christian Century*, he said that unearned suffering is the power of God for individual salvation.[12] So what does this mean?

What this means is that the power of God in unearned suffering is not just applicable to social change or social redemption. But unearned suffering is also applicable to spiritual change, the individual salvation of the souls of people, or the spiritual redemption of people as well. This is what the Apostle Peter was saying to the church when he rhetorically started this very clear revelation from the Holy Spirit by saying,

> And who is he who will harm you if you become followers of what is good? But even if you should suffer for righteousness' sake, you are blessed. "And do not be afraid of their threats, nor be troubled." But sanctify [revere or be in awe of] the LORD God in your hearts, and always be ready to give a defense [an answer] to everyone who asks you [for] a reason for the hope that is in you, with meekness and fear. (1 Pet. 3:13–15)

Peter said that while you are suffering unjustly for righteousness or for what is right—for example, while you are suffering unjustly for the furtherance of the dream—this is a special opportunity (because it is blessed with the power of God) for sharing with others why you believe in Jesus Christ, live the way that you do, and the hope of escaping hell and entering eternal life in the presence of God that you have through your faith in Him.

Therefore, you should embrace the idea that unearned suffering is redemptive and that it is part of the struggle to make the dream a reality. And one of the ways that you do that is to "Always be ready [always be prepared] to give a defense [an answer] to everyone who asks you [for] a reason for the hope [in the promises of Christ] that is in you" (1 Pet. 3:15).

And this is how Jesus affirmed the absolute necessity of using the redemptive power of God that is released in response to unearned suffering to get people saved. He emphatically exclaimed,

> For what profit [what good] is it to a man if he gains the
> whole world, and loses his own soul? (Matt. 16:26)

Along those same lines, what good does it do to help a man or a woman receive all the freedom and justice that they are due—all of their civil rights that they are due as American citizens—and then lose their soul and spend eternity in hell where there is wailing and gnashing or the grinding of their teeth because of the never-ending excruciating pain and suffering that the people will experience down there? What good does it do to help men and women make the dream a reality in their lives for the short time that they will live on planet Earth and then die and go to hell for all eternity? So MLK dreamers must be willing to experience just as much or much more unearned suffering in the procurement of the salvation of oppressed people as they are willing to experience to procure the civil rights of oppressed people.

In other words, what I am saying is that we must never allow our compassion to help people materially, physically, and emotionally override our Holy Spirit–given conviction to help people spiritually or to get saved. We must not let our compassion override our conviction.

Or saying that a little bit differently, our conviction to be compassionate and help people obtain the physical, material, and emotional needs of life should never override our conviction to share the Gospel and what Jesus means to us with people, to help them obtain a personal relationship with Jesus. So what this means is that a significant part of the dream method's element of faith and hope is to be willing to experience unearned suffering to whatever extent is necessary in order to release as much of the redemptive power of God as possible to get as many people saved as possible. Christians must do their best to marinate our culture with the knowledge of the blessings of faith in Christ and hope in His promises. So what I am saying here?

In a nutshell, Dr. King's dream included the revelation of a revival for America and the plans for how the revival must be initiated and conducted until it became a total reality. Therefore, the responsibility of achieving the dream was given to the church. The church must take the lead role in every aspect of the revival.

But more specifically, through Dr. King and the oppression of Black people, God gave the Black church, if you will, or Black believers the very special role of initiating the revival and setting the example of how the plan (dream methods) for making the dream or dream goals a reality. God gave the Black church this responsibility just like He gave the responsibility to Israel to initiate a worldwide revival and to set the example of how the plans to make the revival a reality should be executed. This is explored in greater depth in *The Recovery*, volume 4 of *Hijacked!* And so total justice, freedom, and dignity for Blacks can only come through a genuine revival in America, and the church must lead the revival with the Black church community functioning as the spearhead or lead man, if you will. Any other process to achieve total justice, freedom, and dignity other than a spiritual revival that is led by the Black church and exemplified by the total Black community will tend to destroy America in the process of obtaining these things.

Therefore, Satan has put a target on the back of the Black church and the Black community in general because he is totally aware of the awesome responsibility that Blacks possess—just like the awesome responsibility that was given to Israel. It really isn't rocket science! As Dr. King so correctly stated in "I Have a Dream," the problem in America is a spiritual problem that requires a spiritual solution—a revival! As previously stated, this means that unbelievers can't lead a revival because a spiritual end can only be accomplished by spiritual means. He or she that has an ear, let them hear what the Spirit says to the church.

In summarizing the dream methods, it is obvious that Dr. King's dream is a divine, spiritual revelation that was given to him by God. Therefore, it must not be compromised or hijacked with attempts to implement it, to make it a reality, by using secular or worldly, humanistic means, ways, or methods. Satan will do all that he can to hijack the dream. And so believers, as watchman on the wall, must be aware of this and familiar with all the ways that the hijack can occur. Paul left the following warning to believers that will help to motivate us to employ Dr. King's dream methods and be alert and watchful for the wiles of Satan in his numerous and varied attempts to throw dreamers off and render our efforts ineffective to make the dream a reality:

> "Wake up, sleeper, rise from the dead, and Christ will shine on you." Be very careful, then, how you live—not as unwise but as wise, making the most of every opportunity, because the days are evil. Therefore do not be foolish, but understand what the LORD's will is. (Eph. 5:14–17)

We must make the most of every opportunity to make the dream a reality by consistently employing the dream methods in our quest to achieve the dream goals. For we are living in a time when men and women are calling good things evil and evil things good. But the tragically sad thing about this is that an enormous number of men and women that lack the spiritual discernment to tell the difference between what is good and what is evil are people who say that they are blood-bought believers in Jesus Christ. What I am saying is that today a lot of church folk don't have any more discernment than unbelievers! In fact, instead of the church being the light of the world, the world or human-centered thinking is rapidly becoming the light of the church.

What this means is that the church must employ the dream methods for achieving the dream goals and stop taking its cue from the world or the culture that has the consistent habit of calling good things evil and evil things good. The prophet Isaiah said,

> Woe to those [or much suffering and destruction to those] who call evil good and good evil, who put [or substitute]

> darkness for light and put light for [or in the place of] darkness, who put [or substitute] bitter for sweet and sweet for bitter. Woe to those who are wise in their own eyes and clever in their own sight. (5:20–21)

This is the message that the LORD gave to Isaiah to give to Judah, God's chosen people. And this is also the message that God is giving to the church today.

For this is spiritually where many believers are today, and such believers don't have the spiritual discernment to recognize it. The worldly, humanistic, and politically correct thinking of our culture has so deeply infiltrated the minds of many believers from the pews to the pulpits of America. So many people are calling good evil and evil good that it is a certain and for sure fact that we are living in some critical, uncertain, and unstable times.

You see, our choices and decisions are the divine paintbrush that God gives every man, woman, and nation to design their own future.[13] And if the church doesn't take the lead and promote, support, and exemplify the employment of the dream methods for achieving the dream goals, this will hijack the dream! If dream methods are not employed by both individuals and the nation as a whole, we will make all kinds of bad choices and decisions in our efforts to make the most out of every opportunity to make the dream a reality. What seems like good opportunities to fulfill dream goals will be good opportunities for Satan to employ to hijack the dream. On July 19, 1962, in "An Address before the National Press Club" in Washington, DC, Dr. King illustrated this in his defense for his commitment to nonviolence—which applies to all the dream methods. He said that it was his hope that a deeper dive into the pursuit of freedom would mean a deeper dive into the values or philosophy of nonviolent resistance (six rules for nonviolent resistance). Dr. King warned that first-class citizenship could not be achieved by employing immoral, godless, or second-class methods.[14] Solomon said it this way:

> There is a way that seems right to a man, but its end is the way of death [or results in worthless or destructive efforts]. (Prov. 14:12)

HIJACKED!

Similarly Solomon said,

> There are many plans in a man's heart, nevertheless [it is] the LORD'S counsel—that will stand. (Prov. 19:21)

Now think about this. There are a multitude of people who blame their problems on the circumstances of their life or their lack of opportunities. But the truth is that their lack of opportunities is because of the bad choices and decisions that they keep on making. So don't substitute dream methods with your methods. The times that we are living in are being manipulated by some evil people and by some people who just don't know any better.

This means that there are probably some good things and some good people who, because of a lack of discernment, some people are calling evil. Likewise, there are probably some evil things and evil people who, because of a lack of discernment, some people are calling good. However, if you pray and then employ the dream methods that God gave Dr. King for making the dream goals a reality, you won't make that mistake. You won't unintentionally hijack the dream. You won't delay or hinder the achievement of any of the dream goals or the ability of the dream to become a reality.

So when the enemy tempts you or your organization to lean on your own understanding in achieving the goals of Dr. King's dream, remember and remind others that the LORD said through the prophet Isaiah,

> For My thoughts are not your thoughts, nor are your ways My ways. For as the heavens are higher than the earth, so are My ways higher than your ways, and My thoughts than your thoughts. (55:8–9)

Likewise, the LORD said through the prophet Jeremiah,

> Stand in the ways and see, and ask for the old paths, where the good way is, and walk in it; then you will find rest for your souls. But they said, "We will not walk in it." Also, I set watchmen over you, saying, "Listen to the sound of the trumpet!" But they said, "We will not listen."

Therefore hear, you nations, and know, O congregation, what is among them. Hear, O earth! Behold, I will certainly bring calamity on this people—the fruit of their thoughts, because they have not heeded My words nor My law, but rejected it. For what purpose to Me Comes [your substitutes for what I asked of you] of frankincense from Sheba, and sweet cane from a far country? Your burnt offerings [substitutes] are not acceptable, nor your sacrifices sweet to Me. Therefore ... Behold, I will lay stumbling blocks before the people [I will hijack the dream], and the fathers and the sons together shall fall on them. The neighbor and his friend shall perish. (6:16–21)

So many people and organizations, both secular and religious, have done so many things in the name of the dream or in the name of Dr. King, which have done nothing but hijack the dream, throw it off course, and delay its fulfilment. So the fulfillment of the dream for many oppressed people is stuck in the dynamic forces of the two-steps-forward-two-steps-backward cha-cha-cha, making tracks but getting nowhere. The fulfillment of the dream doesn't need professional, secular, or political help that won't submit to sound spiritual and biblical thinking.

This principle is exemplified in Acts 4:13–14, which tells you that it was not the formal education of Peter and John that made them powerful and effective for the glory of God. The text says that they were uneducated and untrained men. They were "unlettered" and "nonprofessional" men, if you will. It was the fact that Peter and John had been with Jesus that made them powerful and effective and drew the attention of the religious professionals.

Figure 2 is the "I Have a Dream" methods triangle. This visual will help readers to remember the seven dream methods' elements for making the dream a reality and how they are grouped together. Note that the elements are grouped in a manner that expresses that they are closely related, which is how they were presented by Dr. King in his address to the nation.

Also, note that there is a close spiritual relationship between dream methods and the pieces of the whole armor of God recorded by the Apostle

Paul in Ephesians 6:10–18. For example, faith is related to the Shield of Faith; hope and perseverance to the Helmet of Salvation; self-respect to the Belt of Truth and the Sword of the Spirit; nonviolence, unity, and forgiveness to the Shoes of the Gospel of Peace; and righteousness to the Breastplate of Righteousness.

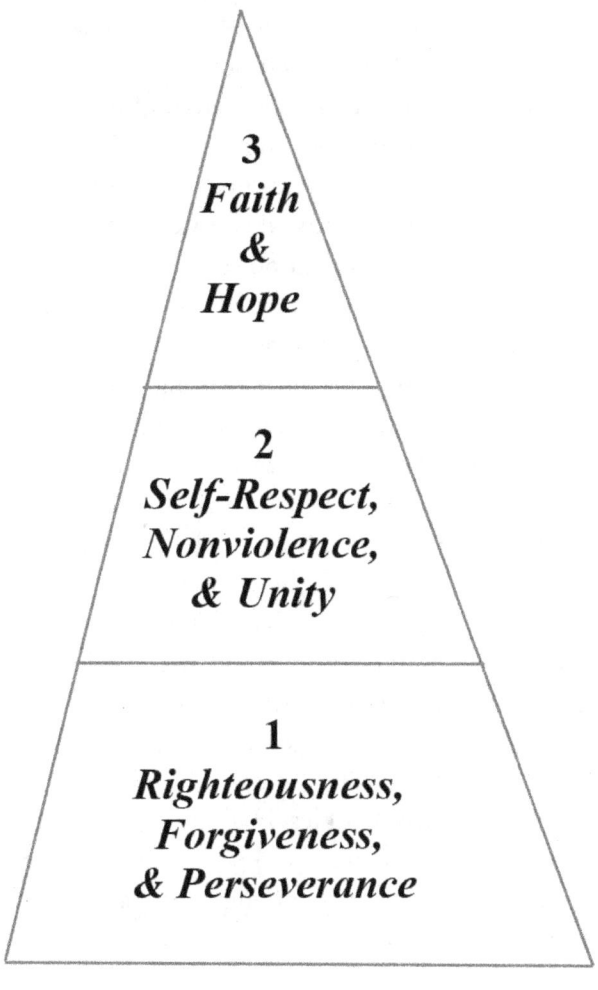

Figure 2

Therefore, I think that it is most profitable for the serious readers of this book to partake of what D. Martyn Lloyd-Jones said below about the importance of possessing all six of the weapons of warfare for immediate deployment in battle. This should remind us of the importance of deploying or employing all eight of the elements of the dream methods in figure 2 and not picking and choosing those that you agree with or those that are convenient and require no sacrifice. This is what D. Martyn Lloyd-Jones said:

> The whole armour of God [all of the dream methods elements] is provided for us. So let us make sure that we are clad with the whole armour of God, which, ultimately, is an understanding and an application of the truth of the Gospel. ... This again is something of crucial importance. It means that we do not pick and choose in this matter. If you are to be a soldier in this army, if you are to fight victoriously in this crusade, you have to put on the entire equipment given to you. That is a rule in any army. You cannot select which parts of your uniform you are going to put on ... You need it all—because your understanding is inadequate. It is God alone who knows your enemy, and He knows exactly the provision that is essential to you to continue standing. Every single part and portion of this armour is absolutely essential ... This means that we take the whole Body of Christian doctrine; we do not concentrate on particular parts of it. It is not surprising that the Christian Church is as she is, forming movements to emphasize one doctrine only. That is a crucial part of our whole trouble today. We must take the complete doctrine [all of the dream methods].[15]

Likewise, the renown Charles Haddon Spurgeon stressed in the following way the need for believers to put on all six pieces of the armor, which also relates to the necessity for employing all eight of the elements of the dream methods shown in figure 2 above:

> Do not merely put on a part of it, but put on the whole of it! ... He [Satan] will attack you sometimes by force and

sometimes by fraud. By might or by sleight he will seek to overcome you and no unarmed man can stand against him. Never go out without all your armor on, for you can never tell where you may meet the devil. He is not omnipresent, but nobody can tell where he is not, for he and his troops of devils appear to be found everywhere on this earth.[16]

Along these same lines, we must always remember that, in the words of Professor David Campbell,

> What distinguished King is not the ends he articulated, but the means [the dream methods] he created, tested and perfected in pursuit of those ends.[17]

This might be a little bit of an overstatement by Professor Campbell, but it does indeed emphasize the absolute necessity of employing Dr. King's dream methods in the pursuit of dream goals.

So in closing this chapter and the exploration of the dream methods' elements and taking into consideration all that has been said, I believe that I can say the following with much confidence. Dr. King's dream—its methods and its goals—is rooted and grounded in the sound biblical doctrine of Scripture. The dream is not based on any humanly conceived social gospel or liberation theology. Such humanistic endeavors to make the dream a reality by perverting the Gospel and making it culturally and/or politically correct or relevant cannot be supported by the sound exegetical interpretation of Scripture.

Therefore, such endeavors could only be relied upon for obtaining freedom, justice, and other goals of the dream to the extent that they are genuinely consistent with the Holy Scripture of the Bible. More simply stated, you can't do God's will your way! Dr. King's dream is not a secular or worldly dream. Remember that the devil is in the details. Be on guard and carefully note that there is only one Gospel of Jesus Christ. And there is only one divinely approved method of correctly interpreting the Gospel or Scripture. You must first determine what a book and passage of Scripture meant to the people it was written to and then apply those principles to contemporary life. For this is how God revealed Himself to His creation in Scripture, whether we like it or approve of it or understand why He did it this way or not. God is God, and we are not.

It is now time to move on down the road and start exploring the goals of the dream or what the specific results of a genuine revival in America will look like according to what God revealed to Dr. King.

4

THE GOALS TO BE ACHIEVED: DREAM GOAL 1—DR. KING'S DREAM IS DEEPLY ROOTED IN THE AMERICAN DREAM

Now that we have explored the methods, ways, means, or tools that must be employed to achieve the goals of Dr. King's dream, what are the goals of his dream? The goal of not being satisfied until "justice rolls down like waters and righteousness like a mighty stream" (Amos 5:24)[1] in America has already been explored. The essential relationship between righteousness and justice necessitated a duality that caused justice and righteousness not to be considered solely as a dream goal but an element of dream method 1 as well.

Hence, the subject of justice and righteousness as a goal of the dream will be expanded upon as the occasion arises in what I defined as the dream goal section of Dr. King's "I Have a Dream," or as it is revealed in other speeches and messages. So what is the first goal that is explicitly proclaimed by Dr. King in his most notable message, "I Have a Dream"? Dr. King, standing on the steps of the Lincoln Memorial, said the following on that hot, muggy day of August 28, 1963, before more than 250,000 people, with hundreds of people cooling off by soaking their feet in the Reflecting Pool.[2] He said that he had a dream that was deeply seated, engrained, or established in the American dream. His dream was that America would step up to the plate and fulfill her responsibility of living out the true meaning of her creed for Black people as she has done for White people. The creed that Dr. King was talking about is the first couple of phrases of the first sentence of the preamble to the Declaration of Independence, which says the following: "We hold these truths to be self-evident, that all men are created equal."[3]

Likewise, Dr. King had previously delineated dream goal 1 in "An Address Before the National Press Club" in Washington, DC, on July 19, 1962. He said that both the destiny of Black people and the destiny of America were inseparably connected. In this address, Dr. King expressed that for two hundred years, Black people had worked without wages to make cotton king and did many other things to help make America the nation that she had become. He went on to say that if the indescribable brutalities that Black people were forced to endure during slavery had not snuffed out our existence, then surely what Black people were facing in 1963 could not. Dr. King used this statement to establish the fact that Black people were simply seeking the same realization of the American dream in their lives as was afforded White people. He said that it was a dream of an America of equal opportunity and privilege, an America where it was clearly understood that the color of a person's skin had nothing to do in determining the quality of their character, an America where all the people were able to live a life with dignity and respect.[4]

Summarizing the above, Dr. King said the following in what I am describing as dream goal 1: I have a dream that the American dream will become a reality in the lives of all the people of this nation—be they Black, White, Brown, Red, or Yellow. The thirteen United States of America made a unanimous Declaration of Independence in Congress on July 4, 1776. The second paragraph of the Declaration of Independence starts in the following way:

> We hold these truths to be self-evident [knowable through right reason] that all men are created equal, that they are endowed by their creator with certain unalienable rights [undeniable, unforfeitable, or inherent rights], that among these are life, liberty, and the pursuit of happiness.[5]

"Life, liberty, and the pursuit of happiness" is a well-known phrase in the United States' Declaration of Independence. The phrase gives three examples of the "unalienable rights" that the Declaration says have been given to all human beings by their Creator, and for which governments are created to protect. Life is the right to enjoy, preserve, and defend your existence on this earth and your liberty. And liberty is the freedom that a person possesses as an American citizen—freedom of religion, freedom of speech, the right to bear arms, and so forth as specified by the Declaration of Independence, US Constitution, and the Bill of Rights. Note also that in 1776, the word *happiness* meant "prosperity, thriving, wellbeing."[6]

The phrase "life, liberty, and the pursuit of happiness" is not found anywhere in the Constitution, which is the legal document of American law. The Fifth Amendment protects our rights to "life, liberty, and property" but not happiness.[7] Happiness is something that the government cannot guarantee. It can only guarantee that everyone has the right or the opportunity to pursue happiness. Only God can guarantee happiness when one follows the prescription for happiness described in the revelation of Himself to His creation—the Holy Bible.

What all this tells us is that when Dr. King said that his dream was deeply rooted in the American dream, this meant that his dream was deeply rooted in the principles stated in the founding documents of the United States. These documents are the Declaration of Independence and the laws and amendments of the United States Constitution. The first ten amendments are the Bill of Rights. To make the American dream and thus

Dr. King's dream a reality, you *must* study and gain knowledge of these founding documents of our nation and how they were divinely *intended* to work.

Therefore, these documents must be studied within the context—the meaning, or the understanding—in which they were given to the people who existed during the time that they were drafted and ratified. For just like the interpretation of Scripture, a text without a context is a pretext, a falsehood, or a misuse of the text of the founding documents of our nation.

So one must be thoroughly familiar with the contents and the original goals or *original intent* of these documents. For if you fail to prepare to achieve *the original intent* of the founding documents, then you are preparing to fail to achieve it, which is what is required to make both the American dream and Dr. King's dream a reality. This is an essential viewpoint of what Dr. King meant when he said that his dream was deeply rooted in the American dream. The Constitution and a description of the Bill of Rights, which is listed below, and its other amendments, articles, and sections can be viewed at the websites http://constitutionus.com/ and https://usconstitution.net/const.html:

- Amendment 1—Freedom of Religion, Press, Expression
- Amendment 2—Right to Bear Arms
- Amendment 3—Housing of Soldiers
- Amendment 4—Search and Seizure
- Amendment 5—Rights of People in Trials and Punishment
- Amendment 6—Right to Speedy Trial
- Amendment 7—Trial by Jury in Civil Cases
- Amendment 8—Cruel and Unusual Punishment
- Amendment 9—Nonenumerated Rights Retained by the People
- Amendment 10—Reserved Powers of the States and People

Yet again, in expressing his appreciation of the American dream and its awesome founding documents—the Declaration of Independence, US Constitution, and the Bill of Rights—Dr. King spoke forth his heart in the commencement address at Lincoln University in Pennsylvania on June 6, 1961. He said in a speech titled "The American Dream" that there was something that uniquely distinguishes the American dream and its democracy and form of government from the "totalitarian" or oppressive dictatorial governments that have existed in history. Dr. King said that the most obviously unique difference is that American citizens have some well-defined, God-given, fundamental rights that the government cannot impose upon or intrude into. And then he dug deeper into the uniqueness of our founding documents by saying that such documents, with their heartfelt and amazingly expressive language on the dignity and worth of its citizens, have very rarely to almost never been adopted by a nation in the history of the world. Dr. King said that the American dream is a memorial that honors the God-given inheritance of the worthiness of all men and women.[8]

Now it is important to note at this point the following. Dr. King in his speeches in both Washington, DC, and Lincoln University in Pennsylvania rebuked a most serious falsehood about him. What he said on these occasions rebuked the deceitful falsehood that Dr. King's civil rights activities were a revolution to change America into a socialist nation or, worse yet, that he promoted communism. This socialist or communist lie—socialism meaning the first stage of Marxism and communism the later stages—has been propagated about Dr. King over the years. This has been done for one of the two following reasons.

First, this has been done over the years to discredit Dr. King's freedom movement. Second, since Dr. King's death, this has been done to provide some credibility to those who are actually engaging in socialist or communist revolutionary activities in America. Such people and groups invoke Dr. King's name to gain sympathy, approval, or support to cover up activities that they know are prohibited by the American dream—or more specifically the United States Constitution—and Dr. King's dream. What is so dastardly deceitful about this is that such people and groups invoke Dr. King's name in an attempt to get approval for things that they know that he did not approve of, things that are outside of the boundary of his dream methods and dream goals.

For clarity about what socialism and communism are, note that Marxism or a Marxist is someone who believes in an economic system where factories, offices, and other means of production and/or making money in a nation are owned by the society as a whole, more specifically by the government or the state. Socialism, as I stated, refers to the first stage of a Marxian society. And communism refers to the later stages of a Marxian society, whose end goal is to establish a dictatorship of the working-class people that will be responsive to and maintain a Marxian society.[9] So it is obvious that neither socialism nor communism describes the American dream that Dr. King said that his dream was "deeply rooted in."[10]

In other words, Dr. King was definitely not a communist. And even if Dr. King himself or others considered him as being a socialist, his God-given dream was definitely not a socialist dream. His dream methods were not socialist methods. His dream goals were not socialist goals. The reason why I know this—for sure and for certain—is that both his dream methods and his dream goals were rooted and grounded in Scripture or the teachings of Jesus, which can in no way be considered as socialist teachings. Dr. King was a man who deeply believed that Scripture—the teachings of the Bible—was an absolute must in order for his dream to become a reality.

Socialism, on the other hand, will always lead to the suppression or the banning of the teaching of the Bible and the death of both the American dream and Dr. King's dream. On January 10, 2019, the very deeply committed Christian Dr. Jerome Corsi, the author of *Silent No More* and about twenty others, emphatically embarrassed this line of thought. He said the following in an interview on the *Eric Metaxas* radio show about the effects of an American socialist or American communist government—Marxism in short—on the teaching of the Bible:

> We are only one generation away from losing liberty. If these ideological purists [socialists] takeover, it's only a matter of time before they band the teaching of the Bible.

And so, is there any evidence of this? Is there any evidence that if what Dr. Jerome Corsi called "these ideological purists"—is there any evidence that if they take over, the teaching of the Bible would eventually be banned? Yes there is. On April 28, 2015, in an article in the online magazine *Charisma,* titled "Hillary Clinton Wants Christians to Give Up on Bible Beliefs," Ron Canton, a Messianic Jew, wrote the following:

> You see just saying, "I am a brain surgeon," doesn't mean I can perform brain surgery. I would need to back it up

with a diploma and years of training. In the same way, no American will get elected president claiming, "The Bible is outdated, it's just a bunch of stories. I am a humanistic socialist at heart!" Sure the left will have no problem with that, but you can't win without independents. So the candidates claim to be Christian—despite having very unchristian positions.

However in a day where anti-biblical behavior is celebrated, where Bruce Jenner is called a hero (not for winning the decathlon, but for identifying as a woman), it is only a matter of time before politicians began to boldly speak against the Bible. Hillary Clinton is testing the waters. It is one thing to take anti-biblical positions, but to publicly call Americans to forsake the Bible is too much. Giving an address at the Women in the World Summit last week, she made this statement:

> Far too many women are denied access to reproductive health care and safe childbirth, and laws don't count for much if they're not enforced. Rights have to exist in practice—not just on paper. Laws have to be backed up with resources and political will. And deep-seated cultural codes, **religious beliefs and structural biases have to be changed.**

It used to be, you were considered compassionate, caring and humble to embrace the values of the Bible. Now you are the enemy ... according to Secretary Clinton and President Obama. It is only going to get worse.[11]

Now let's move on and dig deeper into the fact that Dr. King's dream is deeply rooted in the American dream and what that means. So think about this. There are two things that I can say about all this with great confidence. First, I can say with confidence that Jesus or the teachings of Jesus were neither socialist teachings, nor communist teachings, nor capitalist teachings. Some people want to claim that Jesus was a socialist, and some want to claim that He was a capitalist, but neither is correct. Jesus cannot be correctly defined by either of these societal and political terms. His teachings can only be defined or described by the sound doctrinal interpretation of the truth or His Word—Scripture. Bill Flax, the Christian author of *The Courage to Do Nothing* and a contributing writer for *The Cornwall Alliance for the Stewardship of Creation*, said it most insightfully this way:

> I'm a capitalist and you might be socialists. Christians can be both, but Christ was neither. He was the Author and Finisher of faith.[12]

Second, both the American dream and Dr. King's dream or the dream are not compatible or cannot be sustained by socialism, and definitely not by communism. The only possible chance for the permanency of both dreams is capitalism that is maintained by a God-fearing nation of people. Bill Flax said the following, which helps to better understand this:

> Capitalism is the best platform man has yet devised. However, the Bible consistently condemns its corruption by sinful men and Scripture allows other systems ... No economy can thrive without acknowledging our character [human nature]. Socialism misses that men are inherently selfish ...
>
> *Capitalism is imperfect because man is flawed, but it may offer the only avenue where debilitating qualities orient toward harmonious community* [italics added]. Free markets reward our positive attributes by spurring production without enabling our propensity to only take ...
>
> In socialism, greed shifts from productivity into consumption. Without property rights or opportunities for profit, men quickly descend into mutually destructive envy. Our base instincts betray us. Output plummets. When we see someone slacking and still taking—we

produce less. When we see others hoarding—we snatch more too ... Biblical teaching does not sanction involuntary socialism by governments.[13]

Bill Flax confirmed the historically well-known fact that workers eventually become slaves of the state under socialism. It's the nature of the beast. Adam Smith (1723–1790), the renown Scottish "father of economist," philosopher, and author, said in confirming the slave mentality to which workers are always reduced by socialism, "A person who can acquire no property can have no other interest but to eat as much and to labour as little as possible."[14] Simply put, neither the American dream nor Dr. King's dream is compatible with either the first or the latter stage of Marxism, socialism or communism respectively.

Digging a bit deeper into the issue of socialism versus capitalism for supporting the reality of the American dream and Dr. King's dream, consider the following. Because of the potential flaws of a capitalistic economic system (which, as correctly implied by Bill Flax, is the only permanent platform by which both dreams can flourish), there are numerous spiritually undiscerning people who want to replace American capitalism with a socialistic economic system that ideologically, as well as empirically, has proven many times to possess no possible chance whatsoever of working. Economic failure of a socialistic system is inevitable because of the human nature of man.

In the quote above, Bill Flax stated a reason concerning the inevitable failure of a socialistic economic system because of the fallen human nature of man. His reasoning is consistent with what the prophet Jeremiah said about the heart of man. Jeremiah said,

> The heart is deceitful above all things, and desperately wicked; who can know it? I, the LORD, search the heart, I test the mind, even to give every man according to his ways, according to the fruit of his doings. (17:9–10)

On the other hand, Bill Flax rightly reasons that capitalism has a built-in nature, element, or factor that limits the effect of the flaws that are put upon it by the human nature of man. He said that "Capitalism ...

may offer the only avenue where debilitating qualities [flaws in it caused by the human nature of man] orient toward harmonious community."[15] Capitalism still requires a God-fearing nation to supervise the operation of its economic system so that every effort is made to ensure that it is the most beneficial for all the people of the nation. But what I understand Bill Flax as saying is that capitalism has some inherent or innate dynamics or change-producing forces that help to control the debilitating qualities that are put upon it by the human nature of man. Whereas, this is not true—or I should say the exact opposite is true—in a socialistic economic system.

In other words, the "desperately deceitful heart of man" (Jer. 17:9) has an overwhelming greater negative effect that is available to destroy the establishment and/or the maintenance of the two dreams in a socialistic economic system than it does in a capitalistic economic system. This difference between the two economic systems is implicitly explored in great detail in chapter 5 (the dream goal of freedom and justice) where I expound on the absolute necessity of "the recycling golden triangle of freedom" for maintaining the American dream, which applies to Dr. King's dream as well. Os Guinness in *A Free People's Suicide: Sustaining Freedom and the American Future* described the recycling golden triangle of freedom in the following way:

> Tocqueville called it "the habits of the heart," and I call it "the golden triangle of freedom"—the cultivation and transmission of the conviction that freedom requires virtue, which requires faith, which requires freedom, which in turn requires virtue, which requires faith, which requires freedom and so on, like the recycling triangle, ad infinitum.[16]

And so the difference between the two economic systems of socialism and capitalism is obvious. When the three elements—freedom, virtue, and faith—of the recycling golden triangle of freedom are effectively operating and maintaining the two dreams, this is what it does. It both supports capitalism and negates or greatly diminishes the debilitating qualities of capitalism that are caused by the human nature of man. A capitalistic society likewise supports the effective operation of the recycling golden triangle of freedom from which it so greatly benefits. The two feed on each other.

Whereas, socialism suppresses or stops the automatic operation of the recycling golden triangle of freedom that is needed to maintain the two dreams. For socialism and the three elements of the recycling golden triangle of freedom are contrary to one another, which is the ongoing relationship that exists between the flesh and the Spirit (Gal. 5:17), respectively. And communism of course won't just be a stumbling block but will destroy the *recycling* dynamics of the golden triangle of freedom and its ability to maintain the two dreams.

Moreover, as Paul stated in Galatians, chapter 6, the employment of the humanistic, flesh-driven tactics of any form of Marxism, such as socialism, reaps a different harvest than the Spirit-driven tactics of the recycling golden triangle of freedom. Paul said to the Galatian believers in chapter 6 after he described the war between the flesh and the Spirit in chapter 5:

> Do not be deceived, God is not mocked [cannot be mocked]; for whatever a man sows, that he will also reap. For he who sows to his flesh will of the flesh reap corruption [spiritual decay—Living Bible; destruction—NIV] but he who sows to the Spirit will of the Spirit reap everlasting life [and its abundant earthly benefits]. And let us not grow weary while doing good, for in due season we shall reap [a harvest] if we do not lose heart [give up]. (Gal. 6:7–9)

Accordingly, in *Redeeming Capitalism*, Kenneth J. Barnes said this about how to maintain a capitalist system for the good of all:

> For good or ill, the capitalism we have is the capitalism we have chosen. Capitalism works, and the challenge before us is not to change its structure but to address the moral vacuum at the core of its current practice ... Rather than rushing into solutions, I argue that the only effective way society can overcome the corrosive effects of postmodern capitalism is to consider how we got here in the first place [we rejected the wisdom of the Bible and abandoned prayer]; to celebrate what we got right; to fix what we got wrong; and then set out to redeem capitalism—from the bottom

up and from the top down ... As useful as common grace, wisdom, and the cardinal virtues are to the redemption of postmodern capitalism, three additional virtues are absolutely paramount to our best efforts, and they are the theological virtues of faith, hope, and love ... An old riddle goes something like this: "How does one eat an elephant?" The answer: "One bite at a time." Such is the case with the redemption of postmodern capitalism ... Capitalism can be changed only through a wholesale change of hearts [nationwide revival] and minds as people consciously seek to create an economic system that serves the common good ... To bring about virtuous capitalism, there will need to be a dialogue between all stakeholders—public and private, large and small, rich and poor, secular and religious. The economic problems we face are legion and cannot be solved quickly or coercively ... Redeeming capitalism is a journey, not a destination, but if, like the Israelites, we follow the teachings, values, and commands that have provided the common ground for a values-based culture, we can escape the desert of postmodern capitalism and let those principles pave the way to a new economic promised land.[17]

In summary, the problem is not the principles upon which capitalism is based. The problem is in the hearts of the capitalist. Capitalism without the Spirit of God controlling the hearts of the capitalists will evolve into a nightmare, which is what is slowly happening in America today. It started at the very moment that America began its movement to remove God, the Bible, and prayer from the public affairs of our nation and to replace them with humanistic thinking—secularism.

For we were then forced to seek other principles to control the sin-tainted capitalist hearts of Americans. And as discerning Americans can clearly see, the other principles that are aggressively being sought after to control capitalists are socialism and Marxism. This is what all nations are forced to degenerate to as an alternative to the freedom/liberty that exists in a nation where the Spirit of the LORD is alive and well in the public affairs of the people. Paul said, "Now the LORD is the Spirit; and where the

Spirit of the LORD is, there is liberty" [freedom to live the Spirit controlled abundant life that Christ died to provide] (2 Cor. 3:17). This is explored in much greater depth in *The Hijack!*, volume 2, chapter 2.

Moving on, think about the following, which is also essential to understanding the American dream, in which Dr. King's dream is rooted and grounded. Just as important as the founding documents are in defining the American dream, so also is the motto *In God We Trust*. In the last stanza of our national anthem, which was written by Francis Scott Key in 1814, Key wrote a variation of this motto, which says,

> And this be our motto: *In God is our trust.* And the Star Spangled Banner in triumph shall wave, O'er the land of the free and the home of the brave.[18]

And in 1864, the motto was shortened to *In God We Trust*, which was then applied to US coins. The US Department of Treasury said the following about this:

> The motto, IN GOD WE TRUST, was placed on United States coins largely because of the increased religious sentiment existing during the Civil War. Secretary of the Treasury Salmon P. Chase received many appeals from devout persons throughout the country, urging that the United States recognize the Deity on United States coins. From Treasury Department records, it appears that the first such appeal came in a letter dated November 13, 1861. It was written to Secretary Chase by Rev. M. R. Watkinson, Minister of the Gospel from Ridleyville, Pennsylvania. As a result, Secretary Chase instructed James Pollock, Director of the Mint at Philadelphia to prepare a motto.[19]

You see, history repeatedly demonstrates that America was founded on Christian principles. If you ever travel to Washington, DC, and tour the city, you will notice that the founding fathers acknowledged this fact on numerous buildings, in official documents, and in many historical speeches.

Equally as well, the Pledge of Allegiance to the flag clearly demonstrates that the American dream for decades upon decades was founded on Christian principles. It says,

> I pledge allegiance to the Flag of the United States of America, and to the Republic for which it stands, one Nation under God, indivisible, with liberty and justice for all.[20]

This is a pledge of allegiance to the flag of the United States, which represents America or the American dream. The basic form of the pledge was developed by Francis Bellamy in 1892 and officially adopted by Congress in 1942. And then in 1954, to refute the communist threat of those times, Congress was encouraged by President Dwight D. Eisenhower to add the words "under God."[21] What all this tells us is that the American dream was never intended to function apart from the Christian or biblical worldview.

Furthermore, just like Dr. King's dream, the American dream also cannot become a reality without the biblical worldview being alive and well in the hearts and minds of the American people. It is for this reason—that is, the biblical worldview is not deeply rooted in the hearts and minds of a vast number of Americans—that both dreams are rapidly becoming a nightmare.

President Thomas Jefferson testified about the reason why the American dream is rapidly becoming a nightmare when he wrote this:

> The God who gave us life gave us liberty at the same time. Can the liberties of a nation be secure when we have removed a conviction that these liberties are of God?[22]

And David and his son Solomon, under the unction of the Holy Spirit, put it this way, respectively:

> The fool [The moral degenerate] has said in his [or her] heart, "There is no God." They are corrupt. They have done abominable works ... Righteousness exalts a nation. But sin is a reproach to [brings down] any people. (Ps. 14:1; Prov. 14:34)

So President Jefferson got it so right. The biblical worldview must remain in the hearts and minds of the vast majority of Americans so that the American dream and Dr. King's dream, which is so closely associated with it, do not become a nightmare. It's not rocket science. For—

> Unless the LORD builds the house, they labor in vain who build it. Unless the LORD guards the city, the watchman keeps away in vain. (Ps. 127:1)

Again, Scripture clearly states that the biblical worldview must be employed in our pursuit of the unalienable rights of life, liberty, and happiness that are endowed by the creator. This is the requirement for moving the hand of God to make these things become a full reality in the lives of the American people or any nation.

So examine the Biblical Worldview Chart below and note that the degree to which Americans are living according to the worldview stated therein determines the degree to which the unalienable rights of life, liberty, and happiness will become a reality in the lives of the American people.

The Biblical Worldview Chart

Subject	*Scripture*	*Truth for Today's Culture*
Abortion	Exod. 21:22–25; Lev. 18:21; 20:1–5; Prov. 6:16–19; 31:8; Jer. 1:4–5; 7:6–7, 30–34; 19:1–9; 22:13–17; 26:12–15; 32: 26–35; 2 Kings 21:10–16; 24:1–4; 1 Cor. 6:19–20; 10:5–11	God hates the shedding of innocent blood. There are severe consequences for participants and supporters if there is no sincere repentance and asking God for forgiveness. The writer said in 2 Kings 24:3–4, "Surely these things [the fall of Jerusalem and the 70 years of Babylonian captivity of the people] happened to Judah according to the LORD's command, in order to remove them from his presence because of the sins of Manasseh and all he had done, including the shedding of innocent blood. For he had filled Jerusalem with innocent blood, and the LORD was not willing to forgive."

Homosexual Relationships and Same-Sex Marriage	Gen. 19:4, 9–11, 24–25; Lev. 18:22; 20: 13; Rom. 1:21–29; 1 Cor. 6:9–11; 10:5–11; 1 Tim. 1:9–10	God hates homosexual and same-sex marriage relationships just like He does all other sin. Homosexuality is an emotional and physical addiction that is hard to break, just like the addiction to alcohol and drugs (1 Cor. 6:9–11). There are severe consequences for participants and supporters of such lifestyles—as was the case for the people of Sodom and Gomorrah (Gen. 19:25; 1 Cor. 10:6, 11). Repent and ask for forgiveness from God.
Attitude toward Israel	Gen. 12:1–3; 13:14–17; 17:1–8; Obad. 1–16	God promised that He will bless those who bless or have the right attitude toward Abraham and his offspring (Israel). Likewise, God promised that He will curse those who curse Israel. The implied meaning is that God made Abraham and his descendants so closely identified with His good works that to curse Israel would be like cursing God Himself. Take careful note that God has kept His promise of blessing and cursing people and nations according to their attitude toward Israel since the time that He first made it. The book of Obadiah is a case study of Genesis 12:1–3. It records how the prophet was sent by God to pronounce total destruction upon Edom for their treatment of Israel.
Pornography and Explicit Emotional Intimacy Romance Novels	Prov. 4:23; 5:3–5 (MSG); Matt. 5:27–28; Rom. 8:5–8; 1 Thess. 4:1–10 (TLB)	God did not call believers to be dirty minded or full of lust for people other than their spouses (1 Thess. 4:7 TLB). And so pornography as well as reading explicit, emotional, intimate romance novels is clearly sin (Matt. 5:27–28). They both arouse and feed lust. So what is said for one can be applied to the other.

		Therefore, partaking of either physical or emotional images for sexual arousal makes it most difficult, if not impossible, for a believer to grow spiritually. The lust that each produces hinders brotherly love or the ability to put the welfare of others above your own. And both of them most likely will lead to selfish, self-focused inward habits of self-gratification that are not pleasing to God (Rom. 8:5–8). Likewise, both can lead to fornication before marriage, the selection of the wrong person to marry, and cheating on your spouse after marriage. They are a stumbling block for true intimacy, which impedes the formation of spiritually healthy relationships with the opposite sex. They sabotage the oneness needed for successful marriage relationships. They also sabotage respect for others as well as self-respect, which induces feelings of guilt, self-hatred, and low self-image. They are a genie that is hard to put back in the bottle once it gets out (Prov. 5:3–5, MSG)!
Gambling and Casinos	Prov. 14:31; Isa. 65: 11–12; Ezek. 22:9, 30–31; Matt. 25: 14–30; 1 Thess. 5:21–22	God is a jealous God. He judged the Israelites and said He would slaughter them. The reason is that they tried to split their affection and put their trust in both Him and the idol gods of luck and chance. Hence Scripture defines gambling or worshipping the gods of luck (fortune) and fate or chance (destiny) as idolatry (Isa. 65:11–12). Moreover, the casinos where the idolatry takes place or the home of the idol gods can accurately be considered as the idol's temple or shrine (Ezek. 22:9, 30–31). Luck and chance are anti-God ideas. God controls every detail of everything that goes on in the universe to achieve His own purposes.

		Likewise, gambling is considered as bad stewardship (Matt. 25:14–30), has the appearance of evil (1 Thess. 5:21–22 KJV), and is considered as being a poor tax since most of the victims of addiction to gambling are poor people (Prov. 14:31).
Character and Race	Exod. 18:21; 1 Sam. 16:6–7; 1 Chron. 28: 9; Matt. 15:16–19; 12 :33–35; Acts 17: 26; 2 Cor. 6:14–18; Gal. 3:26–27	God is not a respecter of person or the physical appearance and attributes of people (1 Sam. 16:6–7). Nor is He a respecter of ethnicity or race (Acts 17:26; Gal. 3:26–29). God judges the heart or the quality of our character. This is the example that He has set for us to follow in all our choices, decisions, and selection of people.

"Let us examine our ways and test them, and let us return to the LORD" (Lam. 3:40). Use the chart to examine your personal worldview and the worldview of our nation and see whether you personally and the nation corporately are part of the problem or the solution—part of the hijack or part of the recovery from the hijack!

In concluding this chapter, think about the following final thoughts of emphasis. If the American dream deteriorates through anarchy or lawlessness into either socialism or communism, Dr. King's dream will lose its ability to become a reality. This is a very obvious conclusion because none of the founding documents will support the successful establishment of either a socialist or a communist government. Something would have to change. The plain truth is that the constitution and its amendments would have to be erroneously reinterpreted to support the establishment of a socialist or a communist society, which many on the political left seem committed to today. America would lose such rights as freedom of speech, freedom of religion, and the right to bear arms.

So remember this. Every step toward a socialist government, which is the first step toward a Marxist society, is a step toward the destruction of or the inability to maintain the American dream and also to make Dr. King's dream a reality. *Both* dreams need freedom of speech, freedom of religion, and the right to bear arms. Again I say, *both* dreams are inseparably connected!

Also, think about this. Nikita Khrushchev (April 15, 1894–September 11, 1971) who was the premier (1958–1964) and first secretary of the Communist Party of the Soviet Union from 1953 to 1964, warned the American people of the dangers of allowing socialism to slowly creep into our culture. He quite frankly said:

> You Americans are so gullible. No, you won't accept communism outright, but we'll keep feeding you small doses of socialism until you'll finally wake up and find you already have communism. We won't have to fight you. We'll weaken your economy until you'll fall like overripe fruit into our hands.[23]

In other words, what Nikita Khrushchev was saying to America is that if our people keep on engaging in unsafe sex or keep on dipping and dabbing in socialism, we will eventually wake up and discover that we have become pregnant with communism.

What this means is that Black Americans in particular must always be on guard and never forget that an attack on the American dream is an attack on Dr. King's dream. This will be explored in greater depth in *The Hijack!*, volume 2 and *The Nightmare*, volume 3.

Dr. King said that the founding documents were a promissory note that guaranteed the God-given inheritance or the unalienable rights of life, liberty, and the pursuit of happiness for every American.[24] But the promissory note had not yet been fulfilled. And it is the job of every American—Black, White, Brown, Red, and Yellow—to fulfill it or to keep it working effectively for the American people. It won't keep itself! It is just a piece of paper without the desire of "We the People" to keep it. Life, liberty, and the pursuit of happiness won't keep itself. The preamble to the United States Constitution says,

> We the People of the United States, in Order to form a more perfect Union, establish Justice, insure domestic Tranquility, provide for the common defence, promote the general Welfare, and secure the Blessings of Liberty to ourselves and our Posterity, do ordain and establish this Constitution for the United States of America.[25]

Let us never forget the words "We the People" and the responsibility that goes along with keeping what has been established when we think about the American dream and Dr. King's dream.

You see, the United States Constitution, the Bill of Rights, "The Star-Spangled Banner," the national motto, and the Pledge of Allegiance to the flag are all continuously under attack. But besides the many and various attacks on the first three aforementioned American dream instruments, there is a move afoot to gradually remove the nation's motto, *In God We Trust,* from our currency, both paper and coins. Mark my word, this will happen when the right president is in the White House and enough undiscerning, gullible, or godless men and women are elected to the House and the Senate.

As a matter of fact, this gradualism has already started. It was achieved by claiming that there was not enough room to put *In God We Trust* on the front or the back of the coin. Carefully note in the following quote how shrewdly this was done:

> As specified by Presidential $1 Coin Act of 2005, in order to allow for "larger and more dramatic artwork" on the coins' faces, the new Presidential $1 coins incorporated a few design features not found on other current U.S. coinage, one of which is that elements typically displayed on either the obverse or reverse of U.S. coins—the year of minting, the mint mark, the motto from the Great Seal of the United States ("E Pluribus Unum"), and the current national motto of the United States ("In God We Trust")—were instead included as edge-incused inscriptions. That is, all of these elements appeared on the edges of the new dollar coins rather than on their fronts or backs. With the passage of the Consolidated Appropriations Act of 2008, Congress reversed its previous specifications and instructed the U.S. Mint to move the "In God We Trust" motto from the edge to the front or back of the presidential $1 coins "as soon as is practicable."[26]

Likewise, a similar satanic attack is being deployed to remove "One Nation under God" from the Pledge of Allegiance to the flag. And then there are some school systems that are ignoring the state law that mandates them to start each school day by leading students in the reciting of the Pledge of Allegiance to the flag. On March 21, 2017, Dave Urbanski wrote the following article on the *Blaze* website, which records such a practice:

> It may not come as a surprise that many New York City elementary schools ignore a state law that requires the recitation of the Pledge of Allegiance, according to DNAinfo. But now that one city elementary school has just instituted the practice, the outlet said, some parents of Peck Slip School students are not liking the new routine one bit … DNAinfo reported that other parents were behind the move to get the pledge recited there—the classrooms lacked American flags, too, the outlet said—and began earlier this year pushing the Department of Education to turn things around.[27]

Satan uses the undiscerning, wounded, unforgiving, deceived, and/or easily manipulated people of this nation to bit by bit attack and gradually destroy the effectiveness of the founding documents of the American dream and its promises that hold "We the People" together. These slow-grinding, erosive attacks that are orchestrated by Satan weaken the blessings of God that rest on America, weaken our unity, and drastically weaken the love of the American dream by the people. It destroys us from within—bit by bit—like the erosion of the soil when it rains. And once more I say *an attack on the American dream is an attack on Dr. King's dream!*

So always remember and think deeply about the following. You can't love a nation, you don't really love a nation, that you want to fundamentally change, like some who claim to love America. They claim that they love America, but they say that they want to fundamentally change America. This is nothing but an attempt at deception to cover up the hate that such people really have for America. I say this because discerning Americans know that the fundamentals—the US Constitution, Bill of Rights, and our capitalistic economic system—are not the causes of the problems that America has had in the past. The problem has always been that the fundamentals were not applied equally to all Americans. All Americans did not have equal access or the equal rights to life, liberty, and the pursuit of happiness that are defined by our fundamentals.

Therefore, to correct this wrong, such laws as the Civil Rights Acts of 1964 were passed. America's fundamentals are the greatest in the world. Any change in these fundamentals will be a loss, not a gain! Hence, when someone says that they want to change America fundamentally, that is a red flag that should get your attention. The person(s) bearing this message was sent by Satan to weaken the favor or blessings of God that rest on America, to weaken our unity, and to drastically weaken the love of the American dream by the people. In March 2008, Chris Matthews said, "I felt this thrill going up my leg!" as presidential candidate Barack Obama spoke about fundamentally changing America. What Chris should have felt when he heard this (if he had any discernment) was a severely sharp, excruciating, and almost unbearable pain in the back of his neck.

Such a message to fundamentally change America is indeed an attack on the American dream, which is an attack on Dr. King's dream. The goal of all Americans must always be to equally apply our great God-given fundamentals to all our people—Black, White, Brown, Red, and Yellow. And God will always bless America as we do an excellent job of this.

This is why faithfully adhering to the dream methods to seek and implement dream goals is of the utmost importance. For it is so easy to be deceived into thinking that you are a part of the solution to making the dream a reality when in fact you are a part of the problem; you are an unintentional hijacker! Paul said in Ephesians 5:14–17,

> This is why it is said: "Wake up, sleeper, rise from the dead, and Christ will shine on you." Be very careful, then, how you live—not as unwise but as wise, make the most of every opportunity, because the days are evil. Therefore do not be foolish, but understand what the LORD's will is. (NIV)

5

THE GOALS TO BE ACHIEVED: DREAM GOAL 2—DR. KING'S DREAM IS CHARACTERIZED BY HIS INTENSE DESIRE FOR FREEDOM AND JUSTICE

Dr. King said in describing his second dream goal that he had a dream that one day the decedents of former slaves would be able to come together in genuine loving friendship with the decedents of former slave owners so that America could become a haven of freedom and justice.[1]

Thus, the key elements of this dream goal are freedom and justice, and a genuine experience of loving friendship, brotherhood, or that of a unified family among all Americans will be the result. In the "I Have a Dream" speech, the word *freedom* or something similar, for example *liberty*, is used twenty-one times, and the word *justice* eleven times. Dr. King said in describing his intense desire for justice in his "I Have a Dream" speech to the nation that some people are asking the enthusiastic followers of the civil rights movement about when they will be satisfied with the plight of Negroes in America. He answered this question with the text of Amos 5:24. He said that the devotees of the civil rights movement will not be satisfied with the plight of Black people in America until "justice rolls down like waters and righteousness like a mighty stream."[2]

Observe that the dream goal justice, its importance, and its relationship to righteousness have already been explored in chapter 1 under the section titled "Dream Method 1—Righteousness, Forgiveness, Perseverance." In this discussion, it was revealed that justice and righteousness feed on each other. What this means is that you can't have an abundance of one without an abundance of the other. And of the two, righteousness must be sought after first or before justice can become a reality. This is one of the many things that Jesus expressed when He said in Matthew 6:32–33,

> For after all these things the Gentiles seek. For your heavenly Father knows that you need all these things [the material things of life, of which freedom and justice are prerequisites or needed to obtain them]. But seek first the kingdom of God and His righteousness, and all these things shall be added to you.

During the years of King Solomon's reign when he prayed for a discerning heart and wisdom to govern God's people (1 Kings 3:9), the queen of Sheba visited Solomon, observed his leadership, and said in acknowledgment of his wisdom,

> How happy your people must be! How happy your officials, who continually stand before you and hear your wisdom! Praise be to the LORD your God, who has delighted in you and placed you on the throne of Israel. Because of the LORD's eternal love for Israel, he has made you king to maintain justice and righteousness. (1 Kings 10:8–9 NIV)

The requirement of the inseparable combination of justice and righteousness to make a nation of people happy was in the heart of God from the start of creation.

Moreover, a close observation will reveal that this is also true of all Dr. King's dream methods and dream goals. The requirement of justice and righteousness to be inseparably connected did not start with the expression of this principle in Dr. King's "I Have a Dream" speech to the nation on August 28, 1963.

Furthermore, note in the 1 Kings 10:9 text that a nation's leadership was established by God to "maintain justice and righteousness" in the nation it oversees.

Also, note that the psalmist further confirmed the inseparable connection of justice and righteousness when he said, "The Lord executes [works] righteousness and justice for those who are oppressed" (Psalm 103:6). Observe that the psalmist did not say that the Lord just works to establish justice for oppressed people, but He works to establish both justice *and* righteousness.

Now before we move on, I have a question that I want to ask readers. How many ministers, teachers, and pastors in the churches throughout our nation do you think emphasize the fact that you can't have justice without righteousness? How many pastors do you think teach their people and inform the unbelievers that they encounter in the various secular civil rights movements that they are affiliated with the absolute fact that justice will not roll down through our nation "like waters" until righteousness rolls down through our nation "like a mighty stream"? Think about that.

Digging deeper on this subject matter, note also that no nation of people can have freedom without righteousness and justice. And vice versa, no nation of people can possess righteousness and justice without freedom—freedom of religion, freedom of speech, freedom of assembly, freedom to determine where I will live, what kind of career I will pursue, and so forth.

Concerning the absolute importance of the pursuit of freedom as a dream goal, Dr. King eloquently said in his speech "The Ethical Demands of Integration" that was delivered in Nashville, Tennessee, on December 27, 1962, for a church conference the following. He said that without the freedom to determine how he should live the various aspects of his life, this means that his manhood or the distinctive characteristics of a man has been stolen from him. And thus he is degraded to a lower form of life that does not live but merely exists, an existence that steals from him the ability to effectively bear all the normal personal responsibilities of life.[3]

So think about this in relationship to America today. The gradual absence or deterioration of various freedoms is the exact direction or the kind of American lifestyle that the politically left wing populace of this nation is strongly promoting. Denying Americans who don't agree with them their freedom of speech through intimidation and violence on the issues of our culture is one of the left's tactics being used today. This is thoroughly explored in *The Nightmare*, volume 3, chapter 3.

More and more government control and less and less individual freedom is the name of their game. Moreover, all this is being promoted by the left and supported by liberals—in the name of saving our democracy.

Moving on, as I previously stated, the essentiality of justice in the fulfillment of the dream has been sufficiently covered in chapter 1. This being the case, I want to dig into the dynamics of freedom in greater depth. And since freedom and justice are so inseparably connected, this will also help to understand the importance of an intense concern about righteousness as a nation as freedom is sought after for all the people of a nation—Black, White, Brown, Red, and Yellow.

To achieve this, I will draw on a powerful spiritual insight from Dr. Os Guinness, the author and worldwide lecturer who currently resides in McLean, Virginia. This insight has to do with the dynamics involved in how a nation maintains freedom for all its people—century after century. But first I want to share just a little bit of background about this most outstanding Christian man. He was born in China on September 30, 1941, to medical missionaries who were working there. He returned to England in 1951 to further his education. After graduating from Oxford University, he came to America in 1984. He became a fellow at the Woodrow Wilson International Center for Scholars, located in Washington, DC. Later, Os Guinness became a visiting fellow at the Brookings Institution, which conducts research and education in the social sciences. He cofounded Trinity Forum in 1991, a faith-based, nonprofit, evangelical, Christian organization. He served as senior fellow of Trinity Forum until 2004. Since then, he has been a senior fellow at several prestigious think tanks. He has written or edited more than thirty books, among which is one of my favorites, *The Call*. Os Guinness said in this book,

> What do I mean by "calling"? For the moment let me say simply that calling is the truth that God calls us to himself so decisively that everything we are, everything we do, and everything we have is invested with a special devotion and dynamism lived out as a response to his summons and service.

This truth—calling—has been a driving force in many of the greatest "leaps forward" in world history—the constitution of the Jewish nation at Mount Sinai, the birth of the Christian movement in Galilee, and the sixteenth-century Reformation and its incalculable impetus to the rise of the modern world, to name a few. Little wonder that the rediscovery of calling should be critical today, not least in satisfying the passion for purpose of millions of questing modern people.[4]

You see, Americans in general and Black people in particular who are so desperate for the fulfillment of the American dream and/or Dr. King's dream in our nation—both groups, whether they are the same groups or not—have a calling on their lives from God. On his whistle-stop train ride from Springfield, Illinois, to Washington, DC, on February 21, 1861, to be inaugurated on March 4, 1861, Abraham Lincoln visited the New Jersey Senate. He addressed these supporters and ended it with a most appropriate expression of what he saw as the God-ordained destiny or *calling* on the people of the United States of America. He said,

> I am exceedingly anxious that this Union, the Constitution, and the liberties of the people shall be perpetuated in accordance with the original idea for which that struggle [the Civil War] was made, and I shall be most happy indeed if I shall be an humble instrument in the hands of the Almighty, and of this, his almost chosen people, for perpetuating the object of that great struggle.[5]

Before taking the oath as the sixteenth president of the United States, Abraham Lincoln acknowledged that God had put on his heart that the American people were second in line to Israel as His chosen people. He said that Americans were *God's almost chosen people*, which meant that the American people had an eternal *calling* on their lives for God's glory. It meant that America was indeed a divinely chosen, *exceptional nation* among nations. Eric Metaxas, the erudite and lucid biographer of William Wilberforce, Dietrich Bonhoeffer, and Martin Luther; humorist; and New

York-based talk show host, said the following in his most powerful book that every American should read, *If You Can Keep It: The Forgotten Promise of American Liberty*:

> In the final sentence Lincoln sums up what he thinks of America and the American people. It is there that he calls us God's "almost chosen people," a phrase that is a sparkling distillation of the idea behind what we have called American exceptionalism. This is because it makes clear that Lincoln did not think America's exceptionalism a mere accident of history. Indeed, a few lines earlier he makes it clear that he sees our special role in history much as John Winthrop saw it and as many men in the two centuries connecting them saw it: as nothing less than a holy calling. But this is the point. We were called by God not for ourselves but for the whole world. What we did on our shores would be and was witnessed by the whole world, and it was for them that we did what we did. In what we were doing and in who we would become, we would be a promise to the whole world of a new way of living, something they could reach for as well, something we must help them to do, as we are able. In this way of seeing ourselves, we were to be a sign to the whole world beyond ourselves.[6]

Likewise, as I previously intimated in chapter 1 in maybe a slightly different way, I sincerely believe the following. Black Americans have a very special calling within, in association with, or as a vital part of the general calling that all Americans possess that was described by Abraham Lincoln as *God's almost chosen people*. What I mean by this is that because Dr. King's dream came through Black American history and his dream is so vital to maintaining the American dream, it is most appropriate then that Black Americans should humbly consider themselves as *God's almost, almost chosen people* or third in line behind Israel as God's chosen people. Black people have a calling as Americans but also a calling within a calling that must be performed "so decisively that everything we are, everything we do, and everything we have is invested with a special devotion and dynamism lived out as a response to his summons and service" (Os Guinness).⁷ Like it or not, Black Americans are double agents—called by God to work toward the success of both the American dream and Dr. King's dream.

Dr. King said something worth noting about Black Americans, which should motivate us and make us more aware of our status as double agents or *God's* almost, almost chosen people. In an address before a meeting of the National Press Club in Washington, DC, on July 19, 1962, Dr. King said that because of our history as slaves who suffered the cruel brutality of injustice and humiliation of every sort, Black people should possess the sentiment of being the *conscience of America*. And it is a conscience that should persistently demand that America strives to live according to its founding documents and the will of God.⁸

Moreover, in order for those two callings, those two destinies, those two dreams, which in actuality are one in the same dream—for them to become a reality, Dr. Os Guinness has a word of wisdom from God for us. This insightful word concerns how a free nation maintains its freedom or how the freedom and justice of the American dream and Dr. King's dream are maintained once they are established as the principles by which a nation will exist. Dr. Guinness most insightfully stated this:

> America's deepest crisis is the crisis of sustainable freedom ... Sustainable freedom is urgent for America because freedom is far more difficult to sustain than most Americans realize ... For at the heart of freedom lies a grand paradox: the greatest enemy of freedom is freedom ... Free societies must always maintain their freedom on two levels at once: at the level of their nation's constitution and at the level of their citizens' convictions. The formal structures of liberty and the informal spirit of liberty—or the fundamental laws and the fundamental "habits of the heart"—are both essential to freedom, though in different ways ... In a democratic republic, the rulers and the subjects are one and the same, so freedom depends constantly not only on the character of the nation's leaders but also on the character of its citizens ... The core problem can be expressed like this: Such is our human propensity for self-love—or thinking

> and acting with the self as center—that the virtue it takes for citizens to remain free is quite unnatural ... So law alone will override freedom by its very lack of self-restraint and by its inherent drive to compensate by replacing virtue with regulations. Virtue alone will always be too weak to sustain freedom, yet sometimes virtue alone will be too strong, in the sense that an excess of virtue can itself be an abuse of power.[9]

Neither a nation's constitution alone, no matter how awesomely wise and rooted in fairness and justice it might be—nor the most virtuous people, because of the sin nature of the human race, is strong enough to sustain freedom. Both are required! So what is the indispensable dynamic that must exist to sustain freedom in regard to virtue or the "habits of the hearts" of a nation's people and its leaders? America has some awesome founding documents—the Declaration of Independence, United States Constitution, Bill of Rights, and its other amendments. But some convictions or virtues must exist in the hearts of American citizens in a dynamic relationship with freedom in order to sustain the freedom that is expressly stated in both the American dream and Dr. King's dream.

In Dr. Guinness's book *A Free People's Suicide: Sustaining Freedom and the American Future*, he talks about what he calls "the recycling golden triangle of freedom." This, by the way, confirms the absolute necessity of using Dr. King's dream methods to achieve his dream goals. It likewise provides a more in-depth understanding of the dynamics involved in the process of using dream methods to achieve not just the dream goals of freedom and justice but all dream goals. The reason why this is true is that all dream methods and dream goals are rooted and grounded in virtuous "habits of the heart" (Tocqueville) or righteousness and faith.

Os Guinness described the recycling golden triangle of freedom and how it works to maintain a nation's freedoms for all—which includes justice for all, since both freedom and justice are so inseparably connected—in the following way:

> Tocqueville called it "the habits of the heart," and I call it "the golden triangle of freedom"—the cultivation and

transmission of the conviction that freedom requires virtue, which requires faith, which requires freedom, which in turn requires virtue, which requires faith, which requires freedom and so on, like the recycling triangle, ad infinitum. In short, sustainable freedom depends on the character of the rulers and the ruled alike, and on the vital trust between them—both of which are far more than a matter of law. The Constitution, which is the foundational law of the land, should be supported and sustained by the faith, character and virtue of the entire citizenry, which comprises its moral constitution, or habits of the heart. Together with the Constitution, these habits of the heart are the real, complete and essential bulwark of American liberty. A republic grounded only in a consensus forged of calculation and competing self-interests can never last.[10]

The recycling golden triangle of freedom depicted in figure 3 illustrates the principle that without virtue or character being deeply embedded in an effective faith in God in the hearts of the people of a nation, freedom cannot be sustained. But just as important, without freedom, and more specifically without the unadulterated, unhindered, or unrestricted freedom of religion, virtue based in a genuine faith in God cannot be sustained.

The Recycling Golden Triangle of Freedom

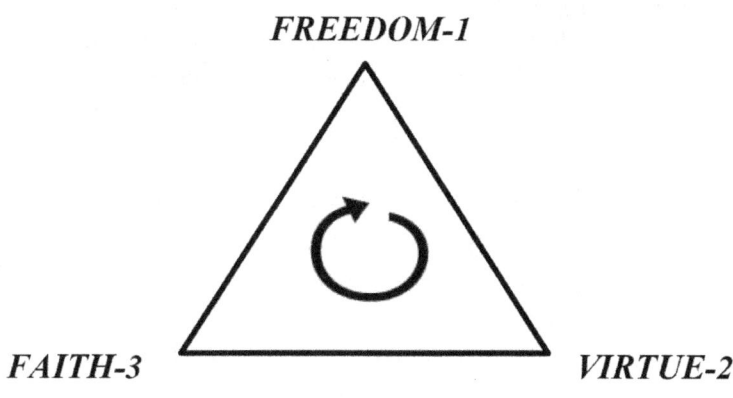

Figure 3

What the golden triangle of freedom tells us is this. For freedom to be sustained by the general populace of a nation, more than the God-given founding documents of a nation, such as the United States Constitution and the Bill of Rights, is required. Such a principle was fairly obvious and well known by earlier Americans. This is true even though early Americans were hypocritical in the application of the principle of constitutional freedom in the treatment of Africans as slaves, American Indians, and American women. In spite of all their hypocrisies, the framers of the Constitution and earlier Americans consistently held fast to the importance of virtue for sustaining freedom. Benjamin Franklin famously said, "Only a virtuous people are capable of freedom."[11, 12]

Also, for more testimony to earlier Americans consistently holding fast to the importance of virtue for sustaining freedom, think about the following. In 1831, twenty-seven-year-old Alexis de Tocqueville and Gustave de Beaumont were sent to America by the French government to study and make a report on our prison system. From his notes, Tocqueville wrote an exhaustive analysis of the successes and failures of the American government in a two-volume work titled *Democracy in America*. And in this most important historical document of the American form of government, Tocqueville made the following of numerous observations. They help to explain the absolute necessity of virtue and faith to sustain freedom in America and our exceptional status from the viewpoint of a gifted political scientist and historian:

> Number 1: I sought for the greatness and genius of America in her commodious harbors and her ample rivers—and it was not there ... in her fertile fields and boundless forests and it was not there ... in her rich mines and her vast world commerce—and it was not there ... in her democratic Congress and her matchless Constitution—and it was not there. Not until I went into the churches of America and heard her pulpits aflame with righteousness did I understand the secret of her genius and power. America is great because she is good

> [virtuous], and if America ever ceases to be good [virtuous], she will cease to be great.

> Number 2: The character of Anglo-American civilization ... is the product ... of two perfectly distinct elements that elsewhere have often made war with each other, but which, in America, they have succeeded in incorporating somehow into one another and combining marvelously. I mean to speak of the spirit of religion and the spirit of freedom.

> Number 3: Liberty [freedom] cannot be established without morality [virtue], nor morality without faith.

And to help explain why America has been in such turmoil over the issue of freedom and justice over the years, which seems to be escalating, when it is not absolutely clear that all Americans are receiving these rights to the same degree, Alexis de Tocqueville said something that should forever ring loudly in the ears of all Americans. He said as he toured America and took notes,

> Americans are so enamored of equality, they would rather be equal in slavery than unequal in freedom.

Therefore, Americans should be equally enamored with virtue and faith in God so that we don't all have to resort to being equal in slavery—or suffer a great loss of freedoms—because we became so unvirtuous and faithless that we could not seriously strive to be equal in freedom with one another. For that is exactly where we are heading as a nation.

What I am saying is that every act or form of behavior that does not conform to Dr. King's dream methods (righteousness, forgiveness, perseverance, self-respect, nonviolence, unity, faith, and hope) hijacks the ability of the dream goals to become a reality in America. As previously noted in dream methods 1 in chapter 1, Dr. King warned us about how freedom and justice can so easily be hijacked when someone leans on their own understanding. He said in his "I Have a Dream" speech to the nation that while we are in the process of getting the promissory note to Black people fulfilled, we must do it in a way that is beyond reproach or in the most *righteous* way. He said that it must be done without bitterness or hatred, which means we must bestow *forgiveness* to America and everyone we feel participated in the failure to fulfill the promissory note to the Negro.[13]

This is an essential principle that many civil rights activists today seem to have conveniently forgotten as they invoke the name of Dr. King in their useless, manipulative efforts to promote freedom and justice in America. Or these hijackers claim that Dr. King abandoned his well-defined methods for implementing his dream later on in his civil rights campaigns. Such an example of the manipulative invocation of Dr. King's name was demonstrated by former attorney general Eric Holder while campaigning in Georgia for Democratic gubernatorial nominee Stacey Abrams in October 2018. David Knowles in an article written for *Yahoo News* on October 10, 2018, titled "Eric Holder's Rallying Cry for Democrats: When They Go Low, We Kick 'Em," reported that Holder said,

> Michelle [first lady Michelle Obama] says, "When they go low, we go high." No, no. When they go low, we kick 'em. ... That's what this new Democratic Party is about. [Holder said] ... Minutes later, Holder qualified his remarks. Now, when I say, you know, we kick 'em, I don't mean we do anything inappropriate, Holder said. We don't do anything illegal, but we got to be tough.[14]

And Aaron Blake in his article for the *Washington Post,* titled "Erick Holder: When They Go Low We Kick Them," added the words of Holder's speech demonstrate how the former attorney general, while supposedly in the quest for freedom and justice, invoked Dr. King's name to support something that hijacked the dream. Aaron Blake recorded the additional words that were spoken on that day by Erick Holder as part of his explanation of what he meant by "When they go low we kick them." Holder said, according to Aaron Blake,

> We don't do anything illegal. But we got to be tough, and we have to fight for the very things that John Lewis,

HIJACKED!

Martin Luther King, Whitney Young—you know, all those folks gave to us.[15]

Former attorney general Eric Holder invoked Dr. King's name in an attempt to justify something that was obviously against all that Dr. King stood for.

However, what was even more grievous to the promotion of Dr. King's dream and the quest for freedom and justice is what prompted Eric Holder to contradict the former First Lady Michelle Obama's high-minded 2016 slogan. Holder was apparently incited to contradict what Michelle Obama said by a statement on the previous day by another First Lady, Hillary Clinton. First Lady Hillary Clinton said the following in an interview with CNN's Christiane Amanpour on October 9, 2018, that was reported by Rachel Ventresca. This would have been most grievous to Dr. King. First Lady Hillary Clinton said,

> You cannot be civil with a political party that wants to destroy what you stand for, what you care about. That's why I believe, if we are fortunate enough to win back the House and or the Senate, that's when civility can start again. But until then, the only thing that the Republicans seem to recognize and respect is strength.[16]

Incivility until you get back in office is the ethics and tactics of the degenerate, sensate culture that we live it today. It is likewise the ethics and tactic of Saul Alinsky's *Rules for Radicles* disciples (*Hijacked!*, volume 2, chapter 1). Such thinking is not even remotely associated with Dr. King's dream methods for achieving dream goals. This is either a most naïve and foolish line of thinking; a most deceptive, manipulative, and calculative line of thinking; or a combination of both. I tend to lean toward the latter. The message of this statement seems to be this: once we use uncivilized mob tactics (violence if necessary) to intimidate conservatives in our efforts to take back control of the government, then we can insist on and enforce a more civilized form of protest. How foolish! I say this because hate begets hate! Incivility begets incivility! Incivility from leftists and liberals will only tempt conservatives to respond in turn with incivility toward them to regain the power to protect what they stand for and care about.

Therefore, what I am saying is that once the genie is let out of the bottle, it is hard to put him back in. Incivility to gain freedom and justice is never the answer. Incivility hijacks the process of making the dream a reality. The *means* are always a predetermining foretaste of the *end*. The *means* are the *end* in the process of becoming a reality.[17] This means that there will always be some unexpected disastrous results when the above Hillary Clinton kind of thinking is employed.

Yes, Dr. King's dream is indeed characterized by his intense desire for freedom and justice. But Christian believers must not allow themselves to be deceived by the uninformed or the intentionally deceptive lies of those who know better. The sound biblical doctrine of Dr. King's dream methods are clearly a faithful and true witness to the immutable or unchangeability of their nature and content. He or she who has an ear, let him or her hear what the Spirit says to the churches—which has the calling to promote virtue, faith in God, and thus freedom, justice, and other dream goals in America.

Thus it obviously seems that the knowledge of the principles of the recycling golden triangle of freedom is increasingly being lost as Americans become further removed in time from the inception of our founding documents. The founding fathers realized that because of the inborn depravity of humans, something more than our awesome God-given founding documents was needed to sustain the freedom that these documents proclaimed.

Note that it was the faith of the founding fathers that was left as a legacy for later Americans to follow that put the principles of the recycling golden triangle of freedom on the hearts of men like Abraham Lincoln and John Brown. These men were forced to acknowledge, as a result of their faith in God, that freedom for the nation could not be sustained without virtue based in faith in God. And thus the civil war was a result of the recycling dynamics or the relationship between the elements of the golden triangle of freedom—freedom, virtue, and faith.

Likewise, the Apostle Paul confirmed the absolute necessity of virtue and faith for sustaining freedom when he said this to the Corinthians:

> But even to this day, when Moses is read, a veil lies on their heart. Nevertheless when one turns to the LORD, the

veil is taken away. Now the Lord is the Spirit; and where the Spirit of the Lord is, there is liberty [or freedom]. But we all, with unveiled face, beholding as in a mirror the glory of the Lord, are being transformed into the same image from glory to glory, just as by the Spirit of the Lord. (2 Cor. 3:15–18)

Similarly, Jesus expressed the relationship between virtue and faith or the Spirit of the Lord for sustaining freedom this way:

The thief [anti-God leadership] comes only to steal, and kill, and destroy; I [virtue and faith] came that you might have life [liberty or freedom], and might have it abundantly. (John 10:10)

The founding fathers understood the essential relationships, the dynamics, that exist between freedom, virtue, and faith to sustain freedom and its associated justice—but so did Dr. King. The evidence of Dr. King's complete understanding of the recycling dynamics of the golden triangle of freedom can be clearly observed in figure 2 on page 69. This is the "I Have a Dream" methods triangle for implementing Dr. King's dream goals. Note that the elements listed on the dream methods triangle are the following: righteousness, forgiveness, perseverance, self-respect, nonviolence, unity, and faith and hope.

Moreover, note that the recycling golden triangle of freedom applies not only to freedom and the American dream but also to freedom and Dr. King's dream. What I mean by this in reference to Dr. King's dream and the dream methods triangle in figure 2 is this. Dream goals (freedom, justice, and others) require dream methods 1 and 2 (virtues), which require dream method 3 (faith and hope), which requires dream goals, which requires dream methods, and so forth and so on, in a never-ending cycle.

Therefore, the recycling golden triangle of freedom can be expressed for Dr. King's dream as shown in figure 4 below, which is titled "The Recycling Golden Triangle of the Dream." More accurately, figure 4 could be called "The Recycling Golden Triangle of Dream Goals."

The Recycling Golden Triangle of The Dream

Figure 4

So just how intense was Dr. King's desire for freedom and justice? He said in his speech "I Have a Dream" that it should be the goal of America to let freedom ring from the magnificently majestic heights of the mountains of New Hampshire, New York, Pennsylvania, and Colorado and every mountainside. But more than that, he said let it ring from the more modest heights of the mountains in Georgia and Tennessee, as well as from every hill and molehill in Mississippi. Dr. King went on to say that, moreover, let freedom ring from every township, parish, city, and state so that we can hasten the day into existence when people of every race and religion will be able to join hands, sing together, and thank the LORD God Almighty for our freedom.[18]

Dr. King said that he had a dream that the permeation of freedom throughout the nation would create a truly unified nation or a genuine United States of America across physical borders, races, cultures, and religious groups.

And what does the recycling golden triangle of the dream tell us about why Dr. King's widespread, intense dream of freedom and justice is being hijacked in America today? In order for freedom and justice to be sustained by a race of oppressed people or people who perceive that they are oppressed, this requires more than the God-given dream goals that were given to Dr. King. It also requires virtue and genuine faith and hope in God, which is the reason why today dream methods are not being effectively employed for the successful establishment of dream goals.

In other words, freedom and justice won't ring from every township and every parish, from every state and every city until virtue and faith in God or Dr. King's dream methods ring from every township and every parish, from every state and every city. We won't be able to hold hands, sing together, and thank the Lord God Almighty until virtue and faith in God or Dr. King's dream methods ring from every township and every parish, from every state and every city.

Accordingly, Dr. King revealed his Holy Spirit–inspired knowledge of the kind of great virtue and its associated great faith in God that universal freedom in America would require in his "I Have a Dream" speech. He expressed the kind of great virtue and faith required to satisfy the dynamics of the recycling golden triangle of freedom.

More specifically, Dr. King used Isaiah 40:1–5 as the context to parabolically express the virtue and faith in God that is required by the American people to "prepare the way" (Isa. 40:3) or to remove all obstacles to universal freedom in our nation. Just like Israel in the day of Isaiah, Americans must believe by faith in God that virtuous living will—for sure and for certain—usher in and maintain universal freedom in America. After stating that he had a dream, toward the closing of his speech, Dr. King quoted the prophet Isaiah, who said in chapter 40,

> Every valley shall be exalted and every mountain and hill brought low; the crooked places shall be made straight and the rough places smooth; the glory of the Lord shall be revealed, and all flesh shall see it together. (Isa. 40:4–5)

Dr. King went on to say that, through faith, the disharmony that exists in America could be transformed into an exquisite synergism of brotherly love. He said that when this happens, all Americans will be able to sing the song "My Country, 'Tis of Thee" with a new meaning, which is a must in order for America to be a great nation.[19]

And so, it should be obvious that the recycling golden triangle of freedom is the key to dream goal 2. For the Christian church in America, this means that we cannot afford to drag our feet in evangelism, preaching and teaching the Gospel of salvation, and injecting the unadulterated love of Jesus into our unbelieving culture.

Thus, both the dream and the American dream are experiencing a devastating hijacking because the Christian church—Black, White, Brown, Red, and Yellow—is not doing that! We the people can't live like devilish, humanistic heathens and then expect an abundance of freedom and justice to permeate our culture. And Black people, Black Christians in particular, whether we want to accept the calling or not, we have been called to lead a revolution of virtue and faith in God in our culture. We have been called by God Himself to lead a dream methods and dream goals revolution in our culture.

And so Americans are losing our freedom because of the loss of virtue or character and faith in God in our political leaders, spiritual leaders, and the people themselves. Freedom and justice requires, feeds on, is strengthened by, or is sustained by virtue. Virtue requires, feeds on, is strengthened by, or is sustained by faith and hope in God. And faith and hope in God requires, feeds on, is strengthened by, or is encouraged or promoted by freedom and justice. And without this recycling dynamic being effectively executed by we the people, we are indeed on the road to hijacking our dreams, resulting in our death by suicide—self-destruction! This will be explored in more depth in volume 2—*The Hijack* and volume 3—*The Nightmare*. It is now time to move on to dream goal 3, which is explored in the next chapter.

6

THE GOALS TO BE ACHIEVED: DREAM GOAL 3—DR. KING'S DREAM IS CHARACTERIZED BY HIS INTENSE DESIRE FOR HATEFUL UNFORGIVENESS TO BE REPLACED WITH LOVING FORGIVENESS

Of all the problems that America has experienced in instituting the principles of the United States Constitution and the Bill of Rights, it seems as though race is the biggest stumbling block. Everything in America seems to be about race. If you want to really hurt someone, all you have to do is play the race card and falsely accuse someone of being a bigot or racist. This automatically causes undiscerning people who hear this lie to mentally check out, abandon logic and common sense, and believe whatever lies are told in connection with the use of the race card.

I am reminded of how the race card was so skillfully employed on August 14, 2012, by Joe Biden at a Democratic rally for the presidential campaign of himself and Barack Obama in Danville, Virginia. Joe Biden said to a diverse audience, which included many African Americans, about their opponents Mitt Romney and Paul Ryan, "They gonna put you'll back in chains."[1] He very intentionally said this in a way that was meant to imitate poor, uneducated southern Black people. He said this about Mitt Romney's economic plan, which in reality would have greatly helped Black people. Joe Biden said this to refresh the memory of Black people about the pain and suffering of slavery and the Jim Crow laws that existed in America for so many years. He said this to stir up hateful feelings of fear and anger in the hearts and minds of Black people and those who have been sympathetic to the plight of Blacks in years past.

This is a common tactic of hijackers whose goal is to gain the political support and the vote of Black people. You see, hijackers could care less that such racially inflammatory words will be a great hindrance to the effort of establishing brotherhood in our nation. All they care about is power or the furtherance of their ideology. The goal of this kind of a hijacker is to manipulate Black people into nursing and rehearsing our pain of the past for their political gain.

What I am saying in all this is that when racial passions are stirred up, then the truth of the matter at hand is in great jeopardy. The reason why this is so effective is that everybody in America seems to believe that everybody is a racist except for themselves or their own particular cultural or social group.

As a matter of fact, I have heard many African Americans ridiculously say that it is impossible for Black or African American people to be racists. And what this is based on is the experience of their ancestors as slaves or during the Jim Crow law era or because of their perceived African American experience in modern-day America.

However, it has been my experience as a Black American that just as many Black people have racist ideas about White, Brown, Red, and Yellow people as some in those people groups have about African Americans. Just because someone is Black does not automatically inoculate or make them immune from being a racist. It probably should, but it quite obviously doesn't.

Therefore, I think that some people really don't understand what it means to be a racist. So at this time, I think it is appropriate to say that a racist is a person who predetermines or decides in advance what a person's character is by the color of their skin or some other physical appearances. Or you could say that a racist is a person who decides that he or she does not want any kind of a real relationship or close interactions with someone because of the color of their skin—their race or the people group to which they belong.

HIJACKED!

This of course makes it clear that racism is indeed one of the most significant ways that Dr. King's dream is hijacked on a daily, almost on a moment-by-moment basis in America. It seems to be what is almost always on everybody's mind in one way or another. Race seems to have a significant influence on the thoughts, feelings, and behavior of people in America toward one another. So what was Dr. King's dream goal for solving the race problem that over the years has been so prevalent in America?

In Dr. King's dream for the people of America, he provided a very simple solution to this apparently complicated problem that seems to be so influential in our thoughts, feelings, and behavior. Dr. King said the following in describing his third dream goal in August 1963. He said that he dreamed that one day America—from coast to coast—would be a place where the quality of a person's character and not their race, ethnicity, or culture would be the means by which we judge one another. He said that he dreamed of the day in America when people of all colors will love one another and live together as brothers and sisters.[2]

Dr. King said that he had a dream of a time when Americans would stop judging people by their outward appearance but instead judge them by what is in their heart, which is how God judges people. The writer of 1 Samuel said the following in confirming this virtuous attitude about life when Samuel was looking for a man to replace Saul as king:

> Then he consecrated Jesse [David's father] and his sons, and invited them to the sacrifice. So it was, when they came, that he looked at Eliab [an impressive young man by outward appearance] and said, "Surely the LORD'S anointed is before Him!" But the LORD said to Samuel, "Do not look at his appearance or at his physical stature, because I have refused him. For the LORD does not see as man sees; for man looks at the outward appearance, but the LORD looks at the heart." (16:5–7)

Summarizing all this, Dr. King said that he had a dream of a time in America when hateful unforgiveness and racial pride would be replaced with loving forgiveness and humility (dream method 1). Dr. King said that he had a dream that a time would come when genuine brotherhood would flow among the people of our nation from east to west and north to south across America, like a mighty raging river that could not be stopped.

In other words, Dr. King had a dream of a time when everybody in America would consider others to be better than themselves—a time when Black Lives Matter signs would be changed to signs that say All Lives Matter. And the only way that this will happen is through forgiveness and abandoning our racial pride. The question now at hand is why must hateful unforgiveness and racial pride be replaced with loving forgiveness and humility in order to judge people by the content of their character instead of the color of their skin?

The reason is that judging people by skin color instead of character is a spiritual problem. And spiritual problems can only be solved with spiritual solutions, which in this case is replacing unforgiveness and pride with the virtues of forgiveness and humility.

Replacing Hateful Unforgiveness with Loving Forgiveness

So first I will present an assessment of the importance of both giving and receiving forgiveness for enabling an individual or a nation of people to start judging by character instead of skin color. After this, I will explore the racial pride aspect involved in wrongly judging people in chapter 7. So, who needs to forgive whom in America, and who needs to ask whom for forgiveness?

Well, African Americans need to forgive America in general and Anglo-Americans of past generations and their descendants in particular. They need to do this for the seventy-two-plus years of the dastardly, shameful deeds of slavery that were perpetrated against their ancestors (1789–1861); the fifteen-plus years of Reconstruction era Black Codes created to restrict the freedom of ex-slaves in the South (1862–1877); the eighty-seven-plus years of the inhumane deeds of the Jim Crow laws in the South (1878–1965); and the insensitive, evil deeds of racism in other parts of the nation during the Jim Crow era.

This also means that slave owners, those who supported the slave economic system, and the Jim Crow law supporters—if there are any still alive—these survivors should issue a genuine public request for forgiveness from African Americans. But they must be forgiven regardless of whether this request is made or not. That's biblical.

On the other hand, African Americans who have anger, hatred, and bitterness toward the Anglo-American descendants of the slave economy and Jim Crow era should abandon these feelings and issue a genuine public request for their forgiveness. Now why do I say this?

I say this because offspring or descendants are not responsible for the feelings, actions, and thinking of their parents or ancestors. This is what the Lord meant when He said in Jeremiah 31:29–30,

> In those days [New Testament days] they shall say no more: "The fathers have eaten sour grapes, and the children's teeth are set on edge." But every one shall die for his own iniquity; every man who eats the sour grapes, his teeth shall be set on edge.

The Message Bible says it this way:

> When that time comes you won't hear the old proverb anymore, "Parents ate the green apples, their children got the stomachache." No each person will pay for his own sin. You eat green apples, you're the one who gets sick. (MSG)

You see, the woke Marxist left and their undiscerning supporters have no awareness of the wrath of God that they will encounter for demonizing all White people or making them to appear to be racists because of the racist actions of their ancestors. These people who are adherents of critical race theory or the religion of wokeism have no perception of the consequences of their wicked behavior. It has gotten so bad in America that White K–12 students and those students, such as Asians, who are perceived as possessing the *White mentality* are being taught by teachers that they and their parents are inherently racist. White students are being taught that they are less than good people because of something they are not responsible for.

Moreover, this does nothing to help Black or Brown people to be successful, but instead does just the opposite. Critical race theory is being ruthlessly propagated by the woke Marxist left to produce spiteful race obsessed robots that they can control in their efforts to reprogram Americans and tear down and start over with a new set of principles of government. And if this kind of hateful unforgiveness that is being spread throughout America is not replaced with loving forgiveness so that the American people are not susceptible to the deception of the woke Marxist left, the results will be just what they are striving for—more racial turbulence and the increasing possibility of a race war. So the question that wokies or member of the woke church must be asked is this. How do you teach people not to discriminate by discriminating?

Thus, it should be carefully noted that critical race theory, which was formulated by the Harvard Law School in the seventies and became a part of the academic and media mainstream[3]—this concoction has hijacked Dr. King's dream and the civil rights movement. Another viewpoint by Christopher F. Rufo, founder and director of Battlefront, a public policy research center, says that critical race theory was formulated in the nineties.[4] He notes that besides being injected into public school systems and teacher training programs, "it has been injected into government agencies, … corporate human resources departments in the form of diversity training programs, human resources modules, public policy frameworks, and school curricula."[5]

This systemic racism concoction, among other things, stipulates that the most important thing about a person is their race or skin color, which is a blatant contradiction of the principles of Dr. King's dream. The woke Marxist left and their softminded, undiscerning followers are propagating the cancerous lie that if you are White or possess the *White mentality*, you are inherently a perpetrator of racism. And if you are a person of color, then you are inherently a victim of all White people because all of them are perpetrators of racism. James Lindsey said the following in the video/article for Prager University titled "What is Critical Race Theory?":

> Critical Race Theory proponents assume racism is present everywhere and always, and they look for it "critically" until they find it. And they always find it. It has to be there because that's how the imperial European powers, and then America, set things up … Critical Race Theory,

therefore, is not a continuation of the Civil Rights Movement. It is, in fact, a repudiation of it ... To Critical Race theorists, Martin Luther King was both wrong and naïve.[6]

On a brighter note, all Americans should observe for the furtherance of brotherhood in America that a confession of sin and the seeking of forgiveness has been sought from African Americans by the descendants of slave owners and Jim Crow law proponents. Now it didn't happen in the Emancipation Proclamation issued by President Abraham Lincoln on January 1, 1863. And it didn't happen in the Gettysburg Address by President Lincoln during the Civil War on November 19, 1863. And it didn't happen in any of the Reconstruction Era documents and laws, such as the Confiscation Acts, the Freedmen's Bureau Act, or the Thirteenth, Fourteenth, and Fifteenth Amendments during the years of 1863–1877.

However, on July 29, 2008, the United States House of Representatives passed a resolution apologizing for slavery and the Jim Crow laws. Likewise, on June 18, 2009, the United States Senate followed suit. But there were differences over the language in the Senate bill. The Senate bill rejected any form of restitution or reparations. This means that the United States Congress has never issued a joint apology. And the issue of reparations is still unsettled.

Nevertheless, it is still most significant that during the presidency of Barack Obama, both the House and the Senate passed a resolution on behalf of the American people apologizing to African Americans for slavery and the Jim Crow laws. I must also add for clarification that neither the lack of an official joint apology or the still unsettled reparations issue are justifiable reasons—in God's eyes—for African Americans not to accept the apology. Nor is it a justifiable reason for African Americans not to be fervent in our pursuit of genuine forgiveness and brotherhood with all Americans.

And so, 146 years after the Emancipation Proclamation, which proclaimed that slaves "shall be then, thenceforward, and forever free," *Essence,* the widely viewed African American magazine for women, reported on December 16, 2009, that the House of Representatives had passed a resolution in which they "expressed regret to African-Americans for slavery and Jim Crow laws."[7] House Resolution 194, titled "Apologizing for the enslavement and racial segregation of African-Americans," passed on July 29, 2008, states in part the following:

> Whereas African-Americans continue to suffer from the complex interplay between slavery and Jim Crow—long after both systems were formally abolished—through enormous damage and loss, both tangible and intangible, including the loss of human dignity, the frustration of careers and professional lives, and the long-term loss of income and opportunity ... Now, therefore, be it *Resolved,* That the House of Representatives—
> 1. acknowledges that slavery is incompatible with the basic founding principles recognized in the Declaration of Independence that all men are created equal;
> 2. acknowledges the fundamental injustice, cruelty, brutality, and inhumanity of slavery and Jim Crow;
> 3. apologizes to African Americans on behalf of the people of the United States, for the wrongs committed against them and their ancestors who suffered under slavery and Jim Crow; and
> 4. expresses its commitment to rectify the lingering consequences of the misdeeds committed against African Americans under slavery and Jim Crow and to stop the occurrence of human rights violations in the future.[8]

Similarly, Russell Simmons—the Black entrepreneur, author, and record producer—wrote an article concerning the United States Senate apology for slavery. Note that Simmons's sentiments must be the sentiments of all African Americans who are serious about making Dr. King's dream goal of brotherhood a reality in America. In June 2009, Russell Simmons, in an article written for the *Huff Post*, expressed his sentiments about the apology of the Senate in the title of that article, which is "The Healing Has Begun." One of the significant things that Simmons said in expressing his sentiments that the apology of the Senate must be seen by African Americans as the time when the healing has begun is this:

> We have finally recognized that in order for us to move forward as a people in this beautiful nation [in order for the healing to begin], we need to acknowledge the pain that we all have suffered because of slavery.[9]

Digging deeper, the article from *Essence* magazine online stated that there are other racial groups of Americans, such as Japanese Americans and Native Americans, that need to both genuinely accept America's apology, remorse, and regret and then forgive and ask for forgiveness just like African Americans must do.

American Indians need to follow this same pattern. They need to forgive America for the many injustices executed against them, such as the forced marches associated with the 1830 Indian Removal Act. In the fall and winter of 1838 and 1839, the United States government forced Cherokee Indians to move west. On this forced march, about four thousand Cherokees died. This forced march became known as the Trail of Tears.

Also, there are Japanese Americans who need to forgive America for what they consider as being unjust forced relocation and incarceration. During World War II (1942–1945), as many as 120,000 Japanese Americans were forced by the United States government to live out the war in West Coast concentration camps.

And then again, there are some Mexican Americans who need to forgive America and follow the same pattern of both giving and seeking forgiveness. For some of them are bitter. They contend that after the Mexican War (1846–1848), the United States government supported the confiscation of land grants given to their ancestors in California, Texas, New Mexico, and Colorado by the Treaty of Guadalupe Hidalgo.

So now the question that needs to be explored in more detail is this: what is the result of all the trauma experienced by the unjust treatment of African Americans, American Indians, Japanese Americans, and Mexican Americans?

The result is that these traumatic events caused many in the populace of these racial groups to be deeply wounded. And the longer the duration of these traumatic events, the deeper the wounds. So it appears that the deepest emotional wounds were experienced by African Americans and then the American Indians.

However, because of the great progress that African Americans have made in their recovery from their traumatic events versus that of the American Indians, some would argue that this order should be reversed. But even with all the progress that African Americans have made, great numbers of African Americans are still experiencing the emotional woundedness that was inflicted upon their ancestors.

The reason for this is that the generations of African Americans since slavery and the Jim Crow era, these past generations have transferred their emotional pain—their woundedness—of their past into the hearts and minds of their children. This modern-day woundedness is evidenced by all the anger, bitterness, and hatred that is expressed toward American values and the Anglo-American people. And the only way that this cycle of recurring woundedness that so many Black people have been stuck in—generation after generation—is going to be terminated is through genuine forgiveness. America and Anglo-Americans must be genuinely forgiven by African Americans for the trauma that we were forced to endure.

This cycle of recurring woundedness that Blacks have been stuck in because of generations passing down the legacy of the pain and suffering that we unjustly endured in our past instead of passing down a legacy of forgiveness that is pleasing to God—this is the biblical principle known as "generational curses" and "generational blessings." But more appropriately, this principle should be called "generational consequences" (Exod. 20:5–6).

The reason is that the principle of generational curses (Exod. 20:5) refers to how the ungodly decisions of parents (refusing to forgive) are passed down to their children, who thus experience the same *consequence* as their parents. And that consequence is the cancer of chronic angry, bitterness, and hatred. These kinds of chronic feelings then result in chronic bad choices and decisions. All these things are the consequences that the generational sin of unforgiveness (Matt. 6:14–15) brings into a person's life or the minds of almost an entire race of people—generation after generation.

Likewise, the principle of generational blessings (Exod. 20:6) refers to how the godly decision of parents (forgiveness) is passed down to their children, who thus receive the same *consequence* as their parents. And that consequence is the healing of their woundedness, which results in chronic peace, joy, success, and prosperity. Moses said the following in his record of the introduction and the generational consequences of the portion of the Ten Commandments that is recorded in Exodus 20:1–2, 4–6:

> And God spoke all these words, saying: "I am the LORD your God, who brought you out of the land of Egypt, out of the house of bondage … You shall not make for yourself a carved image—any likeness of anything that is in heaven above, or that is in the earth beneath, or that is in the water under the earth; ⁵you shall not bow down to them nor serve them [self-worship—an unwillingness to forgive—or racial pride]. For I, the LORD your God, am a jealous God, visiting the iniquity of the fathers upon the children to the third and fourth generations [consequences of ungodly choices and decisions of parents will last for generations after them] of those who hate Me [those who do not keep My commandments], ⁶but showing mercy [healing the woundedness] to thousands [consequences of the godly choices and decisions of parents will last for thousands of generations after them], to those who love Me and keep My commandments [pass down a legacy of forgiveness].

You see, African Americans can say over and over again that we have forgiven America and Anglo-Americans for what we were forced to experience. But the feelings, behavior, and thinking of many who profess forgiveness don't demonstrate an attitude of forgiveness. For these are the same people who claim that living in America is no better for African American people today than it was fifty years ago—which is a boldface lie! How can anyone look around and observe the great advances that African Americans have made unless it is an attempt to justify the current anger, bitterness, and hatred that so many of our people are still experiencing fifty-four years after the passing of the Civil Rights Act of 1964? In other words, it appears that such thinking is an effort to justify the woundedness that has been passed down to so many African Americans by their parents and other influential people in their lives.

What's more, this kind of wounded thinking has been promoted to justify the godless victim ideology that Black and White hijackers have employed to deceive many in the African American community. They do this to promote a continued state of woundedness in African Americans to control us. Their game is obvious because people are easier to control when they are divided into groups that are sorted by skin color.

So the obvious truth of the matter is that most African Americans have not genuinely forgiven America for what she did to us during slavery and the Jim Crow era. African Americans must realize that there are an enormous number of hijackers—both Black and White—who are promoting our continued woundedness instead of our genuine forgiveness of America. They are doing this for their personal, political, and ideological gains. African Americans are the wounded prey of many! And so many African Americans are not even remotely aware of this.

To expand on the idea of woundedness and its consequences, I want readers to think seriously for a moment about what I am about to say. I want to start by saying that a wounded person feels wounded, behaves wounded, and thinks wounded. Knowing this, Satan uses the hurts and woundedness of people by injecting ideas into their thoughts about what happened to them that makes it easy for them to justify their unforgiving, guilt-producing spirit and to be used by others. Bishop Dale C. Bronner stated the reason for the absolute necessity of effectively processing the wounds of the traumatic events of life through forgiveness with the very simple words, "What you don't heal from becomes the thing you act out of!" Forgiveness is indeed the first step toward the healing of one's emotions, the healing of a racial group of people, and the healing of a nation.

In other words, forgiveness is the first and most important step for enabling Americans to do more judging of people by their character instead of skin color. The reason why this is true is that forgiveness sets free both the persons offended or wounded and the offenders.

More specifically, forgiveness sets the offended and the offenders free to unite in genuine brotherhood and in a blessed relationship with Jesus Christ. We Americans are doing much, much better in the area of brotherhood between the races than we did in the past. But from my own personal experience, we still have a long way to go before we achieve the nationwide type of brotherhood that Dr. King described in his many speeches, sermons, and writings on this subject. There are pockets of America that have made great strides toward genuine brotherhood.

But then again, particularly in the urban areas of our nation, there are areas that are greatly struggling to be set free from racial stereotypes—judging by skin color instead of character. There is still a segment of our society that is angry and bitter—full of hate—because of America's past. And the only solution for both the offended and the offenders is forgiveness. There are no other options!

Moreover, there is still a segment of our society that is so full of themselves and racial pride that they can't properly judge and respect anyone whose skin color and social-economic status is considered as being below theirs. These people come in all colors—Black, White, Brown, Red, and Yellow.

However, I must stay on track for the time being with the subject matter at hand, which is enabling Americans to judge by character instead of skin color through forgiveness. The former, racial pride, will be explored a little bit further down the road in this discourse. So again I say, forgiveness sets the offended and the offenders free to unite in genuine brotherhood and in a blessed relationship with Jesus Christ. So how does forgiving someone or a nation that forced you and your ancestors to endure the woundedness of the worst kind of trauma imaginable for almost 175 years set you free to unite with them or their offspring in genuine brotherhood?

Well first of all, without forgiving the person, persons, or nation that wounded you, you become or remain that person's, persons,' or nation's slave and a prisoner of your past pain. A medical doctor by the name of S. I. McMillen, in his book *None of These Diseases*, said the following to explain how important it is to persevere—regardless of how long it takes and how much fasting and prayer it takes—until genuine forgiveness of those who wounded you is a reality. Dr. McMillen said,

> The moment I start hating a man [or people or nation], I become his slave. I can't work anymore because he even controls my thoughts. My resentments produce too many stress hormones in my body and I become fatigued after only a few hours of work. The work I formerly enjoyed is now drudgery ... The man [or persons or nation] I hate hounds me wherever I go. I can't escape his tyrannical grasp on my mind.[10]

Lewis Smedes, in his book *Forgive and Forget,* put it this way:

> Forgiveness is the only way to be fair to yourself. Getting even is a loser's game. It is the ultimate frustration because it leaves you with more pain than you got in the first place ... Suppose you never forgive, suppose you feel the hurt each time your memory lights on the people who did you wrong. And suppose you have the compulsion to think of them, constantly. You have become a prisoner of your past pain; you are locked into a torture chamber of your own making ... The only way to heal the pain that will not heal itself is to forgive the person [or nation] who hurt you. Forgiving stops the reruns of pain.[11]

In *Landmines in the Path of the Believer,* Charles Stanley said it like this:

> An unforgiving spirit binds us to the abuser. We may think that in order for the person to be punished, we need to remain angry, but all we are doing is hurting ourselves even more. You extend forgiveness to another person [or nation] even though he or she may not deserve or ask for this. You are responding like God—like Christ and like the person you were created to be.[12]

You see, you may have to forgive and then relapse into unforgiveness and pray and fast and start forgiving all over again, numerous times, until forgiveness becomes a total reality in your life. But you can't give up. Again I say, forgiving everybody of everything is not optional—regardless of how horrible the abuse or how long it takes before it becomes a genuine reality. For even if you choose not to genuinely forgive someone and just bury the offense or abuse in your subconscious mind so that you are not aware of what was done to you, it will still continue to extract an emotional and spiritual toll on you.

What all this means is that the spirit of forgiveness dwelling richly within you is an absolute must for brotherhood between the offended and their offenders. You must forgive everyone of everything in your heart by (1) giving up your right to get even or for revenge, (2) letting go of the bad feelings about someone because of what was done to you, and (3) working hard through prayer and drawing closer to God to forget what was done to you.

Now think for a moment about what Moses recorded in Genesis 41:51. This will help you to better understand how forgiveness will enable you individually and our nation collectively to process the hurtful things that were done to African Americans and other racial groups. In other words, this will enable wounded American people to better understand the healing process and promote the establishment of a genuine brotherhood between them and the people who wounded them in the past. Moses said,

> Joseph called the name of the firstborn Manasseh: "For God has made me forget all my toil [trouble] and all my father's household."

So what does this text mean when it says that God made Joseph forget that his brothers, because of their jealousy of their father's love for him, had thrown him into an empty water tank; sold him for eight ounces of silver to some Ishmaelites who took him to Egypt and enslaved him; and then deceived their father into believing that he had been killed by a ferocious animal (Gen. 37:24–33)?

Well, first I need to say that Joseph did not forget what his brothers did to him. He knew exactly what each of them had done in great detail. God did not destroy Joseph's ability to remember what had been done to him. But what God did do to make him forget all the suffering that his father's household caused him to experience is this. God took away the sting or the burning pain of what his brothers did to him. He took the sting or the lingering pain out of his remembrance. God enabled Joseph to forgive his brothers, and then He cleansed him of all the emotional hurt and pain that their dastardly acts caused him.

And so, it becomes obvious that genuine forgiveness of everybody for everything they did to you is an absolute must for putting the past behind you, judging people by the content of their present character, and uniting with them in genuine brotherhood. When you forgive, then God takes away the emotional hurt and pain. He heals the emotional woundedness that you were afflicted with. Someone might ask the question, "Where does it say in the Bible that I must forgive everybody of everything?"

After Jesus gave His disciples a model prayer to teach them how to pray, which included asking God to forgive them of their sins, Jesus said to them in Matthew 6:14–15,

> For if you forgive people when they sin against you, your heavenly Father will also forgive you. But if you do not forgive others their sins, your Father will not forgive your sins. (NIV)

Someone might also ask, "Does this mean that, as a believer, if I don't forgive someone for something they did to me, Jesus won't forgive my sins anymore and therefore I will lose my salvation?"

No, that is not the meaning of this text. And the reason is that once a person is truly saved through their belief and a genuine confession of faith in Jesus Christ, all your sins are forgiven—past, present, and future. So there is nothing that you can do to reverse God's promise to you of eternal life in heaven with Him. A person can only receive eternal life one time—or it was not eternal when you received it the first time.

However, what Jesus is talking about in Matthew 6:14–15 is the status of your relationship with Him for determining the extent to which He will answer your prayers and bless you while earth is still your home. The message of Jesus in Matthew 6:14–15 is that if you don't forgive everybody of everything, your prayers and petitions to Him for guidance, provisions, and protection will be greatly hindered. John MacArthur Jr. said in commenting on Matthew 6:14–15,

> Every believer must seek to manifest the forgiving spirit of Joseph (Gen. 50:19–21) and Stephen (Acts 7:60) as often as needed (Luke 17:3–4). To receive pardon from the perfectly holy God and then to refuse to pardon others when we are sinful men is the epitome of abuse of mercy. And "judgement will be merciless to one who has shown no mercy; mercy triumphs over judgment" (James 2:13). There are petitions for the believer to ask from God, but there are also conditions for the answers to be received.[13]

of God, the unrepentant, willful sin of unforgiveness or racial hatred is going to give you some feelings of guilt. So, if you are such a person, how long are you going to loudly hum and ignore the fact that you are judging people by skin color instead of character? What must God do to you to shake you out of your denial?

The Apostle Paul demonstrated the dynamics of how giving and receiving forgiveness sets free both the offended and their offenders so that they can judge each other by character and not skin color and thus establish a genuine brotherhood with each other when he said in Philippians 3:13–15,

> Forgetting what is behind and straining toward what is ahead, I press on toward the goal to win the prize for which God has called me heavenward in Christ Jesus. All of us, then, who are mature should take such a view of things. And if on some point you think differently, that too God will make clear to you. (NIV)

So tell us, Paul, how were you able to be emotionally and spiritually healed and truly forget and put behind you the fact that you were so deeply involved in the wicked execution-style stoning that murdered the godly man Stephen that is recorded in Acts 7:58? And tell us, Paul, how were you able to be emotionally and spiritually healed and forget and put behind you the fact that you persecuted the church before you were converted and saved on the road to Damascus? You dragged off and put into prison and even killed some innocent Christian men and women, as recorded in Acts 22:4 (cf. 9:1–2; 26:9–11).

Well, if the Apostle Paul could speak to us right now, he would say, "Brothers and sisters, first of all, I had to sincerely and genuinely forgive myself for what I did and then ask God and those I hurt to forgive me." This is what Paul had to do after he was converted before he could be cleansed of his guilt and shame for what he had done. He had to do this before he could start his journey of healing, forgetting his past, and becoming all that God had planned and purposed for his life. That was the first step required to be set free to join his Christian brothers and sisters in genuine relational brotherhood.

Digging deeper, it's very safe to say that if you don't forgive everybody of everything, the favor or grace of God won't flow abundantly into your life. And so you must have faith in God that if you obey His commandment to forgive, everything is going to be all right! But if you don't, your unforgiving spirit will take you on a journey to a place that you definitely don't want to go. And it does not make any difference how dastardly you were wounded.

You see, your racial pride might say, "How dare they had the nerve to do that to my people." And Jesus will answer you and say, "If I forgave everybody of everything when those people treated me so heinously unjustly, as they crucified me on the cross when I was perfectly innocent, why is it so hard for you to believe that I want you to forgive everybody of everything?"

I am reminded that many years ago, I heard Pastor Charles Stanley say on a radio broadcast something that I never forgot. He said, "God is responsible for the consequences of our obedience." This means that by faith we must forgive and leave the consequences to God. We must forgive everybody of everything and believe by faith that God is going to make everything all right. This is not always an easy thing to do. But with your genuine willingness to do so and the supernatural help of the Holy Spirit, it can be done. The writer of Hebrews said in 11:1, one of my favorite Scriptures, "Now faith is the substance of things hoped for, the evidence of things not seen."

In other words, faith is what you hold onto when what God has promised you is not yet a reality in your life. And faith is the evidence or the proof that what God has promised you is still on its way into your life when it is yet too far off to be seen. So what are some of the details of the consequences of not being willing, by faith, to forgive everybody of everything? Is it really that bad?

Yes, it is! The lack of the spirit of forgiveness in your life will cause a real sense of separation from God. And this sense of separation always has as its partner—is always accompanied by—feelings of bitterness, hatred, and indifference. And a devastating sense of guilt is sometimes included in the mix of all these feelings. The reason for the sense of guilt is because of the sin of not being willing to forgive the people who wounded you. You can loudly hum all you want, but if you are truly a blood-bought child

But moreover, Paul did not just have to seek or receive forgiveness for what he had done to others before he could forget what was behind him. Paul did not just have to seek and receive forgiveness because of all the people he had hurt and wounded so that he could forget what was behind him and strain toward what was ahead of him. He also had to forgive others for all the wounds that other people had inflicted upon him after he was saved. Now, what do I mean by that?

Paul said, in telling his story (openly and honestly) about his wounded, broken heart; his wounded, broken spirit; and the extreme miseries of his life for which he had received healing from the LORD,

> Five times I received from the Jews the forty lashes minus one. Three times I was beaten with rods, once I was pelted with stones, three times I was shipwrecked, I spent a night and a day in the open sea, I have been constantly on the move. I have been in danger from rivers, in danger from bandits, in danger from my fellow Jews [who plotted to kill him], in danger from Gentiles; in danger in the city, in danger in the country, in danger at sea; and in danger from false believers. I have labored and toiled and have often gone without sleep; I have known hunger and thirst and have often gone without food; I have been cold and naked. (2 Cor. 11:24–27 NIV)

You see, Paul had to forgive all the people who did all those horribly unjust, dastardly things to him before God would heal his emotional woundedness. He had to forgive everybody of everything so that he could be cleansed of all feelings of shame and worthlessness.

Forgiveness! Forgiveness! Forgiveness! It is the key to Paul's ability to say with total confidence to the Philippians and us,

> Forgetting what is behind and straining toward what is ahead, I press on toward the goal to win the prize for which God has called me heavenward in Christ Jesus. All of us, then, who are mature should take such a view of things. And if on some point you think differently, that too God will make clear to you. (3:13–15 NIV)

Forgetting the hurt, pain, suffering, and trauma of your past and straining toward—pressing on toward dream goals by using dream methods—judging people by their character and not skin color is rooted and grounded in forgiveness, both giving and receiving it. Unforgiveness, even not forgiving yourself, will prevent you from walking in the Spirit, in the favor of God, in victory in using dream methods to achieve dream goals. And again, why is this so?

The reason is that the very nature of unforgiveness, which is bitterness and hatred, or at the very best indifference toward someone—if these kinds of feelings dwell within your heart, they will enslave you and force you to walk or live according to your flesh or leaning on your own understanding. If these kinds of feelings dwell within your heart, there is no way you can achieve the dream goal of judging people by their character instead of skin color to establish genuine brotherhood with the people that you hold responsible for the wounds that you and/or your ancestors experienced. If these kinds of feelings dwell within your heart, there is absolutely no way that anyone can expect that God will fight their battles for them and enable them to be effective at making the dream a reality in their personal lives or our nation.

Now think about this. After Jesus told His disciples that each and every time they were hurt or offended by someone, they must always forgive the offender when the offender genuinely repented and asked for forgiveness, their instantaneous response was, "LORD, increase our faith!" None of the many great and awesome miraculous feats that Jesus had performed before their eyes had ever inspired a cry for greater faith for them to believe what they saw and what it meant. But the simple command for the disciples to forgive everybody of every wrong thing done to them, regardless of how many times they were done wrong or how terrible it was—this inspired them to immediately say, "LORD, we need more faith to do this!"

So guess what? That's just what we must do when we are having a hard time forgiving someone for something that they did to us or when we are having a hard time forgiving ourselves for something that we did to someone else.

This as well is what we must do when we are having a hard time judging someone by their character instead of by their skin color. We must go to the LORD in prayer and say,

> LORD, increase my faith! I am slipping back into my old self. I am having a hard time giving this person or that person the benefit of the doubt about their actions toward me because their skin color is different from mine. I am judging them by skin color instead of their character. LORD, increase my faith! I need more faith so that I don't think that my brother or sister who is not the same color as me did this to me or said that to me because of my skin color. LORD, increase my faith so that I can forgive him or her just like I would if they were the same color as me.

Forgiving the person who did you wrong and wounded you sets them free from the guilt of what they did to you. But it also sets you free by starting the healing of your wounds and establishing a relationship with God that will allow an abundance of blessings to flow into your life. Job is a good example of how this works. The writer of Job said in 42:10–11,

> And the LORD restored Job's losses when he prayed for his friends. Indeed the LORD gave Job twice as much as he had before. Then all his brothers, all his sisters, and all those who had been his acquaintances before, came to him and ate food with him in his house; and they consoled him and comforted him for all the adversity that the LORD had brought upon him. Each one gave him a piece of silver and each a ring of gold.

The LORD allowed Satan to take away all Job's great wealth, kill his children, and afflict Job with painful, oozing sores all over his body. The LORD did this to shame the devil and let him know that there was nothing he could do to Job to make him curse God and renounce his faith in Him.

However, Job's longtime friends were certain that Job had done something to deserve what was happening to him. So they turned on Job and hurt and offended him greatly by accusing him of having all kinds of hidden sins in his life with which God was not pleased. Time after time, regardless of what Job said to proclaim and prove his innocence of any hidden sin to defend himself against their accusations, they hurt Job mercilessly. They did this with harsh words of judgment that he did not deserve.

And when the truth of his innocence was revealed, God required Job to forgive all his friends and to pray to Him to forgive them before he restored Job's life. God required this of Job before He healed him of his painful sores and blessed him with twice as much wealth as he had before. The writer said in Job 42:10, "And the LORD restored Job's losses when he prayed for his friends. Indeed the LORD gave Job twice as much as he had before."

You see, Job's forgiveness and prayer for his close friends who verbally abused, misused, wounded, and hurt him really bad with their judgmental, insensitive treatment was the turning point for Job. It was the turning point from sickness to health and from poverty to wealth—from self-pity, sorrow, and woundedness to a blessed life again. Our response to the painful offenses and mistreatment that we receive from other people does indeed determine how God responds to us, which determines our future. When Job prayed and forgave his friends who hurt him, it set him free. It qualified him to have his health, wealth, and the hedge of protection around his life to be restored.

Furthermore, by forgiving his friends who hurt him, it set them free. It set them free to be reconciled with God and cleansed of their guilt for hurting him. Forgiveness! Forgiveness! Forgiveness! It is the only way that any dream goal will ever become a reality in the lives of the American people nationwide.

Traumatized Racial Groups Are Biblically and Legally Entitled to Restitution

Now what about restitution, or the more commonly used word—*reparations*? Are African Americans and other racial groups that have been traumatized and unjustly treated in years past entitled to restitution? In other words, for example, are the descendants of former enslaved African American farmers entitled to the "forty acres and mule" that were promised to our ancestors in 1865 after the American Civil War?

The answer to that question is a resounding *yes*! There are two very clear examples of biblical restitution. The first, which specifically expresses the relationship involved in the enslavement of one person by another, says the following in Deuteronomy 15:12–15:

> If any of your people—Hebrew men or women—sell themselves to you and serve you six years, in the seventh year you must let them go free. *And when you release them, do not send them away empty-handed.* Supply them liberally from your flock, your threshing floor and your winepress. Give to them as the Lord your God has blessed you. Remember that you were slaves in Egypt and the Lord your God redeemed you. That is why I give you this command today. (NIV)

The second more detailed biblical principle of restitution is recorded in Leviticus 6:1–5, and it says this:

> The Lord said to Moses: If anyone sins and is unfaithful to the Lord by deceiving a neighbor about something entrusted to them or left in their care or about something stolen, or if they cheat their neighbor, or if they find lost property and lie about it, or if they swear falsely about any such sin that people may commit—when they sin in any of these ways and realize their guilt, they must return what they have stolen or taken by extortion, or what was entrusted to him, or the lost property they found, or whatever it was they swore falsely about. They [the offender(s)] must make restitution in full, add a fifth of the value to it and give it all to the owner on the day they present their guilt offering. (NIV)

You see, in the past, America was definitely guilty of extortion, stealing, and cheating Black African slaves out of their dignity, freedom, and justice. America was guilty of cheating the ancestors of African Americans out of life, liberty, and the pursuit of a happy, successful, and prosperous future. And after all this unjust treatment, they were "sent away empty-handed."

Therefore, some type of restitution paid by America to African Americans should seriously be considered as an act of goodwill to clear the air and promote brotherhood. So how does the principle of restitution work, as described above in the text of Leviticus 6:1–5?

The principle revealed in the above text is the following. The offender was not just responsible for doing whatever was needed to restore the damage of his offense against his neighbor. But the offender was responsible for restoring the situation to one-fifth or 20 percent *better* than it was before the offense occurred.

In general, *the willingness to gladly make restitution will accompany all true acknowledgments or confessions of wrongdoing.* Since both the House and the Senate have officially made a confession of wrongdoing on behalf of our nation in 2009, the only thing that remains is restitution to African Americans. Ken Sande, in his book *The Peacemaker*, provided the following valuable insight on the principle of restitution:

> Certainly, an injured party may exercise mercy, and in some cases it is good to waive the right to restitution. But in many cases making restitution is beneficial even for the offender. Doing so demonstrates remorse, sincerity, and a new attitude, which can help to speed reconciliation (Luke 19:8–9). At the same time, it serves to ingrain lessons that will help the offender to avoid similar wrongdoing in the future (see Ps.119:67, 71; Prov. 19:19) … As you pray about it, keep in mind that blending mercy with justice is a powerful way to restore peace and glorify God.[14]

Taking these words of wisdom into account, African Americans must not hold our nation hostage—or hijack the dream—by refusing to pursue genuine brotherhood with other Americans because the issue of restitution has not been settled. This must be true even if restitution never happens. That's grace and mercy! That's the kind of grace and mercy that Christian believers were called to exercise and promote in our culture. That's giving someone what they don't deserve and not giving them what they do deserve and then depending on Christ for the consequences of our obedience. This of course provides the very best possibility that the restitution issue will eventually be settled.

But in conjunction with this, Christian believers must pray that America does the right thing when it comes to making restitution to

African Americans—for the sake of our nation as well as our own. So we must know what the problem is in order to be effective in praying for our nation. And as we pray, we will also be able to discern whether it is God's will to continue to pursue restitution from America or to waive our right to receive it, a right that we most definitely possess.

So far as the established precedence is concerned, America has a history of making restitution to racial groups that were unjustly treated by our nation. For example, in 1988, the United States agreed to pay $20,000 to more than 100,000 Japanese Americans because they were unjustly sent to internment camps during World War II. And most noticeably, the relatively mild treatment of Japanese Americans for a relatively short period of time can in no way be compared to the most severe treatment of African Americans for almost 175 years.

So what is the problem? Why has America not made a more serious attempt at making restitution to African Americans? Well, the answer to this question is multifaceted.

First, the issue of restitution or reparation has not ever been given serious consideration because there is a significant segment of the American populace that says to African Americans, "Get over it!" They look at the very successful and prosperous lives that so many African Americans are living and the opportunities that are available in America today for everyone, and they say, "Get over it!" They look at the fact that most African Americans are middle class and better off as a result of being born in the United States than any country in Africa, and they say, "Get over it!"

But this appears to many African Americans as being an insensitive approach to the many decades of extremely harsh physical and emotional pain and suffering under slavery and Jim Crow laws.

There is also the matter of insensitivity toward all the hard work by slaves for which they were never compensated. While other Americans were accumulating wealth for themselves and their descendants to profit from in the future, this was not true for African slaves. In March 2015, ABC News in a *20/20* online post said that the Reparations Coordinating Committee had in their sights the institutions that they claimed had profited from slavery. This group of influential lawyers and scholars was led by the civil rights activist Randall Robinson. Their plan was to bring some massive lawsuits against the government and major corporations.

Randall Robinson very succinctly expressed the reason for the lawsuits and his reply to those who benefited from slavery and are satisfied with just an apology in the following way:

> The principal income mechanism for the United States during the years of slavery was cotton. It made us a powerful country. The people who produced the cotton were never paid ... An apology is not the end of the matter, an apology is the beginning of the matter ... It's not good enough to say, "Yes, we did it, and we're sorry."[15]

Now some have tried to downplay the importance of slavery to the making of America into a great nation, thus downplaying the need for reparations. They say that the Northern cities were mostly responsible for producing the wealth and greatness of America during the time of slavery. They say that "Reparation advocates make the foolish unchallenged argument that the United States became rich on the backs of free black labor" (Williams).[16]

However, in his article "Why Was Cotton King?" Henry Louis Gates Jr. said the following, which soundly contradicts such pretext. It expresses the connection between the wealth of the Northern cities and the cotton that was picked by African slaves in the Southern states:

> The most commonly used phrase describing the growth of the American economy in the 1830s and 1840s was "Cotton Is King." ... But it is important to understand that this was not simply a Southern phenomenon. Cotton was one of the world's first luxury commodities, after sugar and tobacco, and was also the commodity whose production most dramatically turned millions of black human beings in the United States themselves into commodities. Cotton became the first mass consumer commodity.[17]

And so the appearance of such lack of sensitivity toward the plight of African American people as described above has caused many to question the sincerity of the apology rendered by the House and the Senate. This in turn has stifled any significant movement of many African Americans toward genuine brotherhood nationwide. Their perception that America as a nation is insensitive to this very long-standing issue has become their reality—whether such a perception is right or wrong for the majority of Americans.

However, in response to the *20/20* online debate mentioned above, on April 12, 2015, one person did express their sentiments about reparations in a rather insensitive way, which was similar to what a few other people had posted. The edited post reads as follows:

> Please explain to me how it is my fault that people whose names you don't even care to know were kept as slaves by people most likely not related to me and why I should pay YOU for it.

To this and other seemingly insensitivities, I have chosen to take the high road concerning such comments. I personally have chosen to forgive as I must—as I have been instructed by my LORD and Savior, Jesus Christ (Matt. 6:14–15). I have chosen to consider just how hard it must be for others to empathize and identify with someone else's pain when they themselves have never come close to experiencing such.

Second, besides insensitivity or indifference, there is a significant segment of the American populace who sincerely believe that most African Americans have and still are receiving restitution through such things as affirmative action quotas in employment and educational institutions. They see compensation from various programs for public assistance and narrowing societal gaps between Blacks and other racial groups of people as making restitution for slavery and Jim Crow.

Along these lines, Walter E. Williams, the distinguished African American economics professor at George Mason University, who sometimes draws anger toward himself by many in the Black community, thinks that the American people have already provided reparations to African Americans for slavery. He argues that "$6.1 trillion in the name of fighting poverty"[18] to address discrimination has been spent by the American people.

In other words, Walter E. Williams and others who oppose making restitution say that restitution has already been made or is currently in the process of being made.

Moreover, in his book *American Contempt for Liberty*, Williams questions the moral fairness of requiring White Americans of today to pay restitution to Blacks for what was done in the past to their ancestors. Williams said in the article in this book "Slavery Reparations," dated June 18, 2014:

> Punishing perpetrators and compensating victims is not what reparations advocated want. They want government to compensate today's blacks for the bondage suffered by our ancestors. But there's a problem. Government has no resources of its very own. The only way for government to give one American a dollar is to first ... confiscate that dollar from some other American ... What moral principle justifies punishing a white of today to compensate a black of today for what a white of yesterday did to a black of yesterday?
>
> There's another moral or fairness issue. A large percentage, if not most, of today's Americans—be they of European, Asian, African, or Latin ancestry don't even go back three or four generations as American citizens. Their ancestors arrived on our shores long after slavery. What standard of justice justifies their being taxed to compensate blacks for slavery? For example, in 1956, thousands of Hungarians fled the brutality of the USSR to settle in the United States. What do Hungarians owe blacks for slavery?[19]

And these sentiments are passed on to our congressional lawmakers who know in their hearts that they are not valid. But since this is their sentiment also, lawmakers go along to get along with the voters who put them in office. This is evidenced by the fact that lawmakers were very willing to pass resolutions on behalf of the American people to apologize for slavery—but very careful not to assume any responsibility for any kind of reparations in these resolutions. So what do I mean when I said that congressional lawmakers know that such a sentiment as described by Walter E. Williams was not a morally or legally valid argument?

What I mean is this. The debt of a nation is not cancelled when all the people who made the debt have died. The debt lives on after the people who made it have died. The debt that America owes to Japan ($1.09 trillion), China ($1.058 trillion), Ireland ($288 billion), the Cayman Islands ($265 billion), and Brazil ($259 billion) is an obligation that must be fulfilled with payments by our children, grandchildren, great-grandchildren, great-great-grandchildren, and so on until it is marked *Paid in Full!*

Likewise, when people come from a foreign country seeking citizenship so that they can live in America, as a new citizen they are automatically required to assume a portion of our nation's debt that was accumulated before they became a citizen by paying taxes.

You see, although the people of a nation are not individually responsible for the previous sins of the people of their nation who came before them—*they are responsible for the debt accumulated by those people, and so are the people who decide at a later date that they want to partake of the American dream!* The LORD said to Moses concerning slaves in Deuteronomy 15:13–14:

> *And when you release them, do not send them away empty-handed.* Supply them liberally from your flock, your threshing floor and your winepress. Give to them as the LORD your God has blessed you. (NIV)

America's greatness was initiated by the strong backs of cotton-picking African slaves, and then they were sent away empty-handed—without any compensation. And so the debt of America, which must now be paid to the heirs of those African slaves, still remains. Sins are not passed down from one generation to another—but debt in the form of restitution or reparations is. So what's the third reason why reparations have not been given a serious consideration?

Third, no serious consideration has been given because the price tag of reparations to the heirs of African slaves is estimated to be as much as $10 trillion. And so even many of those who support the principle of reparations are struggling with how to pay this. This is an amount that is almost half of America's national debt as of 2018, which is increasing by approximately $3 million per minute. Randall Robinson, the distinguished African American lawyer, author, and political leader, in his book *The Debt: What America Owes to Blacks*, expressed the possibility of reparations as being hopeless. He wrote the following concerning reparations to the heirs of African slaves:

> In the early 1970s Boris Bittker, a Yale Law School professor, wrote a book, *The Case for Black Reparations*, which made the argument that slavery, Jim Crow, and a general climate of race-based discrimination in America had combined to do grievous social and economic injury to African Americans ... The slim volume was sent to me by an old friend who once worked for me at TransAfrica, Ibrahim Gassama, now a law professor at the University of Oregon. I had called Ibrahim in Eugene to talk over the legal landscape for crafting arguments for a claim upon the federal and state governments for restitution or reparations ... "It's the strangest thing," Ibrahim had said to me." We law professors talk about every imaginable subject, but when the issue of reparations is raised among white professors, many of whom are otherwise liberal, it is met with silence. Clearly, there is a case to be made for this as an unpaid debt ... But, I tell you, the mere raising of the subject produces deathly silence ... Derrick Bell, who was teaching at Harvard Law School while I was a student there in the late 1960s, concluded his review of Bittker's book in a way that may explain the reaction Ibrahim got from his colleagues:
>
>> Short of a revolution [which would never work], the likelihood that blacks today will obtain direct payments in compensation for their subjugation as slaves before the Emancipation Proclamation, and their exploitation as quasi-citizens since, is

no better than it was in 1866, when Thaddeus Stevens recognized that his bright hope of "forty acres and a mule" for every freedman had vanished "like the baseless fabric of a vision."[20]

But I content that if it's God's will, regardless of how enormous a sum is owed to Black Americans, and if Dr. King's dream methods are employed at every stage of the pursuit of reparations, it will surely happen.

Finally, there is a spiritual problem that is blocking America from making reparations to African Americans. This spiritual problem is solely the responsibility of African Americans to resolve. And it is, by the way, the greatest hindrance to reparations. The spiritual problem that I am referring to, as you might have guessed, is forgiveness for the things done to us that require reparations. Until African American people genuinely forgive America—in our hearts and minds—for everything that was done to us, there will be no reparations. Until we give up our right to get even, until hateful unforgiveness is replaced in our hearts and minds with loving forgiveness, there will be no restitution or reparations.

To cut a long story short, if you will recall from the text of Job chapter 42, Job's restitution was not just 20 percent as the LORD declared in Leviticus 6:1–5. The writer said in Job 42:10, "And the LORD restored Job's losses when he prayed [when job had forgiven and prayed] for his friends. Indeed the LORD gave Job twice as much as he had before." God gave Job double for his trouble. His restitution was 100 percent! But he had to forgive the people who wounded him with their false accusations about why God let him go through so much pain and suffering—before Job could receive his restitution.

And so this brings the exploration of the issue of restitution/reparations back to the most basic principle of the dream, which as you might already know is this: dream goals can only be achieved by dream methods, of which forgiveness is chief among them.

In closing out this portion of dream goal 3, there is one last thing that I must say, which is this. No amount of restitution or reparations will ever guarantee a positive outcome for or in the individual lives of the people who receive it. I am reminded of the Israelites who received a ginormous amount of reparations after their four hundred years of slavery in Egypt.

Moses recorded the following words of the Lord and some events in the Exodus text about the reparations that the Israelites received from their Egyptian slave masters:

> So I will stretch out My hand and strike Egypt with all My wonders which I will do in its midst; and after that he [Pharaoh] will let you go. And I will give this people favor in the sight of the Egyptians; and it shall be, when you go, that you shall not go empty-handed. But every woman shall ask of her neighbor, namely, of her who dwells near her house, articles of silver, articles of gold, and clothing; and you shall put them on your sons and on your daughters. So you shall plunder the Egyptians. (3:20–22)

> Then he [Pharaoh] called for Moses and Aaron by night, and said, "Rise, go out from among my people, both you and the children of Israel … Also take your flocks and your herds, as you have said, and be gone … Now the children of Israel had done according to the word of Moses, and they had asked from the Egyptians articles of silver, articles of gold, and clothing. And the Lord had given the people favor in the sight of the Egyptians, so that they granted them what they requested. Thus they plundered the Egyptians. (12:31–32, 35–36)

The children of Israel carried with them on their exodus from Egypt a very large number of flocks and herds of animals of all type. They carried off silver, gold, and clothing, which was very valuable at this time in the history of mankind. And when the text says that the children of Israel "plundered the Egyptians"—even though it was done with Pharaoh's permission—it carries with it the idea that they emptied Egypt of its riches. Or it at least indicates that they carried away a most significant portion of the treasures of Egypt. So what did they do with this enormous reparations payment from Egypt? Did it produce a positive outcome for the lives of the children of Israel or not?

HIJACKED!

Moses recorded in Exodus chapter 32 what the children of Israel did with a significant portion of the reparations that they received from the Egyptians:

> Now when the people saw that Moses delayed coming down from the mountain [to receive the two tablets that the Ten Commandments were written on], the people gathered together to Aaron, and said to him, "Come, make us gods that shall go before us; for as for this Moses, the man who brought us up out of the land of Egypt, we do not know what has become of him." And Aaron said to them, "Break off the golden earrings which are in the ears of your wives, your sons, and your daughters, and bring them to me" [which was part of the reparations given to them by Egypt] ... And he received the gold from their hand, and he fashioned it with an engraving tool, and made a molded calf. Then they said, "This is your god, O Israel, that brought you out of the land of Egypt!" So when Aaron saw it, he built an altar before it. And Aaron made a proclamation and said, "Tomorrow is a feast to the LORD. Then they rose early on the next day, offered burnt offerings [also part of the reparations given to them by Egypt], and brought peace offerings; and the people sat down to eat and drink, and rose up to play [drunken and immoral activities]. (32:1–2, 4–6)

Wow! There is so much that can be said about the misappropriated use of the reparations payment of the Egyptians to the children of Israel. But time and space do not permit a long dissertation. What I will say is that worshipping the golden calf did not bring a positive outcome into the individual lives of the people, nor did it promote their national interest. The worldview that the children of Israel had obtained in Egypt overrode and superseded their ability to see the LORD as the person who had led them out of Egypt. They contributed this to Moses.

Even with all the very recent great demonstrations of the LORD's power that they had very recently experienced, the people created for themselves a golden calf to lead them. They said to Aaron, "Come, make us gods that shall go before us" (32:1). And they did this in the name of the LORD! Aaron made a proclamation and said, "Tomorrow is a feast to the LORD" (32:5). The people had little or no discernment. They participated in syncretism. They did this by combining the burnt offerings worship of an idol, the golden calf, with a festive celebration in honor of the one and only true, living, jealous God.

So what were the consequences that the children of Israel experienced when they used a portion of their reparations payment to make a golden calf idol in their most unwise attempt to find themselves another leader? Moses said in the same chapter of Exodus that records their idol worshipping syncretism,

> And the LORD said to Moses, "Go, get down! ... They have made themselves a molded calf, and worshiped it and sacrificed to it" ... So it was, as soon as he came near the camp, that he saw the calf and the dancing ... Then he took the calf which they had made, burned it in the fire, and ground it to powder; and he scattered it on the water and made the children of Israel drink it ... And all the sons of Levi [priests] gathered themselves together to him. And he said to them, "Thus says the LORD God of Israel: 'Let every man put his sword on his side, and go in and out from entrance to entrance throughout the camp, and let every man kill his brother, every man his companion, and every man his neighbor.'" So the sons of Levi did according to the word of Moses. And about three thousand men of the people fell that day ... Then Moses returned to the LORD and said, "Oh, these people have committed a great sin, and have made for themselves a god of gold!" ... So the LORD plagued the people because of what they did with the calf which Aaron made. (32:7–8, 19–20, 26–28, 31, 35)

You see, restitution/reparations is not necessarily the answer to obtaining a positive future or outcome for or in the lives of the people who receive it. It is not necessarily the answer to making dream goals a reality in the lives of Black people. Reparations is a broken cistern that won't hold water (Jer. 2:13) if it is not used in accordance with God's Word to bring glory to God and Him only. Syncretism, trying to worship both God and an idol, will always bring forth a curse, the wrath of God, upon whatever goals an individual or a group of people might attempt to achieve. This is true regardless of how the resources, such as reparations, for achieving said goals were obtained. For God is a jealous God (Exod. 20:5). His name is Jealous (Exod. 34:14). Thus, He will not share His creation, His people, or His glory with anyone or any idol, which has no god in it but is inhabited by a satanic spiritual force.

Along those same lines, until Black people get rid of their golden calves or their golden cows that they are worshipping—or the things that they have given priority above God or above the clear, explicit, unambiguous teachings of God's Word—they won't be able to make their long overdue restitution that they deserve a reality in their lives. So what kind of things, for example, have Black (and White) Christian believers consistently for decades given the priority over God and His Word?

African American Christians have given other things—their golden cows—the priority over what God said about the subject matters of abortion (Prov. 6:17; 2 Kings 24:1–4), same-sex marriage (Gen. 2:20–24; Matt. 19:4–6), and the treatment of Israel (Gen. 12:3; Obad. 1–16). And so, just like Aaron led the people in syncretism, so also are pastors who combine or promote the worship of their golden cows together with their worship of the LORD Jesus Christ. So what are the golden cows on whose altar most Blacks, including most Black Christians and some White Christians, have sacrificed God's teachings on abortion, same-sex marriage, and the treatment of Israel?

Those golden calves that they have given priority over God's teaching on these things are the increasingly far left-leaning, Democratic Party, the NAACP, and the ACLU. All these organizations are pro-choice, which is the same thing as being pro-abortion; and pro-same-sex marriage, and anti-Israel when they should be supporting her.

Accordingly, it is important to note that Dr. Martin Luther King Jr. was not pro-choice. He was pro-life all the way, as has been attested many times by his niece, Dr. Alveda King.[21] And so was Jesse Jackson before he ran for president of the United States in 1984 and needed supporters to finance his campaign.

Likewise, Dr. Martin Luther King Jr. highly respected and fully supported the protection of both Israel and American Jews. There was no rift whatsoever between either Israel or American Jews and Dr. King, as some have misleadingly supposed. In a March 25, 1968, speech to the Rabbinical Assembly, Dr. King said that America must use every resource we possess to protect Israel's right to exist as a nation in the territory that it occupies. He said that he considered Israel as being among those nations that are recognized as a great outpost of democracy. He praised Israel before the Rabbinical Assembly for their spectacular demonstration of how a desolate desert could be converted into a haven of democracy.[22]

Stuart Appelbaum, the current president of the Jewish Labor Committee (reelected in 2018) said the following about the special bond between Dr. King, Israel, and American Jews:

> Today, Dr. King's close bond with the Jewish community is treated only as a small footnote of his life and work. But, toward the end of his life, Dr. King devoted significant time and energy to strengthening what were becoming increasingly strained ties between black Americans and U.S. Jews ... had he lived, Dr. King might have helped heal the divisions between Jews and African-Americans.[23]

As I considered Dr. King's attitude about abortion, same-sex marriage, and Israel, I concluded that it was most appropriate to say the following without any hesitation whatsoever. And that is this. Dr. King would not recognize either the Democratic Party ideology or that of the NAACP as something that he could support as he did in the 1960s. Both of these organizations have so drastically degenerated—spiritually—over the last fifty years. So it's hard to believe that any Christian could possibly concoct in their minds that by supporting such organizations, they were keeping God's command that says, "Therefore, whether you eat or drink or whatever you do, do all to the glory of God" (1 Cor. 10:31).

Nevertheless, I am encouraged that there are still many African American pastors who are not willing to compromise or sacrifice their faith on the altar of the golden calf. What I mean by that is this. After President Obama announced on May 9, 2012, that he fully supported "marriage equality," the NAACP passed a resolution endorsing same-sex marriage. Then about a month later on July 7, 2012, a courageous coalition of Spirit-filled, discerning Black pastors took a public stand against the NAACP's endorsement. Reverend William Owens, the founder and president of the Coalition of African American Pastors (CAAP) said that such an endorsement of same-sex marriage by the NAACP was in opposition to its founding principles. He most appropriately stated that the focus of the NAACP should be:

> Gangs, teen pregnancy, poverty, violence, and the fact that more black men are in prison than in college … Black people face acute and urgent needs, from unemployment to education, family fragmentation, discrimination, and crime. We are calling on the NAACP … to reclaim its mission. The black church founded the NAACP … it is not the organization for the advancement of gays and lesbians … return to your roots and stand with the black church on marriage. The black church in our eyes remains the conscience of America.[24]

Along these same lines, Pastor Owens said the following to the online *Huffington Post*. He said that the NAACP:

> Is supposed to be an organization for black people who were beaten, who were mistreated, and who were enslaved … [Instead it is] advocating for something that's not normal, that's not natural. It's still out of line, it's against moral law. Gay marriage is leading us down a bad path. Our young people are already hurt. They're already damaged.[25]

Moreover, as time went on, Pastor Owens stepped deeper into his role as a watchman on the wall with the following words told to the *Christian Post*. He said that the Coalition of African America Pastors (CAAP) had:

Requested a meeting with President Obama, and until he meets with us, we are going to ask black Christians to withhold their support until he personally hears our concerns ... more than anything, this is an issue of biblical principles and President Obama is carrying our nation down a dangerous road. Many African Americans were once proud of our president but now many are ashamed of his actions ... you have to stand on the Word of God regardless of your race or political affiliation. If the president is serious about his faith then why would he not meet with men of faith of his own race? [That's a good question, but he never did.][26]

And then there was Pastor Keith Ratliff, who made me proud to be an African American pastor. Pastor Ratliff, who was the state conference president of the NAACP for Iowa and Nebraska and a member of the national board of the NAACP, resigned from the organization after it passed the same-sex resolution. Pastor Ratliff said:

Because of his belief in the Bible, if Rev. Martin Luther King were alive today, he would not have supported marriage equality [same-sex marriage].[27]

Moreover, the notable Black Christian leader Bishop Harry Jackson Jr., pastor of Hope Christian Church in Baltimore, Maryland, put the cookies on the bottom shelf in an interview with the *Christian Post*. According to Dave Bohon of the *New American*, Bishop Jackson told the *Christian Post* how deeply disturbing the actions of the NAACP were in passing a resolution endorsing same-sex marriage. Bohon reported Bishop Jackson as saying this to *Christian Post*:

The black community is in an adulterous relationship with President Obama. He is asking us to stray from the most basic tenets of Scripture—that marriage is an institution made by God for man and woman to become one and procreate. He's telling us it's fine to hold onto our beliefs but that it's also okay to accept his stance on a position that goes against that core belief [This is both a golden calf and syncretism].[28]

You see, a golden calf or an idol is anything or the principles of anything that you put above the clear teachings of God. The LORD Jesus Christ said, "Whoever is not with me is against me, and whoever does not gather with me scatters" (Matt. 12:30—NIV). There is no middle ground for compromising God's Word in the kingdom of God. There is lots of love in the kingdom, but there is no middle ground where one can ignore the truth of God's Word without severe temporal and eternal consequences. Paul said in 1 Corinthians, chapter 10,

> Observe Israel after the flesh: Are not those who eat of the sacrifices partakers of the altar? ... I do not want you to have fellowship with demons [spiritual agreement or spiritual sharing with people that don't hate what God hates]. You cannot drink the cup of the LORD and the cup of demons; you cannot partake of the LORD's table and of the table of demons. Or do we provoke the LORD to jealousy? Are we stronger than He? (10:18, 20–21)

Jesus said to the compromising church, Pergamos, and the Lukewarm church, Laodicea, "He who has an ear, let him hear what the Spirit says to the churches" (Rev. 2:17; 3:22). G. Campbell Morgan said that lukewarmness is the worst form of blasphemy. Someone else said that lukewarmness is a way of saying, "God, I believe in You, but You just don't excite me." Not willing to stand for what is right or not willing to separate ourselves from the world or worldly thinking, not willing to stand up and speak out for the things of God, is the greatest form of disrespecting God that a believer can do.

So until Black people—who must be led by Black Christians—become independent thinkers whose choices and decisions are rooted and grounded in the sound doctrine of the Word of God and not on or in conjunction with the godless, humanistic thinking that is dictated by the platforms and talking points of political and civil rights organizations, we won't receive any kind of reparations that will produce a positive outcome or positive future for us. More specifically, until we stop voting for what we perceive as being good for our pocketbooks and our racial pride, we won't receive any kind of reparations that will produce a positive outcome or positive future for us.

In concluding this chapter, I want to share with readers a quote from the powerfully insightful book by Jason L. Riley, who is an African American columnist for the *Wall Street Journal*. He said the following, on the back cover of his book *False Black Power?* It points out the historically uselessness and ineffectiveness of employing syncretism to achieve dream goals. Riley said,

> Black civil rights leaders have long supported ethnic identity politics and prioritizing the integration of political institutions, and seldom has that strategy been questioned … Riley takes an honest, factual look at why increased black political power has not paid off in ways that the civil rights leadership promised. Recent decades have witnessed a proliferation of black elected officials, culminating in the historic presidency of Barack Obama. However, racial gaps in employment, income, homeownership, academic achievement, and other measures not only continue, but in some cases, have even widened. The historical reality for other racial and ethnic groups in America and elsewhere is that political success has not been necessary or sufficient to facilitate economic advancement. Among blacks, the focus on political capital has resulted in the underdevelopment of cultural capital—values, attitudes, habits—that helped to power upward mobility among other groups. Riley explains why the political strategy of civil rights leaders has left so many blacks behind. The key to black economic advancement today is overcoming cultural handicaps, not attaining more political power.[29]

HIJACKED!

This quote should be seriously considered by all who are genuinely interested in making Dr. King's dream a reality in America.

And so in summing up all this, it should be obvious that neither dream goals nor reparations will ever be achieved so long as their reality is being hijacked by the worship of the golden calves of humanistic ideologies. For—

> Unless the LORD builds the house [and Him only],
> They labor in vain who build it;
> Unless the LORD guards the city,
> The watchman stays awake in vain. (Ps. 127:1)

What all this means is this. There is a lot more that is keeping African Americans from making the dream a reality in their lives than reparations or "forty acres and a mule" or "three acres and a cow," which was the British distributist slogan of the land reform campaigners of the late 1880s. A lot more! There are a lot more dangerous things that are hijacking the dream than the lack of reparations given to African Americans by America.

7

THE GOALS TO BE ACHIEVED: DREAM GOAL 4—DR. KING'S DREAM IS CHARACTERIZED BY HIS INTENSE DESIRE FOR RACIAL PRIDE TO BE REPLACED WITH HUMILITY

So now the question at hand is, What about racial pride? How does racial pride instead of humility or a humble approach to life destroy the ability of a person or a nation of people to judge others by character instead of skin color? To begin with, let me say that the installation of the practice of judging people by character instead of by skin color or other physical attributes is hijacked by racial pride. It hijacks our nation's ability to establish genuine brotherhood among the many races of people within it.

And the way that such a thing so easily happens is this. When one race or culture of people believes that they are better looking, more talented, more gifted, more privileged, or spiritually superior to other races, guess what happens? These kinds of false perceptions will destroy the ability of that race or that culture to establish a genuine brotherhood with those races which they perceive themselves as being superior to. The superiority-thinking people—those who think more highly of themselves than they ought to think—will in many cases do everything they can to limit any genuine interpersonal relationship development with those considered as inferior to them. This includes any and everything that might destroy the superiority-thinking people's ability to maintain their separation from those who are deemed inferior. No-holds-barred!

Likewise, I must note that *significant differences* between races in our God-given physical appearances or other attributes are not an indication of the superiority of one race over another—not from God's viewpoint. Nowhere in Scripture will one find the principle that God is a respecter of persons when it comes to race, culture, physical attributes, intellect, or achievements. But what you will find all through the Bible is that God is a respecter of character or the spiritual quality of a person or a nation.

Furthermore, the Holy Spirit, according to Luke the physician, evangelist, and historian, reminds us to be humble. He reminds us not to think more highly of ourselves than we ought to think (Rom. 12:3) of our race, culture, or people group. This was the message when he said in Acts 17:26,

> And He has made from one blood [Adam] every nation of men to dwell on all the face of the earth, and has determined their preappointed times and the boundaries of their dwellings.

We are told in this text that all men are equal in God's sight. But for the Greeks, this was a blow to their national pride. And I am sure that this is also a blow to the racial pride of some in America today. The concept of equality of person was a blow to Greek pride because their perception of life was that all non-Greeks were barbarians. This likewise may be the reasoning of some in America today who perceive the entirety of some people groups to be barbarians.

However, the text "He … has determined their appointed times" makes it clear that God controls the rise and fall of nations (Dan. 2:36–45). What's more, the text "the boundaries of their dwellings" injects the understanding that it was God that established the racial identity of nations, their original geographical locations, and their successful expansions into other areas (Deut. 32:8).

Moreover, in the little booklet *Where Did the "Races" Come From?* by Ken Ham, Dr. Carl Wieland, and Dr. Don Batten, this is stated:

The truth, though, is that these so-called "racial" characteristics" are only minor variations among the people groups [races]. Scientists have found that if one were to take any two people from anywhere in the world, the basic genetic differences between these two people would typically be around 0.2%—even if they came from the same people group. But, these so-called "racial" characteristics that many think are major differences (skin color, eye shape etc.) account for only 6% of this 0.2% variation, which amounts to a mere 0.012% difference genetically. In other words, the so-called "racial" differences are absolutely trivial. Overall, there is more variation within any group than there is between one group and another. If a white person is looking for a tissue match for an organ transplant, for instance, the best match may come from a black person, and vice versa.[1]

What all this means is that so many people perceive these minor differences as being major because they have been programmed by the American culture to see them that way. The Bible says that everyone on planet Earth is from "one blood" or one race. But what about skin color? Why is there such a large variety or large variations of skin color among the different people groups or races? I need to say something about this—even though skin color is only 6 percent of the 0.2 percent genetic difference mentioned in the above quote. The reason is that a most significant number of Americans seem to be obsessed with skin color as their major means of judging people.

So think about this. *Melanin* is a dark brownish pigment that all people groups, all races of people, possess in special cells in our skin. And so albinos are people who inherited a defect that prevents them from producing melanin.

Likewise, if your body produces a little bit of melanin, then your body color will be white like the majority of Europeans. If your body produces a great amount of melanin, your body color will be dark black. And then of course there are all the shades of brown in between black and white, depending on the amount of melanin that is contained in the cells of your skin.[2] I say all this to give inquisitive readers something to think about for further research. The bottom line is that God's plan for people groups or races started way back in the beginning chapters of Genesis.

Then after the worldwide cataclysmic Noahic flood, the LORD confused the languages of the descendants of Noah's sons—Japheth, Ham, and Shem—Noah's family being the only people who survived the flood. This caused the people to scatter from the area of the Tower of Babel "over the face of all the earth" (Gen. 11:5–9). So what was the consequences of the scattering of the people according to their new languages that the LORD gave them over the whole earth? The authors of *Where Did the "Races" Come From?* very succinctly said this:

> In summary, the dispersion at Babel, breaking a large interbreeding group into small, inbreeding groups, ensured that the resultant groups could have different mixes of genes for various physical features. By itself, this would ensure, in a short time, that there would be certain fixed differences in some of these groups, commonly called "races." In addition, the selection pressure of the environment would modify the existing combinations of genes, causing a tendency for characteristics to suit their environment.
>
> There has been no simple-to-complex evolution of any genes, for the genes were present already. The dominant features of the various people groups result from different combinations of previously existing created genes, plus some minor changes in the direction of degeneration, resulting from mutations (accidental changes which can be inherited). The originally created (genetic) information has been reshuffled or has degenerated, not added to.[3]

You see, the myth that Black people are the result of the curse on Ham is a racist lie straight from the pit of hell, and the devil is its author. Nowhere in the Bible does it say that the skin color of Black people is the result of a curse. Black Africans are merely the result of one of the particular gene combinations of the people who migrated to the African continent when they were scattered at the Tower of Babel.

However, a myth does not need truth of any kind to sustain it. It just needs to be accepted by a majority of the people and their leaders for it to become embedded in the culture. In his book *Let's Get to Know Each Other: What White Christians Should Know about Black Christians*, Dr. Tony Evans said the following about the creation of the myth of the curse of Ham. This has been believed about Black Christians for numerous years by many White Christians:

> Now there existed a myth of inferiority with apparent biblical roots. This theological basis provided the raw material necessary to convince the slaves that to resist their assigned inferior status was to resist the will of God. This myth became an authoritative myth because it was rooted in theology, and slave owners used this twisted theology to sustain a perverted sociology. This process is known as *sacralization,* the development of theological and religious beliefs to serve the interest of a particular ethnic or racial group. I knew that something did not sound right about the curse of Ham theory when I first heard it as a teenager. A white minister was giving me the biblical reason why my people and I had to endure the humiliation of American racism. Because I couldn't prove otherwise and because my favorite Bible, the famous Old Schofield Reference Bible, which had become the official version of American fundamentalism, endorsed the curse of Ham theory, I had little recourse other than to accept it. After all, those promoting it were "trained" in the Bible and theology at the finest fundamentalist institutions in our country—institutions, by the way, that at that time would not allow blacks to enroll as students. With the endorsement of the Old Schofield Bible, coupled with the legal status of American segregation, the myth was firmly established and embedded in the American psyche[4] ... They forgot the biblical truth that to be members of the Body of Christ

means that preferences based on class, culture, or race are totally unacceptable to God, and people who make such preferences are candidates for His judgment (James 2:9–13). Such biblical data, however, would not support the inferiority myth. Adding such biblical references would be telling the whole truth, and truth and myth do not mix very well. Therefore, early Americans had to be selective about what Bible verses to use to establish a theological basis to justify slavery and perpetuate the inferiority myth.[5]

The perpetuation of the inferiority myth, as late as the 1960s, did an untold amount of damage on the psyche, inner self, or self-image of slaves. And this slave or "plantation mentality" of inferiority was passed down by some of our ancestors, which unfortunately still influences the self-image of some in the Black community today. However, this is not a legitimate excuse for Blacks not acknowledging that it is their responsibility for bettering themselves.

Likewise, the acceptance of the inferiority myth by the White church has had (and still is in some areas of America) a catastrophic effect on the establishment of genuine brotherhood in our nation. For it is the responsibility of the White church to debunk the inferiority myth that still exists among some White people. But this cannot be done until repentance of this sin is a genuine, heartfelt reality. Dr. Tony Evans made a statement about this in 1995 that I am sure is not as dire today as it was then. But I am also sure that some improvement still needs to be done in this area of race relationships in the church. Dr. Tony Evans said the following about the importance of the White church taking the lead in the debunking process in the White church and the White community in general:

> Many whites claim individual superiority because of the myth's doctrine of group superiority. Therefore, there is a great hesitancy on the part of whites to sit at the feet of blacks with the expectation of learning (as opposed to simply being entertained), because the myth has already defined the relationship as that of a superior to an inferior.

> Unless biblical Christians significantly enter the fray and take over the leadership for resolving the race crisis, we will be hopelessly deadlocked in a sea of relativity regarding this issue, resulting in restating more questions rather than providing permanent answers.[6]

Digging deeper, some people have justified their prideful racist beliefs by holding the unbiblical, unsupportable position that people groups evolved separately. And therefore, different people groups are at different stages of evolution. In other words, they claim that some people groups are more backward or less advanced than others or less human than others. This is the kind of thinking that inspired Hitler to eliminate Jews and Gypsies and establish a "master race."

Now this also is a dastardly lie that Satan places in the minds of emotionally or spiritually weak people or people that are full of pride about who they are as a people. There is really not much more that is worth saying about this. One reason why is that there is absolutely no evidence whatsoever that supports any kind of evolutionary development of the human race or any other form of life. End of story! And so it is more than obvious why Solomon so confidently said,

> Pride goes before destruction, and a haughty spirit [thinking more highly of yourself than you ought to think] before a fall. Better to be of a humble spirit with the lowly, than to divide the spoil with the proud. (Prov. 16:18–19)

The Apostle Peter said it this way:

> Yes, all of you be submissive to one another, and be clothed with humility, for "God resists the proud, but gives grace to the humble." (1 Pet. 5:5)

Humility! Humility! Humility! It is the key to removing the stumbling block of racial pride in our efforts to establish genuine brotherhood with people of other races. But guess what? Some people are so full of racial pride that the only way that they will become a humble person and abandon it is after they have had a near-death experience, a devastating event that happens to them, or a salvation experience such as the frightening events that happened to the Apostle Paul on the Damascus Road (Acts 9:1–22). After Paul regained his sight and accepted his calling as the apostle to the Gentiles, he said the following about how his racial pride as a Jew was changed to humility:

> If anyone else thinks he may have confidence in the flesh [confidence in their racial identity], I more so: circumcised the eighth day, of the stock of Israel, of the tribe of Benjamin, a Hebrew of the Hebrews; concerning the law, a Pharisee; concerning zeal, persecuting the church; concerning the righteousness which is in the law, blameless. But what things were gain to me, these I have counted loss for Christ. Yet indeed I also count all things loss for the excellence of the knowledge of Christ Jesus my LORD, for whom I have suffered the loss of all things, and count them as rubbish, that I may gain Christ. (Phil. 3:4–8)

Paul had some impressive credentials. He was the Jew's Jew—a "Hebrew of the Hebrews"—totally devoted to his Jewish heritage. But on the road to Damascus, when Paul was engulfed by the bright light of the glory of Jesus from heaven, he realized that life was not just about him and his Jewish heritage. It was not just about being a proud Jew.

You see, it's not about you or me or the "race" that we belong to or what we had to go through in life. It's all about bringing glory to God—regardless of what life experiences God has ordained for us or our race. Now I know that some people really don't want to hear such talk as this. The reason is that in their eyesight everything is all about them. And if something does not work to their good or if they can't figure out how something works for the good of the people of their race, then it's not worth considering.

But guess what? A believer must be willing to put in the loss column of their heavenly account all those gains or those things of the flesh that you consider as being an advantage for your self-worth, like what race you belong to. You must consider all such things as being rubbish, garbage, or dung! Just like the Apostle Paul, you must be willing to give up your racial pride "for the excellence of the knowledge of Christ Jesus"—for the incomparable worth of a personal relationship with Him.

This means that a believer must constantly keep in mind that "You are not your own. For you were bought at a price" (1 Cor. 6:19–20). And you were not bought with "corruptible things, like silver or gold … but with the precious blood of Christ …" (1 Pet. 1:18–19). And until the church takes on this kind of an attitude, we won't be able to set an example of how to replace our racial pride with humility for the unbelieving world to follow. In the text below, the LORD gave His people the promised result of judging people by their character instead of by their skin color if Christians would take the lead in the promotion of humility throughout America. He gave us the promised result of nationwide brotherhood if the church would take the lead in promoting humility nationwide. He said in 2 Chronicles 7:14,

> If My people who are called by My name [today—the church] will humble themselves, and pray and seek My face, and turn from their wicked ways [let go of their racial pride and judge people by their character instead of skin color], then I will hear from heaven, and will forgive their sin and heal their land [establish genuine brotherhood throughout the nation].

So for emphasis, *who* must lead the movement to judge people by character and not by skin color and other noncharacter attributes? You're right! The church—spearheaded by the Black church, or more specifically, spearheaded by African American pastors. For you were called for such a time as this by God through Dr. King's dream.

You see, I have heard the words "That's how they are!" in reference to people of another color than the person who said it. Sadly to say, I heard this in a church. More sadly, it came from the lips of the senior pastor of that church. Brothers and sisters, this ought not to ever happen. The church must lead the humility movement to establish brotherhood throughout our nation. We must lead the movement to judge people by the content of their character instead of by the color of their skin. We must first set the example and then proclaim this principle to the unbelieving world. As encouragement to the church to take the lead by example and precept, remember these words of the Apostle Peter:

> For the time has come for judgment to begin at the house of God; and if it begins with us first, what will be the end of those who do not obey the gospel of God? (1 Pet. 4:17)

Charles Grandison Finney (1792–1875) was an American Presbyterian minister. He was a key person in the Second Great Awakening in America. He made a statement that clearly expresses whose responsibility it is from God's viewpoint to lead the humility movement in America for creating brotherhood. He said the following most powerful words to express this:

> Brethren, our preaching will bear its legitimate fruit. If immorality prevails in the land, the fault is ours in a great degree. If there is a decay of conscience, the pulpit is responsible for it. If the public press lacks moral discernment, the pulpit is responsible for it. If the Church is degenerate and worldly, the pulpit is responsible for it. If the world loses its interest in Christianity, the pulpit is responsible for it. If Satan rules in our halls of legislation, the pulpit is responsible for it. If our politics become so corrupt that the very foundations of our government are ready to fall away, the pulpit is responsible for it. Let us not ignore this fact, my dear brethren; but let us lay it to heart, and be thoroughly awake to our responsibility in respect to the morals of our nation.[7]

The pulpit! The pulpit! The pulpit is responsible for it! It doesn't get much clearer than that. It's not rocket science! Someone said that 11:00 a.m.—church time—is the most segregated hour of the week. The reason is that believers go to their church, which is sorted almost 90 percent by race. There are Black churches and White churches and all the other racial group churches. And whose responsibility is it that it is this way? The pulpit is responsible for it!

HIJACKED!

Thus, the church must lead a revival movement of forgiveness and humility in America—by precept and example, by teaching and preaching the Word and by example. And the Black church in America must spearhead or be the point man of this spiritual revival movement of forgiveness and humility that must be carried out by the entire body of Christ. For this is what the Black church has been called to do by God through Dr. King's dream. The Black church has been called by God to engulf this message themselves, "to eat the flesh and drink the blood of Jesus" and then pass it on to the rest of the body of Christ. But most importantly, it is the task of the Black church to pass it on to the unbelieving Black community that is so deeply rooted in an unwillingness to forgive, forget the pain of the past, and humbly abandon any ungodly racial pride. The Black church has been called to take up where Dr. King left off, to quench the hijack and continue the dream. This very special calling on the Black church is explored in more detail in *The Recovery*, volume 4 of *Hijacked!*

Moreover, the pulpit, even more specifically the Black pulpit, is responsible for the fact that weekend after weekend—year in and year out—in Chicago, Illinois, and many other urban cites, large numbers of Black people are wounding and killing other Black people. And the pulpit must claim responsibility for this!

You see, I know that Dr. King's dream has been hijacked by numerous Black pulpits across America, for sure and for certain, because the dream is rigidly based in the sound doctrine of God's Word. Moreover, God Himself confirmed the reality of the hijack that has occurred in Black pulpits when he said this through the prophet Isaiah:

> As the rain and the snow come down from heaven, and do not return to it without watering the earth and making it bud and flourish, so that it yields seed for the sower and bread for the eater, so is my word [so is the dream methods and dream goals] that goes out from my mouth: It will not return to me empty [It will not result in endless Black-on-Black crimes, violence, and murder], but will accomplish what I desire and achieve the purpose for which I sent it. You will go out in joy and be led forth in peace. (Isa. 55:10–12—NIV)

In summary and in closing this chapter, note that Dr. King urged that even though dream goals may not be in full force in our culture today, Black people should not think that they cannot be as high achievers as other citizens while waiting for them to be fully implemented. In his commencement address at Lincoln University in Pennsylvania on June 6, 1961, titled "The American Dream," he gave many examples of this from yesteryears. Since Dr. King delivered this address, we have many more examples of the great contributions of Black people today that confirm this.

Dr. King warned the Lincoln University graduates that they should not use oppression as an excuse to not strive for excellence or a continuous commitment to improvement in everything they did. He reminded them that determination can break the shackles of oppressive circumstances. And that this has been repeatedly validated by men and women like the great leaders Booker T. Washington and Mary McLeod Bethune; the great singers Roland Hayes and Marian Anderson; the great scientist George Washington Carver; the great diplomat Ralph Bunche; the great fighter Joe Lewis; the great runner Jessie Owens; and the great baseball player Jackie Robinson.[8]

Thus, Black people need not wait until the day that the dream becomes a full reality before they are ready to do great things. Dr. King said that these people validated the poet William Cowper in his 1788 poem, "The Negro's Complaint," who said:

> Fleecy locks and dark complexion
> Cannot forfeit nature's claim.
> Skin may differ but affection
> Dwells in black and white the same.
> Were I so tall as to reach the pole
> Or to grasp the ocean at a span
> I must be measured by my soul,
> The mind [heart]is standard of the man.[9]

Accordingly, King Solomon said the following self-fulfilling words in Proverbs 23:7, which will be important in stemming the rising tide of hijackers and reviving the dream: "For as he [or she] thinks in his [or her] heart, so is he [or she]." Our perception of things is indeed our own personal reality. This means that leftist liberal political correctness must be replaced with reality. And so the following attitude changes must take place in order for hateful unforgiveness to be replaced with loving forgiveness, which is a good place to start the revival of the dream:

- Blacks must realize that freedom does not guarantee a positive outcome in life or the Marxist critical race theory doctrine of equity or equal results for all Americans. Freedom only guarantees an equal opportunity for the pursuit of happiness or the pursuit of success and prosperity. A permanent positive outcome requires freedom, virtue, faith, education, training, and hard work.
- Blacks must realize that restitution or reparations from America for the sins of slavery and the Jim Crow laws that we rightfully deserve won't guarantee a positive outcome for the people who receive it. Our focus must be giving and receiving forgiveness and the promotion of brotherhood nationwide; getting rid of our golden cows; and letting God determine how, when, and if restitution is the best thing for us.
- Blacks must stop conflating, mixing, or combining the present with the past (*Shame*, Shelby Steele). We must stop buying into the lie of the hijackers that things are not any better for Blacks in America or that opportunities are still limited for Blacks because of institutional racism. Hijackers have programmed the masses of Black people with the lie that the present American system of education, employment, and housing is structurally aligned against Blacks (*Shame*, Shelby Steele) the same way it was before the civil rights movement that started in the 1960s. Hijackers do this to maintain control of the masses of poor, uninformed, or wounded, hate-driven Black people.
- Blacks must acknowledge that the children or descendants of the Anglo-Americans that executed slavery, Jim Crow laws, and the unjust practices of the rest of the nation during the Jim Crow era are responsible as American citizens for the debt of reparations to African Americans. But they are not personally responsible for the sinful actions of their ancestors.

CLARENCE WASHINGTON SR.

The Dream Concluding Remarks

There are many Black people and Brown, Red, Yellow, and also some White people who are experiencing a nightmare in America today! The reason is that both Dr. King's dream and the American dream, which are intricately connected, are under attack by hijackers. But that nightmare can most definitely be transformed back into the dream that Dr. King envisioned and initiated in the 1960s for all Americans before his death.

In other words, we must look at the dream as not being dead but deferred. It is being deferred until we start deploying the God-given dream methods that are required to achieve the God-given dream goals into our culture. This is what is required to recover from the nightmarish conditions that so many Americans are now experiencing. Some might say that Dr. King's dream was murdered when he was assassinated on April 4, 1968.

However, I think that Langston Hughes (1902–1967), the African American poet, social activist, novelist, columnist, and playwright, can help us to understand that this is definitely not the case. In his poem "Lenox Avenue Mural," his idea in comparison to what others might think is that dreams cannot be murdered. They can only be deferred. Hughes expressed his ideas about the nightmare that occurs when dreams are deferred or hijacked this way:

> What happens to a dream deferred?
> Does it dry up like a raisin in the sun?
> Or fester like a sore—and then run?
> Does it stink like rotten meat?
> Or crust and sugar over—like a syrupy sweet?
> Maybe it sags like a heavy load.
> Or does it explode?[10]

Well, I think that all Hughes's nightmarish questions about a dream deferred but not murdered helps us to understand the dire state that so many Americans are experiencing. The hijacking of Dr. King's dream—the deferment or postponement of the dream—has taken a heavy toll on so many Americans. And as volume 2, *The Hijack*, so clearly expresses, many Americans have participated in the hijack or the deferment of the dream, some intentionally and some unintentionally.

But the good news is that, although deferred, the dream has not dried up so much like a raisin that it can't be watered and brought back to life through the implementation of Dr. King's dream methods. It has not festered so much like a sore that it can't be healed through the implementation of dream methods to achieve dream goals.

Likewise, the dream has not rotted so badly, even though the nightmare that it has become stinks to high heavens, that it can't be restored with a heavy dose of dream methods. Also, it has not crusted and sugared over so badly that the sickening, syrupy, sweet taste of deception and manipulation can't be boiled off with dream methods. It hasn't sagged so badly from the heavy load of hijackers that they can't be thrown off. And if it seems like the dream deferred—the current nightmare—is ticking like a bomb ready to explode, that is a sign of the urgency with which dream methods 1, 2, and 3 must be deployed along with a fervent desire to achieve dream goals 1, 2, 3, and 4!

Therefore, if you are a blood-bought believer, from this time forward for the rest of your life, you *must* remember the dire situation that Black people and Brown people and Red people and our nation in general are currently experiencing. So we must act with a sense of immediacy! For the dream deferred—the current nightmare—is indeed ticking like a bomb ready to explode into a much greater level of rebellion against the principles of the dream and the American dream, which will make it that much harder to recover from if it does.

Nevertheless, we must be of good cheer, cheer up, be brave, and never lose heart (John 6:33). We must think always about what the Holy Spirit said to us through the Apostle Paul in the following text as we faithfully deploy all the dream methods to achieve all the dream goals. Paul confidently and encouragingly said to the Romans, as he is also saying to believers of today:

> And we know that all things work together for the good to those who love God, to those who are the called according to His purpose ... Yet in all these things we are more than conquerors [over or super conquerors] through Him who loved us. For I am persuaded that neither death nor life, nor angels nor principalities nor powers, nor things

present nor things to come, nor heights nor depth, nor any other created thing, shall be able to separate us from the love of God [and His awesome powers] which is in Christ Jesus our Lord. (Rom. 8:28, 37–39)

Dr. King said that he had a dream that was deeply rooted in the American dream, a dream of freedom and justice for all that flowed like a might river throughout our nation, a dream of a nation that was characterized by loving forgiveness and humility. Dr. King's dream contains the goals that *must* be achieved and the methods that *must* be employed to fix what is wrong with America! And guess what? Again I say that this dream can, without any doubt, become a reality in America.

So onward to *The Hijack*, volume 2. I pray that God will sensitize your heart, mind, and spirit to His voice as you partake of it and give you a deep and burning desire to help America recover from the hijack and make the dream a reality. In Jesus's name, I pray. Amen!

APPENDIXES

ENDNOTES

Dedication

1. William Cowper, *The Complete Works of William Cowper: Including His Letters, Poems, and Private Correspondence, with Memoir* (Edinburgh: William P. Nimmo, 1875), 528, 533.

Preface

2. Mike Strain, "The Day MLK Came to Tulsa," *Tulsa World,* January 21, 2019, https://www.tulsaworld.com/news/local/the-day-mlk-came-to-tulsa-we-must-all-live/article_4b0ab51a-8080-568d-a738-5ea6114958e2.html.

Introduction

1. Randal Maurice Jelks, *Benjamin Elijah Mays, Schoolmaster of the Movement: A Biography* (Chapel Hill: University of North Carolina Press, 2012), back cover.
2. *Stanford University Encyclopedia Online,* s.v. "Mays, Dr. Benjamin E. Mays," accessed February 2020, https://kinginstitute.stanford.edu/encyclopedia/mays-benjamin-elijah.
3. Martin Luther King Jr., *Stride Toward Freedom: The Montgomery Story* (San Francisco: Harper Collins, 1958), 84–85, 89, 96–97.
4. King Jr., 102–107.
5. King Jr., 102.
6. Martin Luther King Jr., *Why We Can't Wait* (New York: Signet Classics, 1963), 95–96.
7. King Jr., *Stride Toward Freedom,* 9.
8. Benjamin E. Mays, "My View," *Pittsburgh Courier,* October 25, 1958.

9 Martin Luther King Jr., *I Have a Dream: Writings and Speeches that Changed the World*, ed. James M. Washington (San Francisco: Harper Collins, 1992), viii.
10 *Wikipedia*, s.v. "Rosewood Massacre," August 29, 2019, https://en.wikipedia.org/wiki/ Rosewood_massacre.
11 *Wikipedia*, s.v. "Emmett Till," August 31, 2019, https://en.wikipedia.org/wiki/Emmett_Till.
12 Strain, "The Day MLK Came to Tulsa."
13 "Nikita Khrushchev," Nikita Khrushchev Quotes, accessed October 2019, http://www. azquotes.com/author/7985-Nikita_Khrushchev.
14 Strain, "The Day MLK Came to Tulsa."
15 Eric Metaxas, *If You Can Keep It: The Forgotten Promise of American Liberty* (New York: Penguin Books, 2016), 223.
16 Saul D. Alinsky, *Rules for Radicals: A Pragmatic Primer for Realistic Radicals* (New York: Vintage Books, 1971), 24.
17 Jarrett Stepman, "Unlike the NFL's Colin Kaepernick, Frederick Douglass Loved 'The Star-Spangled Banner,'" *The Daily Signal*, August 29, 2016, https://www.dailysignal.com/2016/ 08/29/ unlike-the-nfls-colin-kaepernick-frederick-douglass-loved-the-star-spangled-banner.
18 Martin Luther King Jr., "The Other America," April 14, 1967, https://www.crmvet .org/docs/otherram.htm.
19 "Black Lives Matter Activists aim to reclaim MLK as Radical," Fox News, January 16, 2017, http://www.foxnews.com/us/2017/01/16/black-lives-matter-activists-aim-to-reclaim-mlk-as-radical.
20 Martin Luther King Jr., *Where Do We Go from Here: Chaos or Community?* (New York: Harper Collins, 1967), 62–63.
21 David J. Garrow, *Bearing the Cross: Martin Luther King, Jr., and the Southern Christian Leadership Conference* (New York: Harper Collins, 1986).
22 Garrow, *Bearing the Cross*.
23 King Jr., *Where Do We Go from Here: Chaos or Community?*, 62–63.
24 David Chappell, "The Radicalism of Martin Luther King, Jr.'s Nonviolence Resistance," *The Washington Post*, January 15, 2018, https://www.washingtonpost.com/news /made-by-history/wp/2018/01/15/the-radicalism-of-martin-luther-kings-nonviolent-resistance/? noredirect=on&utm_term=.70c85c1bef09.

25 Chappell.
26 Michael Eric Dyson, Emmanuel Ocbazghi Video: "A Georgetown Professor Explains How Martin Luther King Jr. Has Been Severely Whitewashed," Business Insider, January 15, 2018, https://www.businessinsider.com/georgetown-professor-reveals-people-wrong-mlk-martin-luther-king-jr-race-black-radical-racism-2017-5.
27 Dyson.
28 Dyson.
29 King Jr., "The Other America."
30 Dyson.

Chapter 1

1 King Jr., *I Have a Dream: Writings and Speeches that Changed the World*, xxviii.
2 Martin Luther King Jr., "I Have a Dream," speech at the march on Washington, copyright 1963, https://www.archives.gov/files/press/exhibits/dream-speech.pdf.
3 King Jr.
4 King Jr.
5 King Jr.
6 King Jr.
7 King Jr.
8 Henry Holloman, *The Forgotten Blessing: Rediscovering the Transforming Power of Sanctification* (Nashville: Word Publishing, 1999), 11.
9 King Jr., "I Have a Dream," speech.
10 C. S. Lewis, *The Joyful Christian* (Nashville: B & H Publishing Group, 1999).
11 Martin Luther King Jr. Quotes about Forgiveness, https://www.azquotes.com/author/ 8044-Martin_Luther_King_Jr/tag/forgiveness.
12 Walter E. Jacobson, https://walterjacobsonmd.com/forgiveness-not-occasional-act-permanent-attitude.
13 Promod Batra, "Your Attitude Determines Your Altitude," *Think Link*, December 12, 2019, http://www.thinklink.in/blog/forgiveness-is-not-an-occasional-act-it-is-a-permanent-attitude-martin-luther-king.

14 Clarence Washington, Sr. *Victory Every Day in Every Way: Kingdom Living According to Nehemiah the Governor* (Bloomington: WestBow Press, 2017), 29.

Chapter 2

1. King Jr., "I Have a Dream," speech.
2. King Jr.
3. King Jr..
4. Jim Taylor, "Has America Lost it's Self-respect?" *Huff Post*, May 25, 2011, http://www.huffpost.com/entry/has-america-lost-its-self_b_691080.
5. Martin Luther King Jr., *A Testament of Hope: The Essential Writings and Speeches of Martin Luther King, Jr.*, ed. James M. Washington (San Francisco: Harper Collins, 1986), 265–266.
6. King Jr., *A Testament of Hope*.
7. King Jr.
8. King Jr., 139.
9. King Jr.
10. Douglas Malloch, "Be the Best of Whatever You Are," https://www.great-inspirational-quotes.com/be-the-best-of-whatever-you-are.html.
11. Martin Luther King Jr. Quotes, https://www.azquotes.com/quote/158999.
12. King Jr., *A Testament of Hope*, 146.
13. King Jr., "I Have a Dream," speech.
14. King Jr., *Stride Toward Freedom*, 156.
15. King Jr., 102–107.
16. King Jr., 97.
17. King Jr., *A Testament of Hope*, 103.
18. King Jr., 86.
19. King Jr., 17.
20. Martin Luther King Jr. Quotes, https://www.azquotes.com/quote/360730.
21. Alveda C. King, "The Meaning of the True Dream," Human Life Alliance, Advertising Supplement, copyright 2010, 2.

22. Martin Luther King Jr. Quotes, https://www.azquotes.com/quote/159056.
23. Martin Luther King Jr. Quotes, http://www.great-quotes.com/quote/10425.
24. King Jr., "I Have a Dream," speech.
25. King Jr.
26. King Jr.
27. Strain.
28. *Wikipedia*, s.v. "Tulsa Race Riot," September 24, 2019, https://en.wikipedia.org/wiki/Tulsa_race_riot.
29. Paul Lee Tan, *Encyclopedia of 7700 Illustrations,* "Guarding the Asylum," No. 3382 (Rockville: Assurance Publishers, 1979), 794.
30. Clarence Washington, Sr., *Victory Every Day in Every Way: Kingdom Living According to Nehemiah the Governor* (Bloomington: WestBow Press, 2017), 254.
31. Washington, Sr., *Victory Every Day in Every Way.*
32. Washington, Sr.
33. Washington, Sr., 255.
34. Washington, Sr.
35. Washington, Sr.
36. Washington, Sr., 257.
37. Washington, Sr.
38. Washington, Sr.
39. Washington, Sr., 241.

Chapter 3

1. Martin Luther King Jr. Quotes, https://www.goodreads.com/quotes/16312, 18063, and 79713.
2. King Jr., "I Have a Dream," speech.
3. Martin Luther King Jr. Quotes, http://www.great-quotes.com/quotes/author/Martin+ Luther/King/pg/2.
4. King Jr., *A Testament of Hope*, 18.
5. King Jr.
6. King Jr.
7. King Jr., 41–42.

8. *Wikipedia*, s.v. "Charleston Church Shooting," September 27, 2019, https://en.wikipedia.org/ wiki/Charleston_church_shooting.
9. Charleston South Carolina Church Massacre Pictures, September 27, 2019, https://www.bing .com/images/search?q=charleston+south+carolina+church+massacre+pictures&qpvt =Charleston +south+ carolina+ church+massacre+pictures&FORM=IGRE.
10. *Wikipedia*, s.v. "Charleston Church Shooting," September 27, 2019, https://en.wikipedia.org/ wiki/Charleston_church_shooting#Officials.
11. John F. MacArthur Jr., *The MacArthur New Testament Commentary, Hebrews* (Chicago: Moody Bible Institute of Chicago, 1983), 287.
12. King Jr., *A Testament of Hope*, 41–42.
13. Mike Murdock, *Seeds of Wisdom Topical Bible* (Denton: The Wisdom Center, 2003), 52.
14. King Jr., *A Testament of Hope*, 103.
15. D. Martyn Lloyd-Jones, *The Christian Soldier: An Exposition of Ephesians 6:10–20* (Grand Rapids: Baker Book House, 1977), 179,180.
16. Charles Spurgeon, "Shoes for Pilgrims and Warriors," *Metropolitan Tabernacle Pulpit* no. 3143, http://www.spurgeongems.org/vol55.
17. Chappell.

Chapter 4

1. King Jr., "I Have a Dream," speech.
2. A Day to Remember: *The Washington Post*, August 28, 1963, https://www. washingtonpost.com/blogs/capital-weather-gang/post/a-day-to-remember-august-28-1963/2011/ 08/24/gIQADeZZbJ_blog.html.
3. King Jr., "I Have a Dream," speech.
4. King Jr., *A Testament of Hope*, 105.
5. Declaration of Independence, http://www.ushistory.org/Declaration/document.
6. *Wikipedia*, s.v. "Life, Liberty and the Pursuit of Happiness," October 11, 2019, https://en. Wikipedia.org/ wiki/Life,_Liberty_and_the_ pursuit_of_Happiness.
7. Columbia Undergrad Law Review, "Constitutional Considerations of Happiness," February 16, 2016, http: //blogs.cuit.columbia.edu/culr/2016/02/16/constitutional-considerations-of-happiness.

8   King Jr., *A Testament of Hope*, 208.
9   Thomas Sowell, *Marxism: Philosophy and Economics* (New York: Quill, 1985), 157, 162.
10   King Jr., "I Have a Dream," speech.
11   Ron Cantor, "Hillary Clinton Wants Christians to Give Up on Bible Beliefs," *Charisma News*, April 28, 2015, https://www.charismanews.com/opinion/49375-hillary-clinton-wants-christians-to-give-up-on-bible-beliefs.
12   Bill Flax, "Was Jesus a Socialist, Capitalist, or Something?" *Forbes*, January 21, 2010, https://www.forbes.com/sites/billflax/2012/01/31/was-jesus-a-socialist-capitalist-or-something-else/#2216ebbb7324.
13   Flax, "Was Jesus a Socialist, Capitalist, or Something?".
14   *Wikipedia*, s.v. "Adam Smith," October 29, 2019, https://en.eikipedia.org/wike/Adam_Smith.
15   Flax, "Was Jesus a Socialist, Capitalist, or Something?".
16   Os Guinness, *A Free People's Suicide: Sustainable Freedom and the American Future* (Downers Grove: InterVarsity Press, 2012), 99.
17   Kenneth J. Barnes, *Redeeming Capitalism* (Grand Rapids: William B. Eerdmans Publishing Company, 2018), front flap, 20, 140, 161, 188, 206, 207).
18   Wikiquote, "Francis Scott Key," https://en.wikiquote.org/wiki/Francis_Scott_Key.
19   In God We Trust, https://www.allabouthistory.org/in-god-we-trust.htm.
20   *Wikipedia*, s.v. "Pledge of Allegiance," October 15, 2019, https://en.wikipedia.org/wiki/ Pledge_of_ Allegiance_United_States.
21   The Pledge of Allegiance, http://www.ushistory.org/documents/pledge.htm.
22   In God We Trust, https://www.allabouthistory.org/in-god-we-trust.htm.
23   "Nikita Khrushchev," Nikita Khrushchev Quotes, accessed October 2019, https://www. azquotes.com/author/7985-Nikita_Khrushchev.
24   King Jr., "I Have a Dream," speech.
25   The Constitution of the United States, http://constitutionus.com.
26   New Dollar Coins and "In God We Trust," https://www.snopes.com/fact-check/ historic-change.

27   Dave Urbanski, "Some Parents Upset that Pledge of Allegiance Being Recited at Elementary School. Here's Why," *The Blaze*, March 21, 2017, https://www.theblaze.com/news/ 2017/03/21/some-parents-upset-that-pledge-of-allegiance-being-recited-at-elementary-school-heres-why.

Chapter 5

1. King Jr., "I Have a Dream," speech.
2. King Jr.
3. King Jr., *A Testament of Hope*, 120.
4. Os Guinness, *The Call: Finding and Fulfilling the Central Purpose of Your Life* (Nashville: Word Publishing, 1998), 4–5.
5. Abraham Lincoln Online Speeches & Writings, http://abrahamlincolnonline.org/lincoln/ speeches/liberty.htm.
6. Eric Metaxas, *If You Can Keep It: The Forgotten Promise of American Liberty* (New York: Penguin Books, 2016), 211–212.
7. Guinness, *The Call*, 4.
8. King Jr., *A Testament of Hope*, 105.
9. Os Guinness, *A Free People's Suicide: Sustainable Freedom and the American Future* (Downers Grove: InterVarsity Press, 2012), 16, 18, 19, 21, 24.
10. Guinness, *A Free People's Suicide*, 99–100.
11. Guinness, 109.
12. Benjamin Franklin, Letter, 17 April 1787, in *The Works of Benjamin Franklin,* ed. Jared Sparks (Chicago: Townsend Mac County, 1882), 287.
13. King Jr., "I Have a Dream," speech.
14. David Knowles, "Eric Holder's Rallying Cry for Democrats: 'When They God Low, We Kick 'Em," *Yahoo News*, October 10, 2018, https://news.yahoo.com/eric-holders-rallying-cry-democrats -go-low-kick-em-192841062.html.
15. Aaron Blake, "Erick Holder: When They Go Low We Kick Them," *The Washington Post*, October 10, 2018, https://www.washingtonpost.com/politics/2018/10/10/eric-holder-when-they-go-low-we-kick-them-thats-what-this-new-domcratic-party-is-about/?noredirect=on&utm_term=.a59d3 bf01d0b.

16. Hillary Clinton, CNN, October 10, 2018, https://www.cnn.com/2018/10/09/politics/ hillary-clinton-civility-congress-cnntv/index.html.
17. Martin Luther King on Dignity Quotes, http://www.searchquotes.com/search/Martin_ Luther_ King_On_Dignity/11/#ixzz56hHfvywl.
18. King Jr., "I Have a Dream," speech.
19. King Jr.

Chapter 6

1. Ben Shapiro, "Biden in 49% Black Danville, Virginia: 'They Gonna Put Y'All Back in Chains,'" Breitbart, August 14, 2012, https://www.breitbart.com/politics/2012/08/14/biden-chains-romney-response.
2. King Jr., "I Have a Dream," speech.
3. James Lindsey, "What Is Critical Race Theory," *PragerU*, April 26, 2021, https://www. prageru.com/video/what-is-critical-race-theory.
4. Christopher F. Rufo, "Critical Race Theory: What It Is and How to Fight It," *Imprimis*, March 2021, https://imprimis.hillsdale.edu/critical/-race-theory-fight.
5. Rufo, "Critical Race Theory."
6. Lindsey, "What Is Critical Race Theory?".
7. *Essence*, "House of Representatives Apologizes to African-Americans for Slavery," December 16, 2009, https://www.essence.com/news/house-of-representatives-apologizes-to-a.
8. Congress.Gov, https://www.congress.gov/bill/110th-congress/house-resolution/194/test.
9. Russell Simmons, *HuffPost*, July 20, 2009, "The Healing Has Begun," https://www. huffingtonpost.com/ russell-simmons/the-healing-has-begunus-s_b_217901.html.
10. S.I. McMillen, M.D. and David E. Stern, M.D. *None of These Diseases: The Bibles Health Secrets for the 21th Century* (Grand Rapids: Revell, 2000), 213.
11. Lewis B. Smedes, *Forgive and Forget: Healing the Hurts We Don't Deserve* (San Francisco: Harper & Row, Publishers, 1984), 132–133.
12. Charles F. Stanley, *Landmines in the Path of the Believer* (Nashville: Thomas Nelson, 2007), 120.

13. John F. MacArthur Jr., *The MacArthur New Testament Commentary, Matthew1–7* (Chicago: Moody Bible Institute of Chicago, 1985), 397–398.
14. Ken Sande, *The Peacemaker: A Biblical Guide to Resolving Personal Conflict* (Grand Rapids: Baker Book House, 1992), 218–219.
15. "20/20: Americans Debate Reparations for Slavery," *ABC News,* January 5, 2006, https://abcnews.go.com/2020/story?id=124115&page=1.
16. Walter E. Williams, *American Contempt for Liberty* (Stanford: Hoover Institution Press, 2015), 197.
17. Henry Louis Gates, Jr., PBS, "Why Was Cotton King," http://www.pbs.org/wnet/ african-americans-many-rivers-to-cross/history/why-was-cotton-king/.
18. Stacy M. Brown, "Five Hundred Years Later Are We Still Slaves?," *Black Press USA,* October 20, 2018, https://www.blackpressusa.com/the-transatlantic-slave-trade-part-v-five-hundred-years-later-are-we-still-slaves.
19. Walter E. Williams, *American Contempt,* 196.
20. Randall Robinson, *The Debt: What America Owes to Blacks* (New York: Penguin Group, 2000), 203–204.
21. Alveda King, *King Rules,* 86–87.
22. Stuart Appelbaum, "A Special Bond," Religious Action Center of Reformed Judaism, accessed October 2019, https://rac.org/special-bond-martin-luther-king-jr-israel-and-american-jewry.
23. Appelbaum.
24. Dave Bohon, "Black Pastors Challenge NAACP's Support for Same-sex Marriage," *New American,* July 17, 2012, https://www.thenewamerican.com/culture/faith-and-morals/item /12094-black-pastors-challenge-naacp%E2%80%99s-support-for-same-sex-marriage.
25. Gene Demby, "NAACP Gay Marriage Position Draws Protest From Black Clergy Group," *Huff Post,* July 12, 2012, https://www.huffingtonpost.com/2012/07/12/naacp-gay-marriage-same-sex_n_1668476.html.
26. Alex Murashko, "Black Pastors Coalition: We're Going to Keep the Heat on Obama," *The Christian Post,* July 12, 2012, https://www.christianpost.com/news/black-pastors-coalition-were-going-to-keep-the-heat-on-obama-78074.

27 Rev. Keith Ratliff, *oneiowa*, March 16, 2011, https://oneiowa.org/2011/03/rev-keith-ratliff.
28 Dave Bohon, "Black Pastors Challenge NAACP's Support for Same-sex Marriage," *New American*, July 17, 2012, https://www.thenewamerican.com/culture/faith-and-morals/item /12094-black-pastors-challenge-naacp%E2%80%99s-support-for-same-sex-marriage.
29 Jason L. Riley, *False Black Power?* (West Conshohocken: Templeton Press, 2017), back cover.

Chapter 7

1 Ken Ham, Carl Wieland, and Don Batten, *Where Did the 'Races' come From?* (Australia: Answers in Genesis, 1999), 6.
2 Ham, Wieland, and Batten, *Where Did the 'Races' come From?*, 11.
3 Ham, Wieland, and Batten, 28–29.
4 Tony Evans, *Let's Get to Know Each Other: What White Christians Should Know About Black Christians* (Nashville: Thomas Nelson Publishers, 1995), 6–7.
5 Evans, *Let's Get to Know Each Other*, 9.
6 Evans, 19–20.
7 Charles G. Finney, "The Decay of Conscience," *The Independent of New York*, December 4, 1873, http://gospeltruth.net/1868_75Independent/731204_conscience.htm.
8 King Jr., *A Testament of Hope*, 212.
9 King Jr.
10 King Jr., *I Have a Dream: Writings and Speeches that Changed the World*, xx–xxi.

CONTENTS

Volume 2

Preface xiii

Introduction: Who Was Dr. Martin Luther King Jr. and Why Is His Dream So Important to People of All Colors and the Survival of Our God-Given American Dream? xvii

    An Overview of the Life of Dr. King xvii

    The Reason Why Dr. King's Dream Is So Important to All Americans xxiv

    The Conspiracy to Discredit Dr. King's Dream xxxii

The Hijack: How Was the Hijack Launched and Maintained?

Chapter 1:   The Saul Alinsky Rules for Radicals Disciples 1

    Saul Alinsky and Some of His More Notable Disciples ... 1

    The Philosophical and Ideological Principles of *Rules for Radicals* 11

    The Eleven Rules and Thirteen Tactics for Radicals 32

    The Rules of the Jew from Nazareth Are Greater Than the Rules of the Jew from Chicago 47

Chapter 2:   The Black Liberation Theology Disciples 55

    The History of Black Liberation Theology and Its Notable Disciples 55

    Black Liberation Theology Is Not a Valid Interpretation or Application of Scripture 71

	Black Liberation Theology Is Established on the Unbiblical Victimology Narrative.......................... 82
	The Dangerous Kinship between Black Liberation Theology and Marxism 102
	Black Liberation Theology Is a Multifaceted, Syncretic Trojan Horse.. 125
Chapter 3:	The Elites, the Greedy, and the Power-Hungry Blacks and Whites with Hidden Agendas.................... 133
	The Hidden Agenda of the Politics of Hate 138
	The Hidden Agenda of the Politics of White Guilt 164
	The Hidden Agenda of the Politics of Race, Sex, Gender, and Social Identity......................................183

The Hijack Concluding Remarks.. 205

Appendixes

Endnotes 211
Table of Contents for Volume 1—*The Dream*....................................... 225
Table of Contents for Volume 3—*The Nightmare*............................... 227
Table of Contents for Volume 4—*The Recovery* 229
List of Bible Versions Abbreviations..231
Index of Authors and Subjects... 233

CONTENTS

Volume 3

Preface xiii

Introduction: Who Was Dr. Martin Luther King Jr. and Why Is His Dream So Important to People of All Colors and the Survival of Our God-Given American Dream? xvii

    An Overview of the Life of Dr. King xvii

    The Reason Why Dr. King's Dream Is So Important to All Americans xxiv

    The Conspiracy to Discredit Dr. King's Dream xxxii

The Nightmare: What Are the Present and Future Consequences of the Hijack?

Chapter 1:   High Rate of Black Abortions 1

    The Dire Consequences of Legalized Abortion in America 5

    The History of Black Genocide in America 27

    The Familiar, the Surprising, and the Contemporary Proponents of Eugenics and Black Genocide in America 38

Chapter 2:   High Rate of Black Single-Parent Families, Poverty, Illiteracy Caused by Ineffective Public Schools, and Black-on-Black Crime and Murder 73

    High Rate of Black Single-Parent Families 73

	High Rate of Black Poverty and Illiteracy Caused by Ineffective Public Schools............................ 94
	High Rate of Black-on-Black Crime and Murder 125
Chapter 3:	Loss of America's Freedom of Speech, Religious Freedoms, Civility, and Right to Bear Arms 157
	The Loss of America's Freedom of Speech and Civility... 157
	Intimidation Examples Number 1 161
	Intimidation Examples Number 2 171
	Intimidation Examples Number 3 180
	The Loss of America's Freedom of Religion 192
	The Loss of America's Right to Bear Arms 210

The Nightmare Concluding Remarks 225

Appendixes

Endnotes 233
Table of Contents for Volume 1—*The Dream*............................251
Table of Contents for Volume 2—*The Hijack* 253
Table of Contents for Volume 4—*The Recovery*..........................255
List of Bible Versions Abbreviations... 257
Index of Authors and Subjects..259

CONTENTS

Volume 4

Preface xiii
Introduction xvii

      Who Was Dr. Martin Luther King Jr. and Why
      Is His Dream So Important to People of All
      Colors and the Survival of Our God-Given
      American Dream? xvii

      An Overview of the Life of Dr. King xvii

      The Reason Why Dr. King's Dream Is So
      Important to All Americans xxiv

      The Conspiracy to Discredit Dr. King's Dream xxxii

The Recovery: How Does America Recover from the Hijack?

Chapter 1   What Are the Vital Elements of the Recovery from
                 the Hijack? 1

                 The First Vital Element Is a Nationwide Spiritual
                 Revival and Reformation of the Government and
                 Other Institutions of Society 1

                 The Second Vital Element Is the Reinforcement of
                 the Principles That Made America a Great Nation 47

Chapter 2   What Is the Role of the Church in the Recovery
                 from the Hijack? 77

                 The Church Must Lead the Nation in a Spiritual
                 Revival and Reformation of the Government and
                 Other Institutions of Society 77

	The Black Church Has a Special Role in Leading the Nation in a Spiritual Revival and Reformation of the Government and Other Institutions of Society ... 123
Chapter 3	What Will Be the Consequences If the Church Fails to Lead America in a Nationwide Revival and Reformation of the Government and Other Institutions of Society?.. 164
	The Recovery Concluding Remarks............................ 223

Conclusion 227

Appendixes

Endnotes 237

Table of Contents for Volume 1 — *The Dream* 251

Table of Contents for Volume 2 — *The Hijack* 253

Table of Contents for Volume 3 — *The Nightmare* 255

List of Bible Versions Abbreviations.. 257

Index of Authors and Subjects 259

LIST OF BIBLE VERSIONS ABBREVIATIONS

AMP: Amplified

ESV: English Standard Version

KJV: King James Version

JB: Jerusalem Bible

MSG: The Message

NASB: New American Standard Bible

NEB: The New English Bible

NIV: New International Version

NKJV: New King James Version

PME: Phillips Modern English

RSV: Revised Standard Version

GNT: Good News Translation in Today's English Version

TLB: The Living Bible

YLT: Young Literal Translation

INDEX

A

Abernathy, Ralph xxiii
Abortion 5, 24, 36, 87, 147
ACLU 147
Alinsky, Saul David xxvii, 107
American Dream 93, 101

B

Barnes, Kenneth J. 83
Batra, Promod 12
Bellamy, Francis 86
Biblical Worldview Chart 87
Biden, Joe 113
Bill of Rights 76, 93, 102, 104, 113
Black Lives Matter xxxiii, 60, 116
Black-on-Black Murder xiii, xxx, 24, 165
Bronner, Dale C. 124

C

CAAP 149
Capitalism 80, 82, 83
Chappell, David xxxiv
Charleston Church Massacre 61
Clinton, Hillary 78, 107
Communism 77, 80, 83, 86, 90, 91
Corsi, Jerome 78
Cowper, William vii, 166
Critical Race Theory 118
Critical Race Theory/Equity 117, 167
Curse of Ham 159

D

Declaration of Independence 75, 102
Democratic Party 147, 148

Douglass, Frederick xxviii
Dyson, Michael Eric xxxv, xxxvi, xxxix

E

Eisenhower, Dwight D. 86
Evans, Tony 159, 160

F

Finney, Charles Grandison 164
Flax, Bill 80, 81
Floyd, George xxxii, 59
Forgetting 127, 130
Forgiveness xviii, xxxiv, 11, 40, 60, 116, 122, 125, 134, 143, 165

G

Garrow, David J. xxxiv
Generational Curses and Blessings 122
Ghandi, Mahatma 33
God's Almost, Almost Chosen People 100
God's Almost Chosen People 99
Golden Calf 146, 147, 149, 151
Guinness, Os 82, 98, 101, 102

H

Ham, Ken and Batten, Don and Wieland, Carl 156, 158
Hate xxvi, xxix, xxxvi, xxxix, 4, 13, 15, 33, 93, 107, 114, 116, 125, 143, 167
Holder, Eric 107
Holloman, Henry 6
Huges, Langston 168

I

Indian Removal Act 121
In God We Trust 85, 92
Institutional Racism xxx, xxxi, 167

J

Jackson, Jesse 147
Jacobson, Walter E. 11
Japanese-Americans 121, 137
Jefferson, Thomas 86
Jim Crow Law 114, 116, 119

K

Kelly, Walt xxvi
Kennedy, John F. 2
Key, Francis Scott 85
Khrushchev, Nikita xxv, 91
King, Alveda 35, 147
King, Alveda C. 36
King, Coretta Scott xxi, xxii, xxiii, 34
King, Jr., Martin Luther xvii, xx, xxv, xxxiii, xxxiv, 2, 11, 13, 19, 28, 29, 31, 37, 52, 53, 55, 57, 59, 62, 66, 74, 76, 95, 97, 101, 111, 115, 147, 166

L

Lewis, C. S. 8
Lincoln, Abraham 3, 99, 108, 119
Lloyd-Jones, D. Martyn 70
Love ix, xviii, xx, xxvi, xxvii, xxviii, xxix, xxxi, 3, 28, 55, 93

M

MacArthur Jr., John 62, 128
Malloch, Douglas 29
Marxism 77, 78, 81, 83, 84, 90
Matthews, Chris 94
Mays, Benjamin E. xviii, xx
McMillen, S. I. 125
Means & Ends xxvii, xxxv, 71, 108
Melanin 157
Metaxas, Eric 78, 99

Mexican-Americans 121
Morgan, G. Campbell 151

N

NAACP 147, 148, 149, 150
Nonviolent Resistance xix, xxi, xxiii, xxvii, xxix, xxxv, 19, 31, 53, 55, 105, 109

O

Obama, Barack 79, 94, 113, 119, 149
Obama, Michelle 107
Owens, Williams 149

P

Parks, Rosa xix, xxiii
Peace 136
Pledge of Allegiance 86, 92
Prayer xxxix, 43, 46, 49, 59, 60, 83, 125, 127, 128, 132, 133
Putin, Vladimir 41

R

Ray, James Earl xviii
Reparations 119, 134, 146
Riley, Jason L. 152
Robinson, Randall 142

S

Sande, Ken 136
Seek the Kingdom 8
Simmons, Russell 120
Six Rules for Nonviolent Resistance xix, 32
Six Steps for Nonviolent Social Change 34
Smedes, Lewis 126
Socialism 77, 80, 82, 84, 90
Spurgeon, Charles Haddon 70
Stanley, Charles 126, 129
Steele, Shelby 167
Syncretism 148

T

Taylor, Jim 24
The Bill of Rights 92
The I Have a Dream Methods Triangle
  Diagram 68
Till, Emmett Louis xxii
Tocqueville, Alexis De 82, 104, 105
Triangle of Freedom 82, 83, 102, 104,
  108, 109, 111
Triangle of Freedom Diagram 103
Triangle of The Dream 110
Triangle of The Dream Diagram 109
Tulsa Race Riot 38

U

Unity xxv, 37, 42, 43
Unity Leveraging 49
Unity Leveraging Diagram 46
U. S. Constitution 75, 77, 90, 92, 93,
  99, 101, 102

W

Washington Sr., Clarence 31, 49
Why Was Cotton King 138
Williams, Walter E. 138, 139, 140
Woke 117, 118
Wokeism 117
Wokies 118
Wounded Broken Spirit 13, 27, 40

This handbook should be on the desktop of every pastor, on the coffee table of every Christian home, and in every classroom where the principles of prayer are being taught and practiced! No other book on prayer is as comprehensive and easy to absorb as *Tools for Effective Prayer*.

Book and e-books can be purchased: www.westbow.com
For more information and to contact author: www.toolsforeffective.com
or www.clarencewashingtonauthor.com

How much of the awesomely abundant life that Christ died to provide for believers do you want—a little bit, a lot, or all of it? If your answer is all of it, then *Victory Every Day in Every Way* was specifically written for you! It will guide you on a journey from wherever you are in life to where God wants you to be, which is victorious in everything you do.

Book and e-books can be purchased: www.westbow.com
For more information and to contact author: www.toolsforeffective.com or www.clarencewashingtonauthor.com